I'm so inspired by the journeys of these incredible women, especially Ilana Goor, a brilliant artist, designer, sculptor, and my dearest friend and creative inspiration. Women carry the weight of change on their shoulders; we create life, we problem solve, we persevere, we collaborate, we communicate, we make change in the world. I am excited for everyone to read *Invincible Women*, be inspired, and continue to share their stories.

DONNA KARAN
Fashion Designer and Creator of DKNY

Remarkable stories of women who challenge our preconceptions, elevate our spirits, and renew our faith in this nation's promise.

RABBI DAVID WOLPE
The Max Webb Senior Rabbi of Sinai Temple
Author of *David: The Divided Heart*

Immigrants have always served to advance the culture, science, and compassion of American society, and Bilha's excellent interviews provide compelling evidence. I will be sure to encourage my students, most of whom are immigrants and children of immigrants, to read and be reassured by the successful women in this book.

MARY C. PEARL, PhD
Dean, Macaulay Honors College of
the City University of New York

Dr. Bilha Fish has given us another look at those who braved enormous obstacles abroad and in the United States to become American citizens. These women are the living testament to why we must be a nation that welcomes potential talent from everywhere, and women from anywhere. Thank you, Dr. Fish, for this gift. We must pass it on to as many as we can, lest we ever forget or ignore the lessons in these pages.

EDIE WEINER
Futurist, Author, President
and CEO, The Future Hunters

This book is a timely and important reminder that Americans cannot afford to shut the door on the millions of immigrants who have made our country great and who continue to do so every day.

DEDE THOMPSON BARTLETT
Former President of the Women's Forum of New York,
Woodrow Wilson Visiting Fellow, and Author

Invincible Women is a celebration. Bilha Chesner Fish's book gifts readers with rich personal interviews with women who came to this country—as she did—as immigrants, confronted multiple obstacles, and rose to positions of influence in many different fields. The stories are powerful and moving. Bilha has done a great service in eliciting and sharing them.

EMITA HILL
Author, *Northern Harvest* and *Bronx Faces and Voices*
Recipient in 2019 of an honorary doctorate
in humane letters from Indiana University

INVINCIBLE
WOMEN

Conversations with 21 Inspiring
and Successful American Immigrants

BILHA CHESNER FISH, MD

HybridGlobal
PUBLISHING

Published by
Hybrid Global Publishing
301 E 57th Street, 4th fl
New York, NY 10022

Manufactured in the United States of America, or in the United Kingdom when distributed elsewhere.

Fish, Bilha Chesner
     Invincible Women: Conversations with 21 Inspiring and
     Successful American Immigrants
     LCCN: 2019914387
     Hardcover: 978-1-948181-74-7
     Softcover: 978-1-948181-73-0
     eBook: 978-1-948181-75-4

Cover design by: Lorie Pagnozzi
Interior design by: Claudia Volkman
Copyediting by: Claudia Volkman and Lisa R. Kosan
Author photo by: Raymond Hamlin
Cover Art: *Riding the Waves* by Bilha Chesner Fish, MD

Quantity Purchases:
Companies, professional groups, clubs, and other organizations may qualify for special terms when ordering quantities of this title. For information, email kbstrauss@straussconsultants.com, or call (212) 913-9894.
www.hybridglobalpublishing.com

For information about speaking engagements with the author, send an email to bilhafish@gmail.com.

www.invinciblewomenbook.com

DEDICATION

This book is dedicated to my parents, Rachel and Dr. Aaron Chesner, for leading by example, showing me the road to reach the impossible, and giving me the strength to follow my dreams. Also, to my daughters, Jordana and Ariel, who continue to enrich my life every day.

Sofia,
This book is very
timely and I
think you'll love
reading it because
you care about many
of the issues described.
And... there is a
little surprise here!
Love,
Safari

CONTENTS

FOREWORD

DEDE THOMPSON BARTLETT

DR. BILHA CHESNER FISH has written a book that seems ripped from today's headlines. At a time when our nation is bitterly debating immigration policy, building billion-dollar walls, and jailing children, Dr. Fish reminds us that the United States is still a nation of immigrants and is indebted to immigrants for many of the advances Americans enjoy today.

Dr. Fish describes some of these contributions in her conversations with twenty-one outstanding women from Asia, Africa, the Middle East, Europe, South America, and the Caribbean. This diverse group includes scientists, artists, teachers, economists, opera singers, engineers, humanitarians, doctors, writers, and philanthropists. Their passion for enriching life for so many has been an incalculable gift to the American people.

Why does it take Dr. Fish, herself an immigrant and a pre-eminent radiologist, to point out what the rest of us who had the good fortune to be born here fail to see? Perhaps it is because she had to work so hard to achieve what "native-born" Americans take for granted—the freedom to live free and to pursue our talents wherever they might take us.

All the women profiled in this book had harrowing journeys to come to this country. They escaped poverty, tyranny, and often abuse. Some arrived as children, others came as adults. All sought to find a place where they could be safe and grow and contribute. In doing so, they have given abundantly to their adopted country.

When Bilha Fish set out to write *Invincible Women*, she could have been writing about her own life as a young Israeli doctor arriving in the United States and forging an outstanding career as a radiologist helping women with cancer and developing wellness programs for adults and adolescents.

She wrote the book about other immigrant women to underscore the debt she and they feel they owe to the United States. Like them, she believes that in no other country would she have been able to flourish and give back as she has been able to here.

However, Dr. Fish fears this opportunity is being denied to other immigrants. Her book is a timely and important reminder that Americans cannot afford to shut the door on the millions of immigrants who have made our country great and who continue to do so every day. While she understands the need to keep our country safe and the importance of developing a rational immigration policy, she says there is room for those who choose to come. Many economists agree with her. They note the United States needs all immigrants to grow the population and the economy and to pay into our Social Security system. Restricting the immigrant pool, they believe, is going to lead to slower population growth, less innovation, and less entrepreneurship.

Bilha Fish asked me to write the foreword to her book because she knows my passion for social justice and that I have a unique historical perspective. My family has been in this country for more than 350 years. Some of my ancestors, on both sides of the Mason Dixon Line, were like the angry "nativists" we hear in the public square today. Yet when my newly arrived poor Irish, German, and Danish-Creole immigrant ancestors married into my aristocratic old English, Scottish, and Dutch family, they revitalized it. It was their children who worked two and three jobs and powered the machinery that built this country.

We must find ways to incorporate newcomers into our society and utilize their hard work and determination so we can continue to prosper. This is the legacy I inherited and the dream Bilha yearned to pursue. I hope it will be there for many years to come.

Dede Thompson Bartlett is a former president of the Women's Forum of New York. She retired as vice president for Altria Group and is the former corporate secretary for Philip Morris Companies Inc. and Mobil Corporation. She has been honored by numerous organizations for her work in helping survivors of domestic abuse. Currently a Woodrow Wilson Visiting Fellow, she is the author of the trilogy *Discovering My Lost Family: The Unexpected Journey of an American Woman*.

**"Eli, Eli
Walking to Caesarea"**

My god, my god
May this never end
The sand and the sea
The rustle of the waters
The lightning of the heavens,
The prayer of man.

—Hannah Senesh (1921–1944)

PROLOGUE

BILHA CHESNER FISH, MD

ISRAELI-AMERICAN AUTHOR, NEW YORK CITY-BASED RADIOLOGIST,
AND COMMUNITY SERVICE ADVOCATE

Photo Credit: Raymond Hamlin

CONFLICTING FORCES DROVE ME TO write this book. Every interview with the fascinating individuals you'll soon meet was encouraged by our glorious women's movement, the universal bonds of sisterhood, and the growing voices of #MeToo. Equally strong was my need to tell powerful stories to refute the policies that stuff certain immigrants into one faceless group. No matter where they come from, how hard they work, or how American they are, we constantly hear that "they" do not belong here.

The indiscriminate targeting of immigrants from certain countries and the uncertainty and lack of protection facing the Dreamers resonated with me. The escalation has continued with the removal of children from their families crossing the US southern border.

While I continue to grapple with the unfairness of the present situation, I understand the times in which we live. We must protect ourselves from terrorists. We must make the United States a safe country. That means being vigilant and aggressive about who is allowed to enter. And that requires responsible and thoughtful policies, education, and practices.

Listening to these stories, as I watched the tears fall and waited for the deep cleansing breaths to pass, I imagined the added fear that immigrants now face. It could just as easily be you, or me, on a different date, coming from a different country.

This reality prompted me to begin the journey of my book. As I met and spoke to these women and dug out their inspiring life stories of struggle and survival, I felt compelled to continue the conversations. I identified with them because parts of my life mirrored theirs. My resolve to write and celebrate their contributions to the world was strengthened daily.

The women I interviewed are all American immigrants who arrived here as infants, teenagers, and well into adulthood. They came as long ago as 1936 and as recently as the 1980s, alone on a snowy evening or clutching familiar hands. They escaped the atrocities of war, or fled wounds of a more emotional nature. Their reasons for leaving the countries of their birth are as varied as their skin tones.

They came from Iran, Pakistan, Haiti, Armenia, Israel, India, Austria, Argentina, Brazil, Rwanda, South Korea, China, Chile, Serbia, Transylvania, Egypt, and Bangladesh.

They are now all United States citizens.

These women have achieved greatness; some are famous and some not so much. You will see how each made her neighborhood, her region, our planet a better place to live.

Their stories, told in their own words, describe incidents of racial and religious discrimination. They quit unwanted relationships, avoided capture, and sacrificed dearly. They learned new languages and new customs and figured out how to live as "the other" yet still retain a strong sense of self.

Back home they tasted the fear of dying as Nazi troops swept through Eastern Europe and death squads invaded Rwandan villages. They felt suffocated by patriarchal societies and rampant gender discrimination. And once here, they were often crushed by loneliness and separation from friends and family.

Though some of the paths are so horrific you may want to look away, I ask that you keep your eyes open. By reading about their journeys, we can learn about their tenacity and what makes a positive influencer and future role model for our children. We can understand what makes a nation stronger and more vibrant.

Some of the women I interviewed found ways to create community by enhancing the performing arts, nurturing the mental and physical well-being of adolescents, feeding the belly and the soul, infusing youth with music and education, and building bridges through art and culture.

Others worked within systems to form coalitions. They strove to improve bureaucratic structures, advance causes, fight injustices, and prevent further erosions of individual and civil rights. Their work was—and continues to be—motivated by personal scars and affronts as well as the desire to improve living situations.

And then there are still more women with positions at top-tier companies, major universities, and international consortiums, who have influenced the world of business, science, our planet's survival, and our knowledge of our bodies and the universe.

Perhaps more subtly, others reveal new worlds that enrich the lives of us all. They write books, design clothes, perform operas, create culinary innovations, and orchestrate philanthropic programs that bring new experiences to diverse public audiences.

Many of these women immigrated to the United States when they were children and had to assume responsibilities well beyond their age by helping their parents with new businesses and translating the language. Later, with their own families, they had to choose which parts of their birth cultures they would bring to the next generation despite the pressures to assimilate.

Each woman in this book does something incredibly noble that establishes connections between people of different nations. I didn't recognize this at first, but as the body of interviews grew, I sensed that these women were validating the human experience by deeming each of us worthy of attention and respect.

Having gone through life challenges, they are keenly aware that all people are vulnerable. We are the same, regardless of where we are in time and space. This ability to see real truths requires tolerance. It requires us to listen to the stories and imagine ourselves walking the same paths.

A few people I interviewed ultimately decided it would be too dangerous for them if their story were published. The fear of deportation on the way to becoming a legal citizen proved too great. Regrettably I cannot share details about the mother who left Iran, an abusive marriage, and her young son. She seized the only chance to build a new life for herself and shed a dark past of surveillance by her husband and oppression under Iran's regime. She escaped to survive, to find her true identity, and offer her son a better future. Today she fights domestic and foreign bureaucracies to help her son immigrate to the United States as she begins a doctorate program at a top American university.

I also cannot share the story of an international journalist whose parents can't leave Syria to visit her. She told me how she left her home when fears of censorship and authoritarian rule became too great, but now wonders if those same seeds of hate and doubt have taken root here, in her adopted country.

The "nation of immigrants" phrase, made popular by President John F. Kennedy's book, was struck from the mission statement of the United States Citizenship and Immigration Services earlier this year. The three simple words that so clearly conveyed this country's multiculturalism vanished with the stroke of a pen. The sense of support and feeling of welcome have either disappeared or eroded.

Part of the solution is to understand that not every "other" is a danger to our way of life. In fact, immigrants are an integral part of our life, and they enrich our country. I wonder what our neighborhoods, our communities, and the world would be like without them.

Would there be fewer scientists, like Nergis Mavalvala, to document the presence of gravitational waves and confirm Einstein's theory, Gordana Vunjak-Novakovic, to be a pioneer in growing new healthy organs to prolong life, and Wafaa El-Sadr, to manage infectious diseases?

Fewer economists and mathematicians, like Graciela Chichilnisky, to consider options for clean energy and basic human needs?

Fewer philanthropists, like Olga Murray, to save children's lives and eradicate poverty, and Monica Yunus, to create an artists' peace corps?

Fewer women who bring distinctive passion to their chosen fields, like Helena Wong in international business, Jacqueline Murekatete in survivor advocacy, and Argine Safari in youth education and music?

Fewer individuals who bring joy and wonder to our lives, like artists Hung Liu and SoHyun Bae, clothing designer Mi Jong Lee, cultural organizer and entrepreneur Aroon Shivdasani, and fashion designer Han Feng?

Fewer world-renowned authors like Chitra Divakaruni and Isabel Allende, whose writing invites us to share their interpretations of immigrant life and culture in America?

Fewer culinary masters to bring us together with tastes of other worlds, like Einav Gefen and Doris Schechter?

And fewer dedicated women like US Army Major Fabiola Wilson, or Judge Ashley Tabaddor, who upholds the US Constitution in her ongoing fight for immigrant justice?

You'll see common threads emerge as you read through their stories. Two of the strongest factors are that these women had solid educations and nurturing families. Their parents embraced curiosity and exploration. And while they might not have been able to provide material treats—and sometimes even food or adequate clothing—they found a way to ensure that their children had an education as a means to improve their lives.

I believe that the driving force for many of these women is the passion to chase the unlimited. It arises from having an enduring capacity to do more and do better. They have ferocious determination, and they take risks, always looking for a way through, up, and over obstacles placed in their way. Overall, I see it as true grit.

The process of writing has enriched me and the protagonists of this book, with whom I developed friendships after coming to know intimate details of their lives. Some of the women told me that the very exercise of revisiting their stories crystallized a full life's circle. Most of us, they said, never really take the time to reflect because we just go through life in the moment.

One day I invited five of the women to my home to get acquainted. But they insisted that I tell my story first! Immediately I understood how they felt when I interviewed them. I got a clear picture of my life, of where I started, and where I am now.

As an immigrant, I had a vision, a purpose, and a mission to become a doctor, like my father. I'm Israeli, and I went to medical school in Italy. This new culture enriched me, offering a broader understanding of religion and pushing me to become a Roman in Rome, to absorb and embrace new people and new ways of life. But this was a temporary world; I was there to learn, study, and move on.

When I came to the United States, I came to stay. Soon after, I enrolled in a residency program that made me feel secure in the sense that I knew my future was determined. Similar to other immigrants, I struggled to learn the language, and in my case, shifts of forty-eight hours contributed to sleepless nights. At the time, I was the only woman in my residency working with physicians from a range of nationalities and cultures.

Following my pediatrics internship, I decided to enroll in a radiology residency and fellowship. I enjoyed the intellectual aspects of this field and the more accommodating hours. This permitted me to expand my life beyond medicine and hopefully become a devoted mother and wife and care for our aging parents. I pursued additional interests in painting and writing.

In America, I felt integrated but different. Here I was welcomed and empowered to maintain my own "self" among so many other cultures and beliefs. Immigrants could feel comfortable—in their own enclaves and within the larger group of Americans—to express themselves and test their voices. Here one could become a citizen and still feel proud of one's mixed heritage.

I also saw that this country is unique in providing opportunities to give back. I can't imagine being able to do in any other country what I did on Long Island: Manhasset Diagnostics Imaging, a multidisciplinary radiology practice; Pathways Women's Health Center, which provided pro bono educational seminars for women; the Unbeaten Path, a seminar series for teens; or Nassau Physicians Foundation, providing financial support for medical research.

To me, the beauty of the United States always lay in its embrace, that here you could be proud of where you came from. You could be an ambassador and represent your duality—or triality.

When I interviewed acclaimed author Isabel Allende, she helped me understand the way some people internalize their fear of immigrants. She compared the uneasy feeling to anticipating the arrival of an elevator in a crowded lobby.

"You're with a group of people, waiting, waiting. Finally, the elevator comes, the doors open, and you get in," Allende said. "Then you don't want anybody else to get in because you're already quite tight in there."

I understand that unease, that claustrophobic discomfort of being too close to somebody. We worry because we *don't know the people* taking up the space next to us in the elevator. And we are great worriers when it comes to the unknown.

Our fears are exacerbated by a constant thrum of tweets, videos, and text alerts. Headlines bombard us with demands for ICE raids and border walls, pushing us back under the covers of our warm beds at night, safe from people we do not know.

The terrorist attacks since 9/11 naturally have contributed to the feelings of distrust in others. We are told that the unnamed strangers threaten our jobs, our way of life, and our children. I hope my book paints a different and more realistic picture of the majority of individuals who come to the United States and are hardworking, honest people. I believe that we will catch a glimpse of ourselves in each of them.

I hope you develop admiration and empathy for the women in this book as you step into their shoes. And I hope you begin to see how grateful we immigrants are to America for the opportunities we have received—and for the chance to share our own talents and passions.

There is room in the elevator. Just take a few steps in and get to know the person standing next to you. You'll be amazed by what you learn. And you might just see a reflection of yourself looking back.

That is my hope.

ISABEL ALLENDE

CHILEAN-AMERICAN *NEW YORK TIMES* BEST-SELLING AUTHOR
AND ADVOCATE FOR THE RIGHTS OF WOMEN AND GIRLS

"I became a feminist without knowing that I was a feminist because the word was not used in Chile at the time. I was fourteen, fifteen, and I was so angry at the world. I could see the patriarchy everywhere, and I was so rebellious against all kinds of male authority. Everything bothered me."

ON SEPTEMBER 11, 1973, FOLLOWING the military coup in Chile, Isabel Allende and her family found refuge in Venezuela. She was thirty-one, a journalist and a relative of Chilean President Salvador Allende. The overwhelming and overnight change of regime from a democracy to a dictatorship associated with torture, death, and the disappearance of many people instilled in Isabel a distrust in government. The fear of being at the mercy of a power that exerts such cruelty inspired Isabel's imagination.

Isabel is considered one of the greatest Latin American writers today. She has published more than twenty-three books translated into forty-two languages and has sold more than 74 million copies. Her books tell human stories as they focus on the empowerment of women who seek the freedom to make choices. These are women who struggle against extraordinary adversity and win through love and perseverance.

Her recent book, *In the Midst of Winter*, evokes suspense and empathy—and a bit of self-reflection. The protagonist, Evelyn, is the ultimate representative of a struggling young immigrant. And one cannot help but recognize that within Lucia, another character, lives Isabel, a strong, creative, and educated woman who takes charge with love and tenderness and hopes to find love at a mature age.

Isabel's first book, *The House of the Spirits*, which was adapted into a movie in 1994, was written when she was a refugee in Venezuela. She had composed a letter to her dying grandfather in 1981 to eternalize stories he had told her. Unexpectedly, this expanded into a book, written in her style of magical realism that takes after real life with its unexplainable and mysterious occurrences: realizing the significance of a dream, or the symbolism of a vision, and the spirits of our lost loved ones that always live within us.

Since then, Isabel's life has changed. She lives in California and spends the majority of her days telling stories that explore expanded and unlimited universes.

Isabel writes in many styles, including stories that were stimulated by real events, children's books, and memoirs. With her storytelling, she makes connections and highlights the similarities of people from different races and different times, emphasizing the commonalities and feelings we share.

Through her life journey, Isabel has encountered injustice toward women and children, places in the world where baby girls are unwanted and women do most of the work yet own the fewest assets. These experiences contradicted her innate sense of justice and created a feminist out of her, ultimately prompting the creation of the now twenty-year-old Isabel Allende Foundation. The foundation cares for the well-being of women and children and supports the Esperanza Grants that are awarded to nonprofits and NGOs that work to secure access to reproductive rights, opportunities for economic development, and freedom from violence. Isabel is following in the footsteps of her mentor, Olga Murray (see page 213), whom she admires, and she admits, "I want to be her at ninety-two." Olga is the founder of the Nepal Youth Foundation, helping thousands of children survive malnutrition and prosper despite the lack of educational facilities.

The funds for Isabel's altruistic endeavors are provided by the sale of her books, including *Paula*, which she wrote to describe the life of her daughter who passed away at the age of twenty-eight. "It is what Paula wants me to do," Isabel says.

Paula's spirit continues to whisper to Isabel: "You only have what you give, and you give till it hurts."

After a military coup in Chile, you found safety in Venezuela in 1973. In 1987 you decided to immigrate to the United States. How did these different situations affect you?

In the first circumstance, I was a political refugee. I left my country because I couldn't stay, and I chose Venezuela because there were not very many choices. Very few countries accepted refugees from Chile. There were no visas given for Chileans in places like Costa Rica, Mexico, and others. Venezuela was a democracy. I could speak Spanish, and being a journalist, language was important for me. It was open for immigrants and refugees and whoever wanted to come to work.

It was very difficult for me because I didn't want to leave my country, and I was always looking back. The experiences at the beginning were like paralysis and nostalgia, and very different from the experience of an immigrant. The immigrant chooses to go, and usually it's a young person who's looking at the future, not looking at the past, not thinking of returning, but thinking of establishing in another place. After all, we had kids and grandkids. So the emotional state of an immigrant is very different than a refugee. I would say that the experience of being an immigrant is much, much easier than being a refugee.

So in 1989, you immigrated to the United States, following your American husband William Gordon, and became a citizen in 1993. Did you feel comfortable right away?

Well, I came to the United States although I didn't like the country at the time. The CIA had been involved in the military coup in Chile, so I had the feeling that America was one of my enemies really. It so happened that when I was on a book tour, I met a man, I fell in love, and I moved to be with him. That facilitated everything, not only my legal status in the US. I came with a tourist visa, but then we married, so very soon I applied for residency and a work permit.

My husband opened all the doors for me. The problem when you are new in a country, like in Venezuela, for example, and actually everywhere, is that you don't know the rules of that country.

Sometimes you don't even speak the language, and you don't know how to get along and how to do things. For example, after living in Chile and Venezuela, I didn't know that you could pay a bill with a check in the mail. I couldn't believe that. It was just extraordinary, and there were many other things, both good and bad. My husband chaperoned me during the first few years until I learned the language and could have a life of my own.

In America, it was really a tremendous change of culture.

Yes. First of all, the language. Then I landed in the most dysfunctional family that you could possibly imagine. My husband had been married twice before, and he had three children, all of them addicts. So we had the problem of drug addiction, which I had never encountered before. I had no idea what that was. I thought it would be just about a few rules and lots of love. But no, forget it.

His life was very chaotic, disorganized, but I was in love, and I'm Chilean, so I take on projects. Chilean women do that. I thought, *I'll handle this*, but it was much harder than living in Venezuela, as I had to learn the language. At the beginning he had to translate the news on TV. I could read in English, but I couldn't understand when people talked. That took me a while and then it took a while to learn to drive here and know the streets and do the things that normal people do all the time.

When you were in Venezuela, you wrote your first book at the age of forty, The House of the Spirits.

It happened by chance. I didn't think I could be a writer, but I couldn't be a journalist in Venezuela. I did all sorts of odd jobs to make a living and support my kids, and I ended up administering a school. It had nothing to do with writing, but my head was full of stories, the stories I brought from Chile and the extraordinary stories you can pick up in Venezuela, which is a crazy and wonderful place.

I had all this that I wanted to tell, but mostly it was that the book was like an exercise in nostalgia. On January 8, 1981, we got a phone call telling me that my grandfather was dying in Chile. I had grown up in his house. He was a substitute father for me, and I couldn't return to say goodbye. So I started this sort of letter that immediately turned into something else. I kept on writing about it, and I wrote till it became a manuscript of five hundred pages. I worked on the kitchen counter because I didn't even have a desk.

Eventually it landed in the hands of an agent in Spain. I was very lucky because the book was published and became an immediate success, which paved the way for other books and made me a writer. Without that, I would still be working in a school in Venezuela.

Your grandfather brought you up after you were abandoned by your father, and he was a very important, beloved figure in your life. What advice did he give you that resonates through your life?

He taught me all the stuff that has helped me to succeed. Discipline. Don't whine. Don't complain. Don't ask for anything. Be responsible for yourself and for others. Life is hard. Don't expect anything.

Those are pretty tough messages.

It was like an emotional boot camp. Much later in life, I have been in therapy to take all that out of my head because I don't need it anymore, but it was really useful during my youth and during the time when I was a political refugee and an immigrant and I needed all those things. That is what my grandfather taught me. He was severe and tough, but he was a loving man, and I hear his voice inside my head all the time.

What can you tell me about the significance of January 8?

I started my first book, *The House of the Spirits*, on January 8. It turned out to be very successful, so I started the second book on the same day the following year, a little bit because of superstition but also because I was working in a school when it was still vacation, so the kids were not back yet. It was very convenient because it was winter, and I had some time. All my books that I started on that date have been somehow successful, but mostly that date works out of discipline because my life has become very complicated. I am pulled in every direction. I have a foundation; I have too much going on. If I don't have a day to start, I would be procrastinating forever. There's always something that gets in the way. I do believe that things happen, weird coincidences that I cannot explain.

When I was working on this interview, I was very focused reading your book Paula, *which you wrote in memory of your daughter who passed away. At that time, a tall, beautiful black woman came to me and asked, "What are you concentrating so hard on?" I explained, "I'm going to have an interview for a book I'm writing about first-generation American women immigrant achievers." She said, "That's very nice, but I have a suggestion for the next book. You should write about mothers who lost their daughters." And she went on to say that she lost her daughter when her daughter was thirty-five and left three children behind. Kathy, the grandmother, is now taking care of them, as well as of her younger daughter who is chronically ill with cystic fibrosis. This was one of those coincidences (magical realism) in life where, while I was immersed in your story, Kathy appeared. I handed her your book about Paula and wished her the comfort that this book has provided to many mothers.*

Thank you. I don't see ghosts, but I feel the spirit of my daughter inside me all the time.

In your mind, what is magical realism?

I think it's accepting that the world is a mysterious place. Things like coincidences and little miracles happen. You're thinking of someone, and the phone rings and that person calls you—that is telepathy. I grew up with a grandmother who spent her life studying the paranormal. When I was a little girl, it was something I could not deny. I don't live in that realm, but I accept it, just like many people accept astrology or hang crystals on their necks or whatever. Everybody has different ways of coping with what we cannot control and what we don't know.

Please tell me about In the Midst of Winter.

The elements of magical realism are somehow explained between the lines. Because the only one who experiences it is the Guatemalan girl, and she comes from a culture where this is accepted and possible. She has had an experience with *ayahuasca*, the drug of the Amazon, when the shaman gives her that tea. That is the equivalent of a very strong LSD, LSD on steroids. She has a trip in which she sees a jaguar. I've done it twice and I know the experience, and it stays with you. She believes in the Virgin Mary and in the jaguar. For her, it's the same thing. I describe the moment she sees a miracle happen as seen only through her eyes, and this vision is used later in the book to build the story.

How did the story come about for In the Midst of Winter?

A couple of things. This was before President Trump, so people were talking about immigration, but it wasn't like now at all. I was in Brooklyn. We had rented a house for Christmas with my daughter-in-law, my son, some friends, grandchildren, et cetera. We were having breakfast, and they asked, "What are you going to write next?" As I mentioned, I start all my books on January 8. "So what are you going to write in two weeks?" I said I had no idea yet.

Somebody said, "Write about this house." They informed me that this had been a Mafia neighborhood in the past. So the idea that there was a body in one of the cars came to mind. I said, "Wait, if you have a body inside a car, you can write anything." With that, it's like a gift. I started thinking about these things, and on January 7 I sat down with some notes and stumbled upon a quote by Albert

Camus that says, "In the midst of winter, I finally found in me an invincible summer."

Beautiful—and often true for our state of mind.

It was like a light in my head because I realized that mentally I was living that moment in which I was in the midst of winter. I had separated from this man that I had loved a lot. I was seventy-two years old and alone. I wasn't complaining or whining about being alone, but I knew that for the rest of my life I would be alone because at that age you don't expect many surprises, do you? Well, I don't.

I was in that mood. My agent died, my dog died, three of my best friends died. My parents were really, really old and had deteriorated. Everything was flat, and I thought, *I am in the midst of winter but there is always an invincible summer inside, and so that's going to be the theme of the book.* Three people are traumatized, are stuck in a sort of winter, and something happens that forces them out of themselves and opens their heart; they take risks, and then friendship, compassion, and eventually love happens.

I love this book, by the way.

Thank you. The character Lucia, a Chilean journalist, of course has a lot of me, but also a lot of other friends of mine who were also Chilean journalists at the time of the coup. One of them they arrested, and his brother disappeared and never appeared again. I took a lot of the story from that. In the case of Evelyn, the Guatemalan girl, I have a foundation and we work with immigrants and empowering women and girls, many from Guatemala, El Salvador, Honduras, so I have cases like her. I didn't have to invent much, and of course the character Richard the professor is based on my brother, who is just as crazy.

I read your memoir The Sum of Our Days, *and I see intertwined magic and realism in your own life because you mentioned that you work with psychics, you listen to spirits, you believe in astrology, you give meanings to dreams, and you're superstitious about the day you start your books.*

Excuse me, but that's discipline.

OK, discipline and a little superstition? You had a dream about two children that you related to your daughter-in-law Lori's resignation to not have kids of her own and to accept her husband's children as her own.

That's one of the only two or three times that I have had a kind of vision because it was so clear and so long. I don't think it was a minute, but it seemed very long, and it was with the light of the clock. In the green light of the clock, these two kids were standing there, and I didn't move. I wanted so badly to see them better, but I didn't dare move because I thought they would disappear, and they did, of course.

And the symbolism of the centrally melting candle that stayed erect like a symbol of strength after Paula's death?

I have it to this day on my altar. I have kept it twenty-seven years now. Yes, it was a sign. My son, who is totally skeptical, said that this is an interesting coincidence and an opportunity. Because why would it stay burning and erect, right after Paula's death? It was a sign.

What moment was it? Right after her death?

We gathered in my prayer group and we had a candle for each one because we were celebrating the end of the year, and Paula had just died a week before. We were meditating, with our eyes closed, and a friend of mine who is a psychiatrist, said, "Isabel, how can we help you? What do you feel?" And I said, "I feel a burning pain inside. I can't get it out of my body, this pain here, this burning thing." And she said, "What do you want?" And I said, "I want a sign. I want a sign that Paula has not disappeared, that her spirit prevails."

And so we meditated, and then I heard the psychiatrist's voice because she was the first one to open her eyes, and she said, "Look at your candle." And I looked at my candle, and my candle was burning in the middle, like the burning here in the middle of my body. It was concave, but it didn't bend.

We waited to see if it would. It ended very, very fast, enough to make a hole, but the candle was standing, and I took that as a sign that Paula had heard me, and that the pain would be there, but I would bear it, and it would not break me.

Your son, Nico, at one point said that you cannot prevent sadness, but you have to learn how to cope with life.

That would have been my grandfather's idea. I mean, if you talk to my grandfather about post-traumatic stress, he'll say, "What the heck is that? You go through suffering and pain and you just bear it." That was the school that I had. It is a good school.

We all want to find the strength to go on through pain. You, for example, find myth to cope through reality.

I work in my foundation with people who have had real trauma. They are survivors from extreme violence, from war, from gangs, from domestic violence, all kinds of stuff, and then they get back on their feet and some of them become leaders, so it is possible. We have a capacity, we have a strength and resilience inside that we don't know we have until we are tested.

Getting back to In the Midst of Winter, *you describe mature love and what you thought was impossible happened. You've found a new love in your life now.*

Yes, I wasn't expecting anything, but a man, a lawyer in New York, heard me on NPR. I have no idea what I said, but he was impressed, and he emailed my office, and my assistant answered the first email. And then the second one I answered, and then he started emailing me every morning and every evening for five months. And then finally I met him when I went to New York for something to do with the Center for Reproductive Rights. We met, and I asked him immediately, "What are your intentions? Because I do not have any time to waste."

Instead of running away, which is what I would've done if someone had said that, he stayed. He got rid of everything he owned and moved to my house with two bicycles and some clothes. We've been living together for two months, and it's working beautifully.

You're both so lucky.

So lucky, because at our age there's so much baggage, so much stuff, but we have families who approve of us and love the idea that we are together. Everything is easy.

It's about time.

Time that something easy happens in my life, that I don't have to fight for it.

At one point you said: "America loves immigration but does not love immigrants." Do you remember that?

Yes. America was formed by immigration, and we love the idea. It has given this country energy, a youth, a sense of future, and vision, and liberation that few other countries have. But every wave of immigrants that has come to this country has been received with hostility, especially people of color, Chinese, Japanese, Hispanics, and also Italians. The poor were never well received, the poor that came from Ireland, the Polish, the Jews—all those people were treated very badly. It takes a while for each wave of immigrants to assimilate.

I always think of an elevator. One is waiting for the elevator. You're waiting with a group of people; you're waiting, waiting. Finally, it comes, the door opens, you get in, and then you don't want anybody else to get in because it's already quite tight in there. You don't want more people inside the elevator. The same thing happens with immigration. You want to come in, but then you don't want anybody else to come in.

This country is huge; you can have millions of immigrants and still the country would be half empty, and still there will be space for everybody.

Your descriptions of Evelyn in The Midst of Winter, *and Alba in* The House of the Spirits *show that both protagonists underwent torture in their own country and represent what could have happened to you if you stayed in Chile during the military coup of 1973. Those memories are as vivid in your mind as 9/11 in America. America has changed since 2001. You experienced more than once the result of a drastic change due to the exertion of power and its effect on the citizens. What are your thoughts about the present times in the United States?*

When I came to the United States thirty years ago, I told the man I loved at the time, "Willy, potentially this is a very fascist country." He said, "What are you talking about? This is the cradle of democracy." I said, "Well, in New York and California." But think about it. Just like in every country, there are pockets of people who are very conservative, nationalistic, live in fear, uneducated, and if the wrong circumstances happen, or the wrong leader appears, democracy can turn into fascism. It always starts with a minority; you don't need the whole country to establish a regime of fear. It happened in Germany, in Italy, in Argentina, in Chile, and it can happen anywhere.

When you ask me about how I see the country today, I am worried, very worried. I am hoping that the solid institutions of this country will bear the assault that they are suffering right now, but we have to be very vigilant. I find it very dangerous.

Can you share the experiences that prompted you to create your foundation that helps women and children?

After Paula died and I wrote the book about her, I didn't want to touch any income that would come from that book. I wanted to save it to pay homage to her in some way, so it went in a separate account. I didn't know exactly what to do with it, and I was confused and still very sad and depressed, so my husband and a friend decided that I needed to get out of my comfort zone, and they took me to India.

A very poor woman in a rural area tried to give me her baby. She gave me this little package of rags, and I opened it and there was a newborn baby. It must have been born the day before. I can't describe how little it was, dark and with the umbilical cord still raw.

I didn't understand that she was trying to give it to me, so I blessed the baby, kissed the baby, and gave it back. And she wouldn't take it. Then the driver who was with us came running and took the baby, gave it to the mother, and just pushed me in the car. A minute later I reacted and said, "Why would that women give me her baby?" And he said, "It's a girl. Who wants a girl?" And that was the moment when I knew what I was going to do with the money that I had saved.

I created a foundation whose mission is to do for women and girls what I couldn't do for that woman and that baby girl I met in India. The foundation has been going on for around twenty years, and I think it's doing a very good job.

Paula's voice, from what I understand, is always with you, and she would want you to do that. She was a very giving person, and in fact she said: "You only have what you give." That is a very, very strong statement.

Very strong for a very young woman. Paula went into a coma when she was twenty-eight. She was recently married, and she didn't own anything; she didn't want stuff, as if she knew that she was going to die. Her husband always said she knew she was going to die young. I remember I wanted to give her a dishwasher, but she said, "No, I don't want it." I said, "But you have the space; why don't you want a dishwasher? You don't have to wash the dishes." "No, no, I wash the dishes." Nothing! She didn't want clothes; she didn't want anything.

I'm sure she's listening to us right now.
I hope so.

You've seen men abusing women in your own close circle. In fact, you had a good friend, Tabra, who was beaten by her husband.
She finally escaped from him, but then she was involved with other relationships in which she was abused verbally and physically. I couldn't understand why it kept happening to her. She went to therapy for a long time, and she said, "It's because of the people I choose. I choose men who will do that to me. The men that would respect me and take care of me, I am not interested in." And so, from where does that come? It comes from her childhood when she was abused by her mother, when she felt she didn't deserve anything. Who knows, but she was raised in a very strict Christian cult, so there are things that mark people.

Finally she's been alone for many years, but she says that every time she sees her kind of man, the threatening dark guy with tattoos, she runs in the other direction.

It's interesting. There's obviously a lack of self-confidence with women who put up with this kind of situation. On the other hand, you had a president in Chile, Michelle Bachelet, who is incredibly strong. What does she symbolize to you?
What women can achieve, what women can do when they have the means, the power, the education. She is fantastic. She's done a lot for women. When she came to the government the second time, her first statement was, "We will try to eliminate domestic violence in Chile." Domestic violence is a secret that is rampant in Chile, absolutely rampant in the way that men abuse women and how parents abuse children. There's

been a campaign denouncing this, and the police who did not intervene in the past now do so because the rules have changed, thanks to her.

In your foundation, your mission is to help women and children, and you support different organizations that believe in women's rights.

After Trump's election especially, we have tried to focus on certain areas so we can be more effective. The first area is reproductive rights, because if a woman has no control over her body, she can't control anything. We also focus on protection from exploitation, abuse, and violence. The other issue has been immigration.

Women's friendships and support are very important to you.

Yes, because I have had it all my life. I have a mother that has been unconditionally loving and present. To this day—she's ninety-seven years old—she writes to me every day, and I write back to her every single day. By the end of the year I put her letters in a plastic box, and I have a room where the boxes pile up by year. Every box has between six hundred and eight hundred letters, so can you imagine that the archive of this thing is her whole life, and my life.

I have worked as a feminist with women and for women all my life. Therefore, I've been accused of making the protagonists in my books very strong women. It comes naturally to me, because there are no weak women in my own life.

I think strong women are attracted to others like them. While I was reading your biography, I learned that you have loyal friends such as the "Sisters of Disorder," and Pia and her prayers.

Those are my companions. My prayer group is made up of six women who have been meeting for more than thirty-five years. I have been in the group for thirty years. We know everything about each other. When Paula died, and they invited me to the group, they held me, and they gave me a safe place where I could really cry, a place where we share our lives and our losses. At one point one of my friends lost her son; her son died in her arms. She's Japanese, and her reaction was very different from mine, but it was such a lesson for me. She believes in the spirit so strongly that she was never sad. Her son was very ill; he was in another dimension, and she's sure that he's a spirit. So, unlike me, who has doubts and misses the presence of my daughter, she does not miss the presence of her son because she's convinced that his spirit exists with her.

My friend Pia is my oldest friend. I see her every time we go to Chile. We write to each other. We could not be more different, and as we age, we become more and more different, and we love each other more. Tabra is now living in Bali and in Costa Rica, and I see very little of her, but we write to each other.

But at one point you ran away to be with her, and at one point she ran away to be with you to find comfort and support.

Yes, well, we helped each other at that stage a lot.

Your loyalty to your friends is remarkable. And of course, you've had specific circumstances in your life where you needed it.

As an immigrant, I don't have an extended family here. My family is very small: it's my son, three grandchildren, and my daughter-in-law. That's my family. I need more, I need way more, so I tend to bring people into the circle of the family, very close friends who stay there. For example, my former assistant, Juliette, and her sons—they are my children. They grew up with my children, and I've seen them since they were two years old. So, of course, they are very close, and so is Juliette. She's living in LA now.

The way you adopted Juliette and her children represents your passion to take care of others with tenderness and love. Besides your grandfather, who are the most important people in your life whose advice you follow? I assume your mother is one.

No, my mother had a very difficult life in many ways. I became a feminist without knowing that I was a feminist because the word was not used in Chile at the time. I was fourteen, fifteen, and I was so angry at the world. I could see the patriarchy everywhere, and I was so rebellious against all kinds of male authority. Everything bothered me. My mother didn't know what the heck was wrong with me.

It took years for me to realize that I was a feminist since I was very young, and I embraced it. I started working on a feminist magazine, and there I started reading feminist books. This anger became articulated in language, in action, in journalism. My mother never approved of that because my mother is a lady, and she was always scared. She was afraid that I would get a lot of aggression, a lot of gossiping, and she cared about what people would say. I told my mom, "So what? That's the price I have to pay. It's a very cheap price; I have no problem with it."

But for my mother, appearance is very important, so you have to do whatever you want but do it nicely. I said the whole point is not to do it nice. Make a fuss, make a fuss. Of course, I didn't follow her advice, but now that she's ninety-seven, I follow her advice in certain things because I understand that her instinct is right.

For example, when I met Roger, my new love, I told her about him and that we had been writing to each other for five months. I sent her a picture, and my mother said, "This is a good man." I went with him to Chile so she could meet him, and she said, "You marry him." I said, "Mom, I've been married twice; I have two divorces. Why would I marry again? That would be crazy." She said, "You should marry him before I die because I want to know that he will be with you forever."

I said, "He will be with me forever if he wants to, and he will not be with me forever, even if we are married, if he doesn't want to."

So, I don't follow exactly her advice, but she's close. I see examples that I want to follow in women around me that are extraordinary, and I can give you a list. But the hero that I can think of immediately is a woman called Olga Murray (see page 213). This woman created the Nepal Youth Foundation, and you should see what she does at ninety-two. I want to be her at ninety-two.

She has all her marbles, and she does a lot for others.
Oh Lord, the strength and the tenderness, and the goodness! She's a big mother to thousands of kids.

I think you are following in her footsteps very closely.
Oh, no.

Let's talk about your relationship with your son.
It's an extraordinary relationship; it always has been. But since Paula

died, we have been really close. We live close by and now he works with me since my divorce from Willy. Nico's in charge of everything—the contracts, the money, the taxes, the management of the office, the hiring and firing people, everything.

I don't have to worry about anything because he's there, and the beautiful thing is that his wife, Lori, is my buddy. She and I, we are accomplices; we travel together, we do all the book tours together, and she manages my foundation completely. I don't even ask. She decides. We see each other every single day because we are all here together.

You discovered Lori with your matchmaking for Nico.

Oh, I lucked out twice in my life—with *The House of the Spirits* and with Lori.

You've been the recipient of many awards. In 2006 you represented South America in the Olympics, and in 2014 you received the Medal of Freedom from President Barack Obama, which is the highest civilian honor in the US. It appears that both your birth country and your adoptive country claim you as their own. What do you think were the most important moments in your life?

I've always said that carrying the flag at the Olympics were the four most important minutes of my life. But that is not true. The most important ones in my life are when I gave birth. When I had the newborn baby in my arms, I cannot tell you what I felt. I felt that my life had changed forever, that I would never be the same person again, and I never was. After the kids were born, every decision I made and make in life is made thinking about them. Where are they, where will they be. I cannot be in a place where they are not.

I feel the same way. I have two girls and four grandchildren. They're seven, five, four, and one and a half. I love them so much.

Oh, wow. Enjoy them. Wait until they reach the teenage years.

Tell me more about the Olympics experience.

It was just a joke. I was representing South America, and we were eight women carrying the flag. But it was the same week when a Danish illustrator made an illustration of Muhammad or something, and there was this horrible outrage against the Danes. Therefore, there was high security in the Olympics, and the Italians hired German security, who were these guys all dressed in black leather! Very scary. Part of the security was that you have to get to the stadium very early, eight hours before the event. We were locked in the green room in the stadium, so I spent eight hours with Sophia Loren and the athletes. It was quite an experience. They gave us a uniform; they had emailed me before and asked for my measurements. Oh Lord, what a humiliating experience! Everything was too big, so they had pins to hold the skirt, and whatever. They had to fill the boots with newspaper because everything was meant for Sophia Loren, not me, but she was the only one who had high heels, and she's very tall, plus the hair.

All the rest of our boots did not have high heels, so I appeared in all the photographs, carrying the flag between Sophia Loren's legs. There was the flag, and there's Susan Sarandon, and all you can see is my feet because that's all that was seen of me. But of course, my son and my daughter were there, and they said that I was beaming, that I was so happy.

What was your feeling when President Obama awarded you with the Medal of Freedom? After all, you were an immigrant in the United States, and now you were getting the nation's highest civilian honor.

I think that at that point, it was a statement because I was an immigrant. I was a Latina immigrant, and there was all this noise against Latina immigrants, so probably that was part of the choice.

You're very modest. I don't think so. You're one of the most important writers today, and you're talking about issues that are so humane in your books. So that award was well deserved. Do you feel gratitude toward the United States?

Yes! Yes, yes. I feel gratitude; this is my country also. I have a foot in Chile, and a foot here. I have participated in everything, in politics, in the foundation; I have friends, I have a home, my grandchildren are Americans. Of course, I feel great gratitude as most first-generation immigrants feel, because even if it's very hard to adapt and to make it, your children make it.

When I see Nico and the grandchildren, I realize that they have a life here that they would not have in Venezuela, and probably not in

Chile either. At the time that I immigrated to the USA in the 1990s, I could've returned to Chile, but my kids would not come with me. They were grown up, and they had their own lives. So I did not go back either, even though by that time, Chile was a democracy again.

Do you think that we are "in the midst of winter presently with an invincible summer" in the United States? In other words, do you think things are going to get better?

Yes. They will get very, very dark first, and then eventually we will overcome it. Governments pass, countries and people stay—that was my experience in Chile. Seventeen years of the dark brutal dictatorship, and then we had an even stronger democracy because we learned a lesson.

Thank you for this encouraging statement.

Isabel Allende is the recipient of dozens of awards, including these most recent: National Book Award Honorary Medal for Distinguished Contribution to American Letters (2018); *The Times* (London) names *The House of the Spirits* one of the Best 60 Books in the Past 60 Years (UK, 2009); Lawrence Sanders Award in Fiction, Florida International University (USA, 2012); Carl Sandburg Literary Award (USA, 2013); Latino Book Award for *Maya's Notebook* (USA, 2014); Gabriela Mistral Foundation Humanitarian Award (USA, 2014); PEN Center Lifetime Achievement Award (USA, 2016); California Hall of Fame Inductee (USA, 2016); CA Latino Legislative Caucus, Latino Spirit Award, Achievement in Literature (USA, 2017); Premio Sicily (Italy, 2017).

Isabel Allende and Aretha Franklin at Harvard

Postscript: Since this interview was conducted, Isabel Allende lost both her mother and father-in law. Her ex-husband also passed away. Happily, she married her companion, Roger Cukras, in July 2019.

SOHYUN BAE

KOREAN-AMERICAN ARTIST

"The challenge for me as an artist is to walk the narrow path toward recognition without sacrificing hunger. Complacency equals death."

SOHYUN BAE WAS SEVEN YEARS OLD when her father was wheeled to the hospital, his skull bleeding from a riot at Donga head-quarters in South Korea. The mass-media giant was under tremendous pressure from dictator Park Chung-hee to censor the news. SoHyun's father, a Donga newspaper editor and radio producer, had received a phone call in the middle of the night and rushed out to try to ease tensions between the journalists and the company owner.

Soon after he recovered, the family sought haven from the political unrest and moved in with relatives in America. SoHyun rapidly acclimated to her new life. But her parents, well-respected members of the Korean society, struggled to make ends meet, becoming low-income merchants subject to bullying by Americans and Koreans alike. SoHyun picked up English quickly and became her parents' translator and mediator. She helped them navigate their American lives, painfully understanding the slurs that were directed at her highly educated and refined parents. She had to determine whether to translate each slight or not. Often she kept silent.

As a child immigrant, art was the language with which she communicated and made friends. SoHyun earned a full scholarship to the Rhode Island School of Design (RISD) where she received a Bachelor of Fine Arts. From there, she earned her Master of Fine Arts at Boston University, where she found inspiration from her mentors: internationally renowned British painter John Walker and Nobel Laureate, Holocaust survivor, and international ambassador of peace, Elie Wiesel. She completed her second master's degree, in Theological Studies, at Harvard Divinity School.

It was a spring morning in New York's West Chelsea when SoHyun, now forty-nine, attractive with long, wavy brown hair and dressed casually in blue jeans and a white t-shirt, gave me a tour of her studio. "It is like opening a gift box," she whispered as she opened the door. "The painting that I left last night will be a surprise in the morning." SoHyun's studio is airy, with large windows flooding light onto her stacked canvases. "Those who know me best know me through my work," SoHyun explained.

Our journey transformed into a conversation about how SoHyun has conveyed her deepest thoughts through her brush strokes in her paintings. She is one of the most prolific and respected Korean-American artists of her generation, bridging East and West through her experiences and giving presence to women of the past, present, and future.

America formed SoHyun and gave her a home, but South Korea's memories and stories stayed with her long after she left, and ultimately gave SoHyun her art.

This painting looks unfinished.

It may look unfinished at first glance, but if you take your time, you will see that it is finished. The painter has to recognize when to lift her hand. This comes with experience. This painting is complete.

When did you start painting?

It isn't so much that I started to paint; I never stopped painting. All kids draw and paint, and then they stop, but I simply continued.

I'm staring at this magnificent work of a woman's head. She is serene, and her gaze is downward.

I painted this series in 1997–1998. It's titled *An Ode to the Women of the Josun Dynasty*. This one is part of the *Colossal Head* series. The Joseon Dynasty refers to nearly five centuries of Korean history where Neo-Confucian philosophy and customs prevailed. They are my mother, my grandmother, and many generations of my family way back who paved the way, ordinary/extraordinary women who were never depicted in art.

What inspired the Colossal Head *series?*

When I spent the year abroad in Rome as an art student, I came across a painting by Piero della Francesca called *Madonna del Parto*. I was impressed by the repetition of sacred circular spaces. The pregnant Madonna stood inside of a round tent with curtains parted by angels with matching wings and socks. The painting itself was placed in a round architectural space. The pregnant Madonna's dress reminded me of the round bulge of the Korean traditional dress called *Chima Jeoguri*. I imagined the round traditional dress to be a vessel. Then I started to fill it metaphorically with such things as "dead leaves rustling about" (an expression used by Professor Elie Wiesel) and blood and fertile soil. I began to dig and dig and discovered heads inside of the dress.

This specific painting called Colossal Head I, *which you're telling me you're not selling, is very dear to you. It appears to convey the characteristics of Korean women of this time. Her eyes are downcast; it talks of humility, suffering, and strengths.*

As you can see, the surfaces of the colossal heads are reminiscent of early Korean pottery. I love the Korean ceramic tradition. By the way, this head I made in one day. My hands were bleeding because I didn't use a brush. I really believe I was in a kind of shamanistic frenzy. At that time, I was crazy about *Pansori*, which is a Korean epic-telling. It is a guttural opera with shamanistic roots. A lot of women sing *Pansori*. As part of their training, they go to the waterfall and compete with the sound of the waterfall. They create these guttural sounds to a point where their throats start to bleed, like ballerinas and their toes. It is really better than rap. It has a strong percussion element.

That is a beautiful image of a colossal head enclosed in a lotus flower with falling leaves.

This one is long gone. It is the only one of the *Colossal Heads* that has a proper name. She is *Shim-Chung*. Back in Korea, we grew up listening to a Neo-Confucian tale about a beautiful, courageous girl who offers herself as a sacrifice to the river god in order to ensure the livelihood of her blind father. As she drowns, the river god sees how beautiful she is and decides to make her his wife. She is happy with him but longs to see her blind father, so he sends her back up encased in a lotus flower. This is the moment of her rise.

The other one that you have here is called Little Sister.

It is a continuation of the *Colossal Head* series but made in Italy. I noticed that Italian women are no different than Asian women when it comes to societal pressures. I depicted a head of a woman wearing her hair in a *binyeo* (chignon). In the Joseon era, the way in which a woman wore her hair signified her social status. Here, with her hair made up like this, she was a proper married woman. The term *Little Sister* comes from a verse in the Song of Solomon.

Your work has won numerous awards, has been exhibited in multiple museums, and is a part of highly respected collections. How do you deal with recognition, as well as the downtime when it is not there?

Recognition fosters the growth of an artist. Naturally, being recognized encourages us in more ways than one. I've had plenty of recognition thus far. When I say recognition, I don't mean fame and fortune as the world seeks. I read Ecclesiastes as a child and learned very early of its futility. The recognition I seek is far greater than that. At a certain point, however, recognition can stunt the growth of an artist. That is why the early works of artists are so compelling. They are full of hunger and whatever else it was that originally drove them.

So what is your challenge?

The challenge for me as an artist is to walk the narrow path toward recognition without sacrificing hunger. Complacency equals death.

Tell me about your immigrant experience.

My parents went from being in the upper echelon of Korean society in Seoul to being immigrants. At that time in the '70s, Korean immigrants of downtown Cleveland took over stores run by the Jews who catered to the African-American community. They felt completely disoriented because America was not the America they imagined. My parents worked like dogs just to put food on the table for us. There is nothing like seeing your parents suffer . . . for a child.

I see tears in your eyes. Those are painful memories.

(Silence)

I have many sweet memories from my childhood in Seoul. I think of my nanny, Yogo Unnie, who raised me. My mom was busy going here, going there, taking lessons in flower arrangement, learning calligraphy, and teaching at the university. Yogo Unnie was always home. I am told that she loved me like her own. She wasn't always treated well by my Tiger Auntie, who once kicked her out of the house.

She was forced to leave but couldn't. She would linger by the house, unable to leave me crying.

Life was beautiful. I was surrounded by all forms of art, as my parents loved being around artists and writers, one of whom was Pak Tu-Jin Sunsangnim, the poet laureate of Korea. My father told me that he was often imprisoned for the political content of his poetry. He had kids to feed and never enough money. Once his wife told me that she used to put a smaller rice bowl upside down into her rice bowl before filling it up so that the kids would think that she, too, had a full portion. Since then, I never equated class with money.

So here in America, you experienced the difficulties of a first-generation immigrant through your parents?

Yes. I do not remember direct discrimination against me from my peers. Although kids can be cruel, I made friends easily. On the other hand, my parents were taken advantage of left and right.

When you went to school in Cleveland, you were eight years old, and you were an immigrant. Didn't you have difficulty adjusting, making friends?

You know, I learned the language very quickly. I taught myself English. I remember reading a children's book all by myself and feeling good about it. Then I read another, and another until I couldn't count how many I had read.

In school, I had a tiny Korean-to-English/English-to-Korean dictionary. This fascinated all my classmates. They wanted me to look up bad words in Korean. (She smiles.)

Since my English was poor, the way I made friends was through drawing. They could see that I drew very well, and they accepted me, even admired me. The teacher, too, gave me special privileges. She allowed me, and no one else, to draw on a hot pan with oil sticks. She would put a sheet of paper on top of a heated pan so that when I drew with the oil stick, it would bleed and create this incredible effect.

Then a very significant thing happened. Without my knowledge, my teacher submitted one of my drawings to an art competition. The class was asked to make drawings of musical instruments. I decided to make a collage, which had never been done before in class. I just kind of pieced things together and made a harp. It was accepted into the competition and won first prize. The competition was co-sponsored by the Cleveland Orchestra and the Cleveland Museum of Art, two very well-respected institutions. It was a big deal to be a part of this competition and to win the prize. We were invited to a concert by the Cleveland Orchestra at Severance Hall. They projected my artwork onto a large screen during intermission. You can imagine how proud my parents were. After that, there were many other awards that I won, all which helped me get through school without burdening my parents financially.

Where did you go to college?

I was accepted to the Rhode Island School of Design (RISD) with a full scholarship. I couldn't believe it! I had a full ride, to the amazement of my parents, who were so proud.

Did you have a good experience at RISD, and how did it contribute to your artistic success later?

Since it is based on Bauhaus principles, we learned to understand the harmony between functionality and the beauty of things. The philosophy is that the idea comes before the form. Then everything else is a means to that idea. It was a great foundation.

After completing my freshman year of RISD, I went to Seoul for the summer to improve my Korean at Yonsei University. I lived with the poet laureate, Pak Tu-Jin, whom I mentioned before, and his wife. They were good family friends whom my parents greatly admired. I was trying to be well-behaved and to adhere to the proper ways of a Korean girl. I sat with my legs fully bent while listening to him speak. Pretty soon, I started to feel pins and needles, so I shifted my weight to one side, then to the other, subtly but over and over, when the dear man said to me, "Feel free to stretch your legs out and just relax." With that comment, he made me feel so at home.

He showed me how to love river stones. He had a beautiful collection of them for which he had cedar bases made. He would rub oil onto their surfaces in order to enhance their natural colors. Some resembled body forms, while others had nature's drawings on the surfaces. To me, they were nature's sculptures and very much alive. He also used to play the *piri* (Korean flute) for me in the moonlight. He made several sheets of calligraphy especially for me and gave them to me as gifts.

The last year of RISD I spent in Italy. I was accepted into the European Honors Program in Rome. There I saw so many masterpieces. My only obligation was to roam Rome and to sketch. One particular sketchbook, which I filled with my best drawings, was stolen at the opening of our candlelight exhibition in a cantina. I usually write and draw in my sketchbooks, but I had filled this one only with drawings, my very best! I put so much heart into this sketchbook.

Why did you choose Boston University for your Master of Fine Arts?

I wanted to study with John Walker. He is one of the best painters of his generation. He also has a huge heart. While studying painting with him, I met Elie Wiesel. Who would've ever guessed? I hit the jackpot at Boston University!

Tell me about Elie Wiesel.

Well, while working on a Master of Fine Arts, I had to fulfill a liberal arts requirement. I found a class that interested me: Franz Kafka taught by Elie Wiesel. I thought to myself, *Elie Wiesel . . . Elie Wiesel, that name sounds familiar.* Then it hit me! He was one of the authors I read in a course I took at RISD called the Jewish Narrative. I tried to sign up for this course, but the class was full. However, his secretary found out that I was an art student and told me that Professor Wiesel loved artists and that I should come anyway just in case someone dropped out. And sure enough, someone did. So there was an empty seat for me in the small seminar.

Up until then, I was hungry for something, but I didn't know for what. Many of my friends from RISD were rushing to New York to become artists, but I knew I wouldn't find what I was looking for in New York. In walked a small, frail man with wiry hair. He spoke so softly that I had to strain to hear, but the moment I heard him speak, I knew that I was at the right place at the right time.

He made it a point to meet with every single one of his students, one on one. When it was my turn, I walked to his office and introduced myself. "Professor Wiesel, I sit on the left-hand side of the room." He responded, "I know who you are, SoHyun. You are a very good writer."

I was stunned. I always thought that the teaching assistants read our reflections, but apparently, he read them too.

He asked me why I paint, and I asked him why he writes. We spoke heart to heart about art. He then asked me if he could come to my studio to see my work, and I was shocked! At that time, he was flying all over the world as a political activist, and I wasn't about to remind him of our studio visit. Again, to my amazement, his secretary came up to me on the second-to-the-last day of class and said, "Professor Wiesel would like to know when it would be convenient for you to have him visit your studio."

I didn't tell him, but I had painted a scene from his book, *Night*. The scene was based on the execution of the three who were found guilty for stealing bread. They were to be hanged. Two died instantly, but the third struggled because he was just a boy and the lightness of his weight got in the way. I happened to be teaching figure drawing to undergraduates and telling one after the other not to cut off the feet because the figure will simply fall off the page. Many students who didn't yet understand proportions couldn't place the figure correctly on the page. After repeating it several times, it hit me that I should do that myself. Unfortunately, the painting was torn apart in the group critique. But when Professor Wiesel came to my studio, he stood for a long time in front of that painting and said to me, "There is something in this one. There is something about this little boy with the old man's face." That's all I needed to hear. I felt that he saw me. He was the first person to see who I was through my work.

From then on, Professor Wiesel was a constant support. He was the one who encouraged me to study, and he introduced me to Jewish mystical thought. This is why I ended up at the Harvard Divinity School. It was not my original plan. Of course, I always wanted to read and to learn, but I didn't expect to be enrolled in such a rigorous program. In fact, I completely underestimated the program. I thought that basically I was going to continue to paint and read a few books on the side. Little did I know, we were assigned one thousand pages a week!

How have your studies in Jewish mystical thought influenced your work?
Like anything I suppose . . . through a distillation process. First of

all, Professor Wiesel, being who he was as a human being, transformed my life. He introduced me to Jewish mystical thought through the tales of Rabbi Nachman with "The Princess in Exile." Of course I studied the scholarly texts. What drew me the most was the Lurianic Myth of Creation and the image of *tzimtzum*—the Mystery of the Breaking of the Vessels. The Jewish mystics believed that there was a cataclysmic shattering of the vessels whereupon the Divine Presence of God, sometimes called the Female Presence of God, was shunned into exile. As long as the Godhead remains separated, there will be suffering on this earth. It is up to every individual to reconstruct the vessels. This could be interpreted on so many levels. Regardless, I chose to leave the shards as they were because they better reflect our world. That's how I began a series of paintings called *The Wrapped Shards*.

Why are the shards wrapped?

The painted shards are poetically "wrapped," referring to the practice of common women of the Joseon Dynasty who gathered up bits and pieces of existing cloths to create patchworks (*bojagi*) large enough to wrap gifts or to cover individual lacquer dinner tables. The idea of "wrapping," in this sense, introduced a feminine quality, specifically Korean, to the Jewish vision of the shattered world.

Particularly in *Wrapped Shards: The Egg Woman II*, I attempted to portray the strength in vulnerability which I recognize to be a true human strength. When I was a child back in Korea, the *gaeran-ajumma* used to come to our home every week to deliver eggs. She was tiny, old, and frail and yet carried an enormous basket on her head. Somehow she came to symbolize the plight of women, of mankind, as we attempt to walk life's balancing act with somewhat of dignity.

Can you show me this painting?

It is in the Permanent Collection at the Asian Art Museum of San Francisco.

Can you tell me about your time living in Italy?

I fell in love with an Italian geologist. His name is Leonardo Gherardi from Bologna. After getting married here in New York City and having our first child, Jacopo Inseok, we decided to live in Italy. That was in 2003.

When I arrived in Bologna, the first thing I noticed was that all of the colors I had associated with Giorgio Morandi were simply the colors of Bologna. He, like most of us artists, had simply painted the colors around him. I was mesmerized by the austere elegance of this medieval city rich in Italian history. I was proud to know that I could call such a place home. I biked everywhere with our baby. We went to Piazza Maggiore to see the bas-relief sculptures of Jacopo della Quercia in the center portal of San Petronio or to San Domenico to admire the candlestick made by the young Michelangelo Buonarroti. I lifted my son up onto the lip of *Fontana del Nettuno* and pointed out the *sirene* and the *putti* to him. We visited just about every church and museum in the city and walked endlessly down the *stradine* lined with the *portici*. Often I walked staring at the ground as I found *pavimento veneziano* as beautiful as any fresco. I was busy looking up, down, and all around. I savored the sheer beauty of Italy, the breathtaking landscape in the hills of Bologna, especially in the spring, colored with blossoms of every hue, and I learned how to cook *tagliatelle al'ragu, i tortellini in brood,* and *le lasagne—la cucina Bolognese* from my Italian family and friends. Within six months, I was pregnant with our second son, Michelangelo Jiseok Gherardi.

On the other hand, life in Bologna would prove to be a struggle. I had been exiled for the second time. I often found myself in situations that I could only call . . . twilight. In Jewish mysticism, twilight is described as the moment in which it is hard to distinguish between a dog and a wolf. I, myself, could not distinguish between a dog, a she-wolf, and a Korean tiger.

It is difficult to define the absurd but easy to recognize it. I began my *Folly* series. I painted the *Five Foolish Virgins, Amphigory, Assumption* and *Due Palle.* I painted *Romulus and Remus* suckling the she-wolf now transformed into a female Korean tiger. I also painted my *Bow* series, where my *Women of Josun Dynasty* bow through a labyrinth.

I also painted *Agatha I* and *Agatha II.* I heard about the legend of a beautiful young maiden from Catania, Sicily, who was sent to a brothel by the rebutted town official, then to prison where he ordered to have her breasts cut off. She eventually earns her sainthood and in our modern world becomes the Patron Saint of Women with Breast Cancer. I decided to take "Saint" off of her name and call her simply Agatha, the girl that she was. I painted *Solitude, Quietude, Beatitude* in search of dignity as a woman, as a human being.

Why did you choose to come back to New York?

I never felt so American as I did while living in Italy. And I missed New York like crazy. I missed the diversity, the freedom, and the opportunities.

Art is the greatest communicator.

Yes, art is about building bridges. It is about finding common ground and bringing people together. And I believe in Elie Wiesel's notion of redemption—friendship. It sounds elementary, something we learn as children playing in the sandbox. But it's really true, because it is only when we consider someone a friend that we're willing to look beyond our differences or give him or her the benefit of the doubt. This really is redemption. Organized religion to me, in many ways, misses the whole point. It underestimates God's sense of humor and creativity.

A Woman of Josun Dynasty Colossal Head III Shim Chung

SoHyun Bae is an American painter living and working in New York. She is the recipient of numerous awards including the John Simon Guggenheim Memorial Foundation Fellowship in Fine Arts, 2007; The New York Foundation for the Arts Fellowship, 2002; The Pollock-Krasner Foundation, Inc. Grant, 2000; and The National Endowment for the Arts Fellowship, 1996. She has been a resident artist at: Montalvo Art Center, 2019; The Corporation of Yaddo, 2000; Virginia Center for Creative Arts, 1996; and Skowhegan School of Painting and Sculpture, 1993, among others. SoHyun Bae received a Bachelor of Fine Arts from the Rhode Island School of Design, 1990; a Master of Fine Arts from Boston University, 1994; and a Master of Theological Studies from Harvard Divinity School in 1997, having studied with the Nobel Laureate, Elie Wiesel. Her works have been exhibited worldwide in galleries and museums including the Asian Art Museum of San Francisco, Peabody Museum of Archaeology and Ethnology at Harvard University, Seoul Arts Center Hangaram Museum, Museo Nacional de Artes Visuales in Montevideo, Queens Museum, Sotheby's New York, and Phillips, de Pury & Luxembourg. She collaborated with Martha Graham Dance Company in 2018 as a guest artist for Graham + Google, drawing dancers in 3-D using Google technology. In 2019 she was invited as a guest artist in the first of the studio series *GrahamDeconstructed: Steps in the Street with SoHyun Bae.*

GRACIELA CHICHILNISKY

ARGENTINIAN-AMERICAN SCHOLAR
AND CLIMATE CHANGE INFLUENCER

"The only genuine source of happiness in life is the feeling of being useful to others."

I'M LUCKY I ARRIVED a little early for my interview with Graciela Chichilnisky. I spent a lot of time wandering past the front door, never thinking the unassuming entrance could belong to such an illustrious woman. When I finally rang the bell and walked in, I was surprised by the elegance.

And then came Graciela, who in my mind was a larger-than-life figure with scientific and academic achievements and the honor of being part of a Nobel Prize-winning team. I was enchanted even more when this lovely person revealed that she was dressed so very casually because she had had a sleepless night, taking care of her six-month-old son at a time of life when most women have long retired.

Graciela, a professor of Economics and Mathematical Statistics at Columbia University and the CEO and co-founder of the company Global Thermostat, rarely followed the typical path, even from a very early age. From her high school in Argentina to the lecture halls of top schools in the United States, Graciela learned the hard way that it is lonely at the top. But neither the fear of alienation nor the gender discrimination she continues to fight has deterred her from her goal.

In 1976, after a military coup in Argentina, Graciela immigrated to the United States. She was seventeen, a high school student, and a single mom, who, through an American professor's help, found herself at MIT. Always a sharp and hardworking student, Graciela studied mathematics because, she says, it is the language used by the brain to communicate with itself. She moved to sociology and economics with a goal of helping the world. Over the next few years, she earned two doctorates from UC Berkeley: one in mathematics and one in economics.

The wide divide she saw between the developing and developed countries awakened her global consciousness. Graciela was driven by her philosophy: "Justice is not a choice; it is a moral imperative that is critical for survival." While at UC Berkeley, Graciela and her team formulated what is known as the Bariloche Model to alleviate poverty and use the earth's resources wisely. The model introduced the radical concept of Basic Needs for developing countries and defined the minimal resources needed for long-term well-being. In 1992, more than 150 countries adopted the concept of Basic Needs in the UN Earth Summit of Rio de Janeiro as a cornerstone effort to define sustainable development.

Graciela is an innovator in mathematics economic theory and policy regarding climate change. In 1997 she introduced tradable markets for CO_2, which became international law as a key part of the United Nations Kyoto Protocol in 2005. Graciela was a US Lead Author of the Intergovernmental Panel on Climate Change (IPCC), which won the Nobel Peace Prize in 2007 along with Al Gore. Graciela has produced 360 publications, 14 books, and 120 seminars. She's worked as a director for research with the United Nations Institute for Training and Research in New York, OPEC, THE IMF, and the World Bank. Today, Graciela's company, Global Thermostat, purifies the air of carbon dioxide at low cost and uses the extracted CO_2 commercially.

Graciela did not reach where she is by playing it safe. Several times in our interview, she referred to her ongoing battle with Columbia University over gender pay disparity, which began in the 1980s. She raised the question of equal pay long before the issue gathered momentum.

Graciela's persistence has paid off, but she's still questioning what it means to win.

"The only genuine source of happiness in life is the feeling of being useful to others," she says. Graciela has been recognized by the American Association of University Women, which reaches about 170,000 women in the country and uses her example as a landmark case of victory for gender equality. She was selected in 2016 as the CEO of the Year in Silicon Valley, and she was chosen by the Carnegie Foundation of New York as a "Great Immigrant and Great American" in 2017.

I got a sample of her honest and intelligent mind as she sat down to candidly talk about her journey to America, her economic model to erase poverty, her stamp on the Kyoto Protocol, and raising a baby at this stage in her life.

———•◦•———

You said, "Justice is not a choice; it is a moral imperative that is critical for survival." Is your belief in moral justice based on your experiences growing up in Argentina? What was your life like there?

I was born in Buenos Aires, to Jewish Russian immigrant parents at the end of World War II. My father was Salomon Chichilnisky, who was an extremely intelligent man, a neurologist MD. He was the first

Jewish professor at the University of Buenos Aires. Later, he became a minister of public health for the government of Perón, and he was also the doctor for First Lady Eva Perón. He built dozens of hospitals all over the country and even developed the public health system in Argentina. He did what President Obama did in the US. It was very, very hard because the anti-Semitism sentiment at that time was brutal. My parents had escaped Russia because of the pogroms and the anti-Semitism, and they fell into a country that was full of Nazis. So I was really growing up aware of anti-Semitism and the discrimination against Jews. That's where my quest for moral justice began.

My mother, Raquel Gavensky, was very beautiful, kind, and intelligent, and came from a wealthy fur-exporting family. My father and mother eloped and had three children. I was the middle child.

I remember that there was discrimination against Jews everywhere. I attended Instituto Nacional de Lenguas Vivas, which was an all-girls school. I was the top student, but that was never enough. I was treated differently in school. I remember that I was selected to raise the morning's flag in school, but the schoolmistress found an excuse to have someone else do it. Once she said there was a small spot on my white uniform, and when my mother rushed to get me a new one, she found another excuse and said that a button was missing. In that confusion, I wasn't able to make it to the morning ceremony. Everyone thought I had done something wrong for which I wasn't allowed to raise the flag. That's where I learned what it meant to blame the victim.

I was always passionate about sociology and studying social organization. But I chose mathematics because it seemed easier to me. I intended on going back to social issues later on. I wanted to solve the issues of society through mathematics. By the time I was in high school, I had given birth to Eduardo José. My babe, I call him Gordito, which means "little fat one," was indeed pretty chubby and cute. Gordito is now the Chair Professor of Neurobiology and Experimental Physics at Stanford University. Two days ago somebody said to me, "You know, there is a famous institute at Stanford University on Neurobiology. And a professor there has your name." I said, "Yeah, he's my son."

Your studies were interrupted in Argentina as a result of a military coup in

1966, known as the Night of the Long Baton. How did you proceed with your education?

I was finishing high school at the time. There was a coup d'état and the military closed down the university of Buenos Aires. There were a few American professors from MIT in Buenos Aires, one of whom, Professor Warren Ambrose, was hurt in the Night of the Long Baton. He complained through diplomatic channels about an American citizen being beaten up by the police in Argentina, and he decided to leave. But before he went, he picked his six best PhD students to study at MIT. I was one of those students.

I was not a PhD student. In fact, I was not even a college student. I had not even finished high school, but I was already taking college courses. Professor Ambrose proposed that I join the other students. I thought to myself that there was nothing to lose, because at the time there was nothing to do in Argentina. The universities were closed; the libraries were shut. So I took my year-and-a-half-old baby with me and went to MIT.

How did you adjust as a young immigrant student and a single mother to a new life in America? Did you feel secure?

I wasn't a college student then. I was nothing. I was admitted as a special student, and the first year was my "test year" at MIT. I had faced discrimination in Argentina before, but after I came to the United States, I realized that being Jewish was not the biggest problem. The biggest problem in America for me was being a woman from Latin America, but basically it was the same type of problem.

My advisor at MIT, the excellent and late mathematician Norman Levenson, told me I was not going to be able to graduate with a PhD in mathematics in a new country, with a baby, and without having gone to college. He meant well. But with the help of the Ford Foundation, I received a scholarship. I completed classes, came in first in my class, and became an official PhD student at MIT without ever going to college.

Eduardo José was almost two years old and was my source of joy. Although I struggled financially and worked hard in my academic pursuit, I feel like having him enriched my life and filled it with joy. He was my greatest accomplishment. I wasn't looking to feel secure. I was looking to do something that I considered important to my life. Eventually I was accepted at UC Berkeley, and I completed my PhD in mathematics in 1971 from MIT. Afterward I completed my second PhD in Economics from UC Berkeley.

To bring up a child while studying at such competitive schools is extremely creditable.

I'm bringing up a child now. I have a seven-month-old baby. And today the nanny canceled. So I had a bit of a nightmare, you know. But I feel blessed. I wanted to have a baby. I had a daughter, who was wonderful, brilliant, and kind, but I lost her. And I couldn't recover, so I decided to have another baby. It is my baby, and he has my DNA. He is beautiful. He's growing up so fast! Last evening there was a big party here, and my guests wouldn't leave until midnight. That's why I'm so tired. This morning he and I had a good time in the Jacuzzi on the sixth-floor terrace overlooking the river.

When I tell people about my baby, they say, "You're crazy." But let me explain. It's because I do what I think is important even though other people may think it's strange. To me, it was important to do a PhD in mathematics even though I didn't go to college.

Likewise, it's important to me to have a baby now even though I have so many things in my life that make it almost impossible. But it is what is important to me and what is good for me. As for others, as Eleanor Roosevelt apparently said, "I have no business being concerned with the opinions of others."

You gave life to a new son at this time in your life, and it makes you happy. However, this would be considered unconventional.

Yes. The convention is not that successful anyway, right? So, if you told me that using the convention, you have this life of happiness and everything goes well, I will say, "OK." But if you look at these conventions and what's happening all around you, you realize you're better off not following them.

As a first-generation immigrant in America, did you adjust quickly?

No, I didn't, but I didn't need to. I didn't expect to adjust. I was never expecting to become part of any group. I knew I was going to be different and separate. It was OK with me.

Different and separate? Could you please explain that?
It was because of my background. It was so completely different from anybody else's. First of all, coming from Argentina, being a woman in mathematics and studying in a male-dominated school. On top of that, I had a baby when I was a teenager. And on top of *that*, I was taking PhD courses when I hadn't even been to college. I knew I had broken all the links to normality. I was not expecting anybody to accept me as part of their group. If they accepted me, I was very grateful, because I am very sociable, and I like people.

When I arrived in America, I lived in a house rented by a Russian lady. She was very nice to me. So I wasn't alone. I found a family who babysat for my son when I was at school at MIT. Some of the other students in my school were also nice to me and helped me out. Although that quickly disappeared when I became top of the class. The other MIT students, all male, didn't like me anymore. I lost all my friends.

They say it's lonely at the top.
It didn't matter to me. I was living with who I wanted to, and I loved MIT. They had a library that was open twenty-four hours a day. In Argentina, they were closing the universities. At MIT, it was heaven.

You've written about gender discrimination against you in American schools. Tell me about that experience.
I worked with prominent professors while I was in school, such as Jerrold Marsden, Stephen Smale, and Moe Hirsch. While submitting my dissertation on "Group Actions on Spin Manifolds" at UC Berkeley, I found that other students had attributed my dissertation to Marsden. This is a very bad story. Marsden was very good, but he died a little bit young. He just died two years ago, which is really tragic. But he was a wonderful professor and friend. The record was cleared, but after that, the problems of gender discrimination in their Mathematics Department became known. It is ferocious.

While at UC Berkeley, I also worked to help student mothers with small children—like myself—and created the university's first child-care center within the Berkeley campus with the help of the United Automobile Workers Association. Eduardo José attended the center himself at the time. This center is still working and has been imitated at other universities.

Why math and economics?

I felt that mathematics was the natural language for the brain to communicate with itself. However, I took a second PhD in economics because I wanted to be useful and get trained enough so that I could essentially make up my own mind about things without needing anybody else to translate them.

I completed a master's degree in economics and proceeded to pursue a PhD from Harvard in 1974. My second dissertation proved even more difficult than my first. I was paired with Gerard Debreu for my thesis. Debreu did some horrible things. He gave copies of my dissertation to other people. So, when I finished my dissertation, he said to me, "It's not new anymore. Other people have done it." And I said, "That's impossible. How could that be? I was talking with you about it, and nobody else was doing it." And he said, "Well, I gave them copies because I believe in competition." I decided it was a waste of time to talk with this man.

At one point, I had an offer to go to Harvard as a young professor working with Professor Kenneth Arrow, another Nobel Laureate who became an important mentor for me.

I went to Harvard and completed my PhD while I was teaching there. I couldn't get tenured in Harvard because another young male professor accused me of sleeping with a professor at Berkeley to get my Berkeley dissertation done. Kenneth Arrow confronted him and stood up for me. The other professor apologized to them, but he never apologized to me. That created such a bad situation and prevented me from getting tenure. I left Harvard and came to Columbia.

What did you learn from these experiences and how did you proceed?

I learned a lot about how the intellectual property of women was treated in the world of academia. I became familiar with women from other Ivy League schools who had their work duplicated or stolen from them.

Although at the time I won the battle and completed my second PhD, in economics, I may have lost a war. It was a war that I did not know existed. I was simply trying to do my best. I was unaware of the glass ceiling. Things do not get easier as you progress and prove yourself—they get more difficult. As a woman, the more you succeed, the more you are punished. These facts became reality again when I got my tenure at Columbia University.

The former United States Congressman and current Washington State Governor Jay Inslee said about you: "Her leadership in the global community has been legendary." What were your innovations that led to that recognition?

While I was finishing my PhD at UC Berkeley, my father became ill. I started visiting him in Buenos Aires. But I needed to support myself, so I started working in Argentina part-time. I took a job as a director of Mathematical Modeling at Fundacion Bariloche, located in the town of the same name in Patagonia, the south of Argentina. My job was to create a mathematical model of the world economy, which would later be called the Bariloche Model. In collaboration with an interdisciplinary team of prominent Latin American scientists, including geologists, sociologists, population experts, computer scientists, political scientists, and economists, we created the Bariloche Model, a mathematical model of the world economy aimed at helping developing countries and helping to increase the earth's resources.

My concept of development based on the satisfaction of basic needs led to important publications on that subject. "Basic Needs" became my first real contribution to economics—it was a somewhat radical concept at the time. It was nevertheless adopted by more than 150 nations in 1992 at the Earth Summit of Rio de Janeiro, Brazil, and voted as the cornerstone of efforts to define sustainable development. Eventually Basic Needs penetrated the United Nations system and the World Bank, becoming a world standard in rethinking fair and sustainable economic development.

Why was a new radical model for global economic change necessary?

When I was at MIT, there was a discrepancy between the growing population and the natural resources of the planet. The developing nations, which house 80 percent of the population of the world, could not thrive without the fear that it would destroy the availability of natural resources. My purpose there was to come up with a model that would promote the developing countries without hurting earth's resources. I developed the idea that the solution was to satisfy basic needs of the poor nations. Nobody had said it before. But I insisted that the solution was based on satisfying the basic needs and not on maximizing the GDP, as everyone else was suggesting. I fought for it, and it was accepted. I invented the term Basic Needs and proved that the world economic resources will suffice if we follow the satisfaction of basic needs.

In Rio de Janeiro, in 1992, the concept of Basic Needs was voted in by 150 nations. And then Gro Harlem Brundtland, the Norwegian prime minister, said that we needed an environmental principle that was then called sustainable development. That meant satisfying the basic needs of the present without depriving the future generation from satisfying its needs.

In 1993 I presented a formalized mathematically sustainable development model. In 2009 the G20, which is a group of the twenty most important nations that dominate the world economy, decided that sustainable development would be their main objective of the development of economic progress. It became clear that following the structure of satisfying of basic needs, which leads to sustainable development, is essential for survival.

Are there any countries particularly following the Basic Needs model?

Well, there are many, but the one that comes to mind is Brazil. One of the participants of the Bariloche Model produced a book called *Catastrophe or New Society?* It says that either we follow the Basic Needs structure, or it's going to be a catastrophe in terms of resources and the environment.

Are you relating this issue to climate change as well, and the basic needs to live in a healthy environment?

The hurricanes in Florida and the Caribbean are a direct cause of what the economy is doing because it's the result of burning fossil fuels. The fossil fuels are heating up the atmosphere and the water, and that produces additional energy that blows out these hurricanes. And that's what we're observing now.

So now you're convinced more than ever that manmade CO_2 is contributing to climate change?

It is not just me who is convinced. There are thousands of scientists in a United Nations organization that was created in 1996 called the IPCC, Intergovernmental Panel on Climate Change, which is part of the United Nations framework convention on climate change, that say so and say it without equivocation.

At one point you said that manmade CO_2 is just a "risk" for climate changes. You compare it to insurance on one's house.

Let's say that I'm going to cross Riverside Drive. And I take a piece of cloth and tie it over my eyes, and then I cross. Am I sure that I'm going to be hit by a car? No, I'm not sure. But I can assure you that if I do that every day, I will be hit by a car. I don't know when, but the risk is very high. And that's the type of uncertainty of not knowing when it is going to happen with our precision and meter. But it will happen. Because you're increasing the energy in the atmosphere and in the bodies of water in the oceans, when a hurricane is produced, instead of being category two or three, it becomes a five or six. This also causes record storms, droughts, and wildfires as seen in California this year. The sea level is rising, and the warming oceans are inexorably engulfing coastal areas and entire island states.

Getting back to Brazil, the Bariloche group that I worked with was made up of very distinguished political and physical scientists in Latin America. One of them was a man who then became the president of Brazil, Fernando Henrique Cardoso. So, of course, he implemented the Basic Needs strategy with great success when he was president. And there were others in Bolivia, in Colombia, in Venezuela, in all of Latin America. I believe if we implemented the Basic Needs strategy in the United States, we would have a much better result.

I became the UN Advisor in the United Nations Institute of Training and Research in New York. I proceeded to apply the Basic Needs for international research projects to pursue the development strategies for the Third World.

In the fall of 1977, I joined the Columbia faculty, and by 1980, I became a tenured full professor of economics at Columbia. Shortly after, I took a year off and worked as the Keynes Chair of the Economics

Department, University of Essex, in England. At that time, I was an advisor to OPEC visiting several countries in Europe. Thereafter I returned to Columbia University.

Can you talk about the friction that was created in the academic space when you began teaching at Columbia University? Was the glass ceiling phenomenon intensified?

Yes, and my situation was complicated by my gender and by my national background. I did not fit the image of a woman scientist in a man's world. Columbia gradually interfered with my ability to teach my expertise in international trade and economic theory. Teaching was one of the most important reasons I had joined Columbia University. And being deprived of this privilege was painful. My work was ignored, and my funding to publish articles was revoked. I believe that the better my work was, the more hostile the environment became. I no longer had an office to work from. I could no longer teach, and my salary was lowered substantially compared to the male professors. The university denied me a proper hearing. I then discovered that similar circumstances had occurred in other universities. In 2001, this led the MIT president to create a commission of nine university presidents, which publicly acknowledged the problem of gender discrimination. I filed a lawsuit. In 1994, Eduardo Macagno, the Dean of the School of Arts and Sciences at Columbia, called to initiate a reconciliation on behalf of the university, promising among other matters to double my salary. It led to a settlement of the lawsuit between the end of 1995 and early 1996.

In Columbia University, as a woman, the higher you climb in academics, the higher is the salary disparity with male professors. Although I won lawsuits against Columbia University twice, huge salary disparities by gender persist. And there is no Equal Pay Act for women in the USA.

It makes me think about how women's rights are violated on a wider spectrum.

Yes, while I was completing my second PhD, I lost my father in Buenos Aires. Circumstances were such that I wanted to go to Buenos Aires to attend to my sick and dying mother. However, the legal system in Argentina prevented me from taking Eduardo with me because the law gave all the rights to the father of the traveling child. I couldn't leave my son alone, and my parents passed away without meeting Eduardo José again, their beloved grandchild. I realized that men take over women's rights regarding the life decisions of the children. That's when I decided to fight for women's rights.

You ventured from academia into founding your own company. Despite the opposition and suppression, you never stopped working on your mission.

Yes. In 1985, with Geoffrey Heal, Eduardo José, and Jeff Bezos, I founded a company called FITEL, which offered financial services to support international trading of securities. It became a successful company, and we worked around the world in New York, London, and Tokyo. This way I was able to break away from the dependency on Columbia University, paving the way to my own success. I became independent and was financially rewarded without being punished. A few years later, after the birth of my daughter, Natasha Sable, in August 1987, I decided to dedicate myself to care for this beautiful, happy child, and gave up the role in the company.

I continued to work on global environmental problems at the United Nations and created the tradable market for carbon emissions that I wrote into the Kyoto Protocol in 1997 and that became international law as the European emissions trading system in 2005. China has adopted my carbon market at a national level, and in the US, so has the state of California.

I understand that you are a Nobel Peace Prize winner.

I was not awarded the Nobel Prize myself. My work with the team on the IPCC in 2007 won the Nobel Prize "for their efforts to build up and disseminate greater knowledge about manmade climate change, and to lay the foundations for the measures that are needed to counteract such change."

We didn't really reach the goal we set out to achieve, following the guidance of the Kyoto Protocol. What do you think about the Paris Protocol? Is it going to work?

The Paris Protocol has no mandatory provisions. It has no teeth. It is just about good intentions—voluntary goals to reduce carbon emissions. The Paris Agreement tried to have all nations agree on a minimum common denominator. And as soon as it was agreed, the United States left the Paris Agreement. So it was somewhat of a wasted effort, and actually it was destructive because people think that we have an agreement to do something. But that agreement has no obligations, no mandatory force. It's not an agreement. It's an expression of hope. An expression of hope is valuable but will never fix problems.

In 2010, you founded Global Thermostat, a company that uses a unique technology to cleanse the air of CO_2. Can you tell me about the company?

By 2014, the fifth assessment report of the UN IPCC and other environmental bodies had concluded that it is no longer sufficient to just decrease carbon emissions. What is now needed is to remove existing CO_2 from the air in massive amounts; otherwise we face the risk of catastrophic climate change. Together with Dr. Peter Eisenberger, I invented the technology that would remove carbon from the air directly at low cost. We take carbon from air, cleanse it, and use it to make commercially valuable products such as polymers, desalinated water, synthetic fuels, carbonated beverages, dry ice, all while making economic profits. It's a win-win solution.

Global Thermostat has obtained thirty-four patents and raised $51 million in investments so far. We have already built two Global Thermostat plants, which look just like small buildings, at SRI, which is the leading Silicon Valley Technology Campus where the internet was first introduced. These plants operate based on the Global Thermostat technology. We're currently building a commercial Global Thermostat plant in Huntsville, Alabama, to provide low-cost CO_2 for classic carbonated beverages. The carbon that we extract is used to power markets such as water desalination, synthetic fuels, building materials, and others. Our technology is low cost and carbon negative™, which means that operating our technology decreases the CO_2 concentration of the atmosphere. Carbon negative technologies are now needed to avert climate change, and our company can remove enough CO_2 from the atmosphere that it can indeed avert climate change. Our patent policy encourages developing countries to use our carbon negative technology.

You've fought for women's equality almost all your life. What is your advice for women immigrants discouraged by the political environment today?

I was asked the same question in Abu Dhabi in a presentation I gave for women in 2017. I said, "My advice for women is to be patient . . . especially with men." They all laughed. I didn't want to criticize men. Not in another country, when I was invited. It is a double-edged comment to tell women to be patient: To tell them to be patient with men implies that men require special patience.

What does it mean for women to be patient?

It means to keep on doing your work, and when you get trampled on and discriminated against, you should not let it destroy you.

Your famous recipe for continual success for women is to turn dung to fertilizer. We should follow that advice.

What I meant to say was that throughout this arduous process, my inner path has actually strengthened. My internal peace and happiness were fortified. I learned to see more clearly what was important in life and in my work. I achieved compassion for other women, many of whom had lives much more difficult than my own, and I found gratification in helping them out.

Graciela Chichilnisky is a professor of economics and of statistics, the director of the Columbia Consortium for Risk Management at Columbia University, CEO and co-founder of Global Thermostat, and the architect of the Kyoto Protocol Carbon Market. She is the author of several books, including *Saving Kyoto: An Insider's Guide to the Kyoto Protocol, The Evolving International Economy, Oil in the International Economy,*

Graciela Chichilnisky with Al Gore at the 2015 China US Clean Air Conference

and *Sustainability, Dynamics and Uncertainty.* She is the author of the essay "Sex and the Ivy League," a portion of which is included in this interview.

CHITRA DIVAKARUNI

INDIAN-AMERICAN AUTHOR AND WOMEN'S RIGHTS DEFENDER

"I think that it's important for women to see that you can be a fine woman, and you don't have to be perfect. It's not natural to expect anyone to be perfect. We are human with our imperfections, and that is part of what makes us humane and beautiful."

IN HER BOOK *THE PALACE OF ILLUSIONS*, Chitra Divakaruni writes about the fierce Princess Panchaali from the Indian epic *The Mahabharata*. History's Panchaali was a warrior princess married to five warriors who fought the greatest battle in India's history. Chitra's Panchaali is a quick-witted, intelligent, and strong woman who challenges the patriarchy of the world she was born in, who demands she be educated in the same manner as her brother, and who questions the role of a woman and a princess in the world.

In Chitra's collection of stories, *Arranged Marriage*, she paints a portrait of young Indian women and the complex psychologies of marriage, like the new bride who becomes a young widow, or the middle-aged divorcee who moved to the United States to start fresh. In *The Mistress of Spices*, Chitra writes lovingly about a mysterious Indian woman named Tilo, who with her knowledge of magical spices, is helping people with their ailments as well as their alienation as new immigrants in the US.

Chitra's books have global appeal, having been translated into twenty-nine languages and adapted into movies. Whether through Panchaali or Tilo, Chitra is the unfaltering voice of the modern Indian woman, a strong ambassador for the Indian immigrant woman in the United States. Her words bridge two cultures.

Born in the literature-rich city of Kolkata, now known as Calcutta, Chitra grew up reading the dusty hardcovers in her grandfather's study. Her love for writing took her to the United States when she was nineteen, where she began her life as an immigrant student in Ohio. She graduated with a master's degree from Wright State University and a PhD from the University of California, Berkeley.

The author of about seventeen books, Chitra writes about the themes that are closest to her heart: the immigration of Indians and their diaspora, the complex social and cultural dynamics of women in the modern and post-modern age, and the deep mystical roots of her homeland. Additionally, Chitra's stories trace the lives of immigrants, from their struggles of adjustment to the hard work and sacrifice they dedicate to their new land. "It is something I try to show in many of my immigrant stories, the coming together of immigrants who come here and who work hard and who really prosper, and how they help society to prosper," Chitra says.

During the aftermath of Hurricane Harvey in Houston, Chitra opened her house to victims of the natural disaster. For her, service to the community begins at home. The author and poet also lends her time and resources to the causes of child literacy and women's equality.

In a deeply thought-provoking and personal interview, Chitra talks about her love for books and writing, her commitment to her family, how she is honored to tell the stories of women, and how she remains unafraid to lend her voice on behalf of the dreamers and immigrants in today's America.

Tell me about your upbringing in India.

Kolkata is a very old and cultural city, so reading, writing, and listening to classical Indian music was a big part of growing up. I came from a very middle-class family. And my family's roots are in the village. My grandfather lived in the village, about two-and-a-half hours outside of Kolkata, so I spent a lot of time during my holidays with him. That was wonderful, and that has influenced my writing a lot. I write a lot about rural scenes as well.

All my grandparents had passed away except my mother's father, so he's the only one I knew growing up. He was a doctor. And when I was born, and by the time I got to know him, he had retired from his medical practice and was doing free service in the village. I think I really learned the whole idea of service and giving back from him. He is the one who told me the stories of my culture—the old folktales, and the epics, and the fairy tales. And all of those have been woven into my work. I think he was a big influence.

My father was an accountant. At a certain point of my growing up, he just left the family and moved away. So my mother is the one who brought us up. She was my role model. She's taught me to be a strong woman and to stand on my own feet. I think in my writing there are a lot of strong female characters.

Was it common for a woman in India to raise children on her own?

No, that was not usual. A lot depends in India on the family background you come from and how influential your family is. When I was growing up, women who were from more influential families had a stronger position in society and often had a better education. But as you went down the socioeconomic ladder, the position of women became worse and worse. Poor women did not get a good education, and as a result, they were not able to stand up for themselves often.

But my mother realized early on that education was the way to regain power, so she started a free school in her village. And she especially encouraged girls and women to come and study with her.

You write about strong women in your books. In Palace of Illusions, *you write about Panchaali, who has not been given a voice in history. She's told that the highest purpose of a woman is to serve a man. And she says very simply, "I plan other things with my life." She's so mythical and divine, but there's something so human about her.*

That's one of the reasons I wanted to tell her story, because I felt she was very timeless as a woman. She was doing all these very modern contemporary things. That book is my most popular book in India. Women just love her character, and they are always writing to me about how much they relate to her. And also how reading about her gave them strength to make some difficult decisions in their lives.

And I wanted to show her as a complex character with her faults, because I think it's important for women to see that you can be a fine woman, and you don't have to be perfect. It's not natural to expect anyone to be perfect. We are human with our imperfections, and that is part of what makes us humane and beautiful. A lot of times women—especially in India, maybe here too and in many cultures—are held to some really impossible standards. And if they fall from those standards, if they make one mistake, they get a bad reputation. Through Panchaali, I really want to show that that's not true. Panchaali makes mistakes, but she's a good woman. She still has admirable values, but she has her own faults and problems. Everybody has them. People accept them in men, but they want to knock them out in women.

There's a magnificent moment in the book where Panchaali is insecure about the color of her skin, and Krishna tells her, "A problem becomes a problem only if you believe in it to be so." And also "Often, others see you the way you see yourself." And then she goes to an event, and she projects confidence and she feels better about herself and becomes the hit or the 'belle of the ball.' This is such deep psychological insight. Is there color and gender discrimination in India today?

Yes, color and gender discrimination still exist in India. Although there are strong female organizations in India, the fight for equality is going on. Awareness is being raised about these issues. These organizations inspire women to realize that their inner beauty is more important than the color of their skin. There is still quite a bias about fair skin in India. There are a lot of skin lightening creams that are very popular.

Especially in the urban areas, a lot of these ideas are changing faster. But there's still a real bias for fair-skinned women. We see that even in the Indian popular movies. The actresses who are most popular and are highest paid all have very fair skin.

Are arranged marriages still going on in India?

Yes. They're a big part of Indian culture, and it's more prevalent in the rural areas. But the nature of arranged marriage is changing. So in many cases it's a nice mix of how parents will introduce you to people. The parents are involved in the process, but then you get to go out with your partner for a few times, and you can make a decision.

Now many more women are working, especially in the urban areas. They don't want to be forced into an arranged marriage. And they feel they have many options.

Were you introduced to your husband through an arranged marriage?

No, I met my husband when I was going to school in this country. He's Indian, but he was from a different part of the country. Our language is different; our food is different; the festivals are different. And because the language is different, the movies he likes to watch, the Indian movies, are different from what I like to watch.

Religion is a big similarity. And then family values. That's a big thing that we share. I think there's a lot of compatibility between us in terms of wanting to give back to society. And we both believe very highly in education. He has several higher-education degrees. And he always supported me to go for my PhD and do whatever I wanted in my career. So I think those values we are lucky to have in common.

But religion is a big deal? I mean that's common to both of you. And it facilitates the way you bring up your children?

Yes. That is a big plus. That really helps to keep us together. We have two boys, who have both graduated and now have started working. And I think one of the interesting things about living in America and bringing up children here is that I had to make a very careful decision about which Indian values to bring them up with, and which American values to incorporate into our lifestyle.

What Indian values are you raising your children to follow?

I think two are most important to me. One, I really made an effort that they should have a spiritual education. I made sure that they went to Indian Sunday school and were introduced to the main spiritual ideas of Hinduism. And the second thing is the importance of family, and family commitments. We've talked a lot about that, and we've talked about how important it is to be close to your family. And I think that value is really a human value more than Indian or American. I think that both in India and in America, good people have that value, and like to give back to society.

Yes, America is very philanthropic.

Yes. Right now in Houston we are seeing so much philanthropy. It's very heartwarming how people are just coming up to help the victims of the hurricane and the floods.

Is that going to inspire another book? Like you did with your book, One Amazing Thing, *where nine people are trapped at the Indian Consulate after an earthquake hits an American city. It reminds me of Boccaccio when he wrote a story about young women getting together during the plague. I thought you went classical when you chose to write about it.*

Yes. I had Boccaccio in my mind.

Let's speak about another important woman in your books, Tilo, from The

Mistress of Spices. *She's torn between two worlds, as immigrants often are. She's maintaining her tradition but turning to modern resources.*

Yes, she's traveling the two cultures. Like any successful immigrant has to do, right? In my mind, a successful immigrant is one who takes things from her culture that are useful and powerful and meaningful to her. But she also looks at the world that she is inhabiting, and she uses what's there. I think, as immigrants, we must be aware of what's around us, what are the resources. And we must be willing to hold on to things that are important and change when we need to. And make use of other things that we can lean on.

You talk about immigrants bringing their own culture to America. I think that's what makes America beautiful.

I completely agree. What makes America beautiful is that so many cultures have come together here, and we have an opportunity to learn from each other; the cultures influence each other, and therefore, America is enriched by that.

Because once we start saying "America is only for certain kinds of people," we have lost the whole idea of America. Really this is what made America strong. And that is something I try to show in many of my immigrant stories—the coming together of immigrants who come here and work hard, who really prosper and help society to prosper.

I believe that the obstacles that immigrants are facing today are bigger than ever. Apart from the problems of adapting to a new country, they have external problems that the government brings upon them. Just like the young male, Jagjit, in your book The Mistress of Spices, *who has been bullied in school for wearing a turban. He is experiencing being the "other," which is a feeling now emphasized by higher authorities that indirectly promotes this behavior.*

Right. When you have the threat of being deported from this country, like the dreamers have through no fault of their own, it promotes racism; it influences other kids to feel that it's OK to express racism and to think that America is for white people only. I think there's a whole group that feels they could not have said it before, but now they feel it's OK for them to say it. And so that's why immigrants' stories are so important now, because of the anti-immigrant sentiments. People don't really have information about immigrants. They don't talk to them, and they don't know what their life is like in America. They have this racial stereotype picture of what is an immigrant, which is untrue.

Everyone came from somewhere else, and everyone struggled at one point. When they came, they were all in the same place. They had hardly anything. They set goals, and they made their lives, and they made America what it is. Just like immigrants are doing now. It's not different.

So in The Mistress of Spices, *you have a Native American and an Indian-American falling in love. Why did you put the two together?*

Well, a lot of times things happen in my books that I don't consciously think of, but Ravan just appeared in the book. But later when I thought of it, I think that Tilo, the Indian woman coming from another ancient culture, needed to connect with something in America that was ancient, spiritual, and connected to the natural world. But her crowd is made up of many people who have lost it. Ravan is no longer in touch with his culture. He has cut himself off from that culture like many Native Americans who feel that in order to succeed, they must crucify that part of themselves. So he's missing something, which Tilo can provide. And Tilo needs something that he can provide. And I thought those two characters together made a beautiful whole.

When you came to America, you were already educated. How would you describe your struggles as a new immigrant?

To a great extent, I was in a protected environment while I was studying and in school. However, I have had my experiences with racism as well. And that's why I'm very sensitive to it and write about it often. When I went outside the university, not being rich, walking on the streets and taking public transportation, or shopping at less expensive places, I was not protected. I came across a lot of negative emotion every once in a while.

Traditionally Americans have been very welcoming, but I'm afraid it is changing now. I hope that it'll come back to the kind of America that we're longing for.

When I talk to my friends who went to other countries, maybe in Europe, and they compare their experiences with mine, I've had a much better time. I think overall Americans were much more accepting and welcoming.

And I really feel this was what was wonderful about America when I arrived—that in general, people made me feel very welcomed, which helped my success in this country. Because it wasn't like I was always struggling just to be accepted; I could focus on other things. And that's why it's so important that this particular part of American culture should not disappear. This openness to immigrants should not disappear from our culture.

I also understand that you are interested in rehabilitating women who are victims of abuse and investing in children's education as well.

Yes, those are my two passions. I'm very involved with this group called Pratham; they do literacy work in India. They work in slums; they work in rural areas. They work with underprivileged children. And now they've started working with women by giving them vocational training so that they can open their own small businesses. Maybe a beauty salon, or they can learn computers, and then they can go into that field. So they're teaching women how to stand on their own feet and get a good livelihood. And they're also teaching children, because education, as you know, is the first step.

So I'm very involved with them and have been for a number of years. And then I'm involved with a couple of domestic violence organizations. I helped to found one in the San Francisco Bay Area when I was living in California. And now in Houston, I'm on the advisory board of another one.

And why did you choose those two causes? Was there any personal experience about that?

Well, for a long time I felt that women should be treated with respect, and they need to be allowed to live the life they want. Every woman is deserving of happiness. I think every human being is deserving of happiness, and safety in their homes. But I think what happened is that when I was in graduate school, at the University of California in

Berkeley, I started volunteering at the women's center. And through the women's center, I got to know about domestic violence organizations.

I met some of the women who were in domestic violence situations. I think that really just hit me hard. Why should a woman have to be afraid in her own home? What gives another human being the right to hit her or abuse her? I thought that was very wrong. That's how I got into that field, realizing that men can be so violent toward women—often their wives, or their girlfriends.

You are an extremely prolific writer. You've been included in the Best American Short Stories and the O'Henry Prize Stories, and you have won an American Book Award. Do you feel that this country has given you the opportunity that you would not have had otherwise?

I think America has given me a lot of opportunities. It's hard to know what my life would have been if I had lived in India. And who knows if I would have become a writer in India. I only started writing after I came here. In some ways I think being an immigrant gave distance from my own culture. And I saw it more clearly. Also being an immigrant, I was exposed to a whole series of other experiences that were very strong. And I felt the importance of writing them. Though I really do think that being an immigrant woman in America has contributed to making me into a writer. And contributed to my success as well.

What were the experiences that compelled you to start writing?

I think there were two major experiences. One was personal, which is that my grandfather in India passed away when I was here in this country. I was doing my PhD at that point. Sadly, I could not go back for the funeral. I felt a great need to write about him, to immortalize his memory for myself. And I think that pushed me into writing. So that was the first stage where I was writing personal things. I was writing poetry at that time—poems about my grandfather, for example. But I was really writing them for myself.

And then when I came in touch with women in abusive situations, I felt that their stories and their dreams and their hopes needed to be shared with people. I think that was what really pushed me and made me want to become a professional writer. Because I felt stories would be the way to touch people's hearts. Stories about women, like the immigrant women and the reality of their lives.

So what do you do for fun?

I love teaching; I love writing. Actually, everything I do is fun for me. But things I love doing are gardening, meditating, reading books, and watching movies. I also have a meditation practice which I try to do every day.

Chitra Banerjee Divakaruni is an award-winning and best-selling author, poet, activist, and teacher of writing. Winner of the American Book Award and the Premio Scanno, also known as the Italian Nobel, she was chosen in 2015 by the *Economic Times* for its Twenty Most Influential Global Indian Women. Her latest novel is *The Forest of Enchantments*.

WAFAA EL-SADR, MD

EGYPTIAN-AMERICAN PHYSICIAN AND INFECTIOUS DISEASE SPECIALIST

"When I hear people making judgments about doctors who are foreign graduates, I think to myself: Just wait and see. You don't know what that person is capable of or what they will accomplish one day, if given the chance."

WHEN DR. WAFAA EL-SADR WAS doing her training after graduating from medical school in Cairo, Egypt, she decided to specialize in infectious disease. This was motivated by growing up in Egypt where infectious diseases were prevalent and where dealing with them was a day-to-day reality. She was also inspired by the fact that most infectious diseases were preventable, and most were curable. They were unlike neoplastic or noncommunicative disease such as heart disease, diabetes, and other illnesses where patients require lifelong care, or where there were limited options for prevention and successful management.

In the early 1980s, the first cases of AIDS were identified in the United States. It did not take long before tens, hundreds, and thousands of young patients presented to hospitals and clinics with an array of mysterious symptoms. During those early years of the epidemic, Wafaa remembers the sense of helplessness she and others felt as they desperately cared for these young patients, watching them fight the host of opportunistic infections that followed, and ultimately losing many people to AIDS.

Wafaa continued her training at Harlem Hospital, a hospital situated in a community that served a vibrant but economically and socially disenfranchised population. She had long known about the importance of community service, thanks to the example set by her parents, both of whom were physicians. They had a keen commitment to making a difference in the lives of those who were less fortunate. It was at Harlem Hospital where she saw how that community would also bear the brunt of the new epidemic.

Early on it became obvious that HIV carried a social stigma that caused shame, marginalization, and isolation. A more inclusive approach had to be taken. Wafaa initiated a program that involved the patient's family and the community at a time when the cause of the disease was unknown, and when supporting and caring for the patients were key strategies.

In 1995, effective medications for the treatment of HIV were discovered. Almost overnight, gravely ill patients felt better, and HIV became a chronic condition requiring lifelong medication instead of a death sentence. As long as they stuck to their regimen, people could live healthy and productive lives.

In the early 2000s, Wafaa became convinced that the successful approach she and her Harlem Hospital team took toward HIV could work globally. This was at a time when millions of people living with HIV in poor countries around the world had no hope of getting treatment. Facing intense skepticism, she created ICAP at Columbia University, a global health center at the Columbia Mailman School of Public Health. This international AIDS program reached vulnerable regions of the world like sub-Saharan Africa, where HIV was the leading cause of death. ICAP's mission is to work with local institutions in countries around the world to respond to public health challenges. It focuses on the global response to HIV and bringing hope to those who had none.

Today, almost four decades since the start of the HIV epidemic, with a brilliant smile Wafaa humbly but proudly stated, "We reached the unreachable." I think she meant that the world had achieved an unprecedented victory over an infectious disease. Then began the hard work of how to reach people in the most remote places in the world who needed these services. Those are pretty amazing accomplishments and goals, and Wafaa has been right there, doing the hard work, from day one.

In the 1980s, the world encountered HIV and AIDS. You were a young doctor in New York City, and you found yourself in the midst of an epidemic that soon became a pandemic. It became your life's goal to join the army of doctors and researchers to fight this disease. You became a world leader in your effort to reach "the unreached" with a goal to control the disease. How did you feel as a young, enthusiastic doctor specializing in infectious disease as you faced this unknown entity?

I can start at the beginning. I had just finished my training in infectious disease at the time when we started hearing about the very first cases of AIDS here in the United States. It's interesting to think back and reflect on the reason why I picked infectious disease as a specialty. It was for one important reason—that infectious diseases were often preventable and usually treatable. Then came HIV/AIDS.

Part of the initial fear associated with AIDS was that no one knew what caused this disease and how it was transmitted. In those early years, we essentially just watched young people who were dying from AIDS, and all we could do was to provide support and to keep them comfortable. We tried to treat the symptoms and alleviate the suffering, but we really didn't know fundamentally that it was caused by a virus.

This was a period with a lot of uncertainty and fear. Some people were afraid of catching this condition, while others made judgments about people affected by the disease. At the same time, for many of us in the trenches, there was a profound sense of camaraderie. Many of us who were there at the beginning and faced those early difficult years became a close community that remains deeply connected to this day.

People ask me all the time, "Weren't you afraid?" I don't remember being afraid. I remember feeling challenged, being in the midst of something bigger than myself. I remember the deep connection to the patients, their families, and their loved ones. This could have been because of who was affected by HIV; these were really the most disenfranchised people in our society, racially, socially, or economically. We felt that these individuals needed somebody who would advocate for them and who was willing and eager to take care of them through very difficult times.

You were really being challenged as a doctor, and in front of you was the exact reason you went into medicine. In 1985, the first drug for HIV was discovered, zidovudine (AZT), and in 1987 it was approved for treatment. Then in 1995 came the discovery of a combination treatment, and almost overnight, a sick patient was up and ready to carry on with life. What did that mean for you?

The discovery of AZT, but more importantly the discovery of the combination treatment—the three drugs together that some people call "the treatment cocktail"—could really have a major impact on peoples' lives. We saw this beneficial effect almost overnight. HIV was transformed from a death sentence into a chronic disease. For people living with HIV, they were now able to live healthy lives. The availability of treatment also transformed the way society looked on people with HIV. Before you could tell if somebody had HIV, and thus, some could stigmatize such individuals. People began to realize that there were people living with HIV among them who were living productive healthy lives. This had a profound societal effect beyond the individual benefits of treatment.

For my patients in Harlem, our goal was to try to get the treatment to as many people who needed it, as quickly as possible. However, many in the community had a deep mistrust of the health system because of the legacy of abuse and discrimination. We had to gain their trust so they could feel confident to come and get the treatment. It was a slow process, but ultimately by reaching out and building community partnerships, we were successful in bringing together people living with HIV, families living with HIV, and providing them with the treatment they needed. That was in the mid- to late-1990s. After that my colleagues and I started being interested in what was going on globally.

You conceived of ICAP, the center you established at the Columbia Mailman School of Public Health, in 2003. You actually were a part of Columbia since the late 1980s when you started to work in Harlem, which was affiliated with Columbia. Was your work in Harlem Hospital a model for ICAP and your work globally?

Thinking back to the early 2000s, it became very obvious to me and to my colleagues that in rich countries like the US, we had at our fingertips these treatments that could save peoples' lives. But in countries in sub-Saharan Africa, where most people living with HIV resided, those people had absolutely no access to treatment. Millions were dying. That disparity of having treatment for the people who were able to get it versus no treatment for people who couldn't get it was disturbing and deeply unethical.

This was what motivated me to establish ICAP at Columbia. I really was convinced at that time that what we were able to accomplish in Harlem, where we brought treatment to people who were disenfranchised, to poor people, to families with a wide mistrust of the system, could be done globally. I felt very confident that if given the opportunity, we could do the same in Africa. With that in mind, we worked very hard to take the lessons we learned in Harlem and adapt them to this new context.

I'm curious about your life growing up in Cairo. What was it like—the

town, your environment, and your family when you were a child? I think
all of that impacted your choices in life and who you became.

My parents were both physicians. They were very socially conscious
people, both of them, very much involved beyond their day work in
supporting youth and serving the poor. As a young child, my brother
and I spent a lot of time with them observing and noting what they
were doing. This gave me an early appreciation of how this type of
commitment needs to be an important part of one's life, and that it is
critical to embed this into one's day-to-day existence. I believe that was
part of what motivated me to go into medicine. It was a way of doing
service, giving back to society.

Growing up in a developing country like Egypt, infectious diseases
used to be and still are quite common. They have a profound effect on
a lot of people's lives. I grew up at a time when polio, rheumatic fever,
and tuberculosis were rampant in the country, and cholera and typhoid
outbreaks were not uncommon. So infectious diseases were palpably
present in people's lives. I think this motivated my later interest in
infectious disease, and particularly my interest in public health. If you
want to have an impact on the broader community, you must embrace
public health.

You had a nice childhood?

I had an interesting and unusual childhood. I had unusual parents
who had fulfilling careers. In retrospect, it was important, and it was
enriching in many ways.

Why did you move to the United States?

Part of it was because I was the daughter of two prominent
physicians. You are expected to take a certain path. I wanted to go to
a place where I would have different kinds of opportunities, be on my
own, where you're just who you are and it doesn't matter what your
name is, who your parents are—a place where you can carve your own
path. I think there's something attractive about that, and the US offered
me the opportunity to do so.

Not that it's easy for everybody, but to me it offered a different kind
of opportunity, more options. I think that's why I came.

Was there any political change or difficulty in the country itself that made you want to improve your life? Or was it just the idea of coming here and growing as a doctor?

I came to the US largely for the opportunity to grow. But I'm of the generation that had Anwar Sadat and Hosni Mubarak. There were years, and years, and years of uncertainty, economic difficulties, political difficulties, societal constraints; these were difficult years for the country overall.

Gloria Steinem said that "we women are like immigrants in our own country." You're a woman and you're an immigrant, so you were double-challenged in a male-dominated profession and society.

I feel most people would assume that in Egypt it was more difficult for a woman to go to medical school or to become a doctor. Actually, that was not the case. In my medical school class, 50 percent were women. My mother was a doctor, so she went to medical school in the 1940s. I think there's a disconnect between the professional opportunities and the traditional, societal expectations in Egypt. I was actually quite surprised coming to the US to hear of how few women were accepted in medical schools at that time. It seemed to me very odd, that here was a society that perceived of itself as more progressive, while at the same time women had more difficulty entering medical school when compared to women in Egypt.

Over my career, I think that certainly women faced—and continue to face—enormous professional challenges. And I believe even though you can rise—and I certainly feel fortunate to have attained leadership positions—I think there are still moments when you feel that you're not heard. It is not unusual, for example, for the observations made by a woman to be unacknowledged until a man repeats the same observation. That happens all too frequently. You have to speak loudly and fight to be heard so that your idea is not assumed to be somebody else's idea.

I'm also an Arab-American, and Arabs have never been the most welcomed immigrant group anywhere. That's part of who I am. It's part of my personality and forms my foundation. Fortunately, once you belong to a professional group and you succeed, I don't think people look at you and think about where you came from anymore.

I find it amusing though, when I hear people make negative comments about foreign medical graduates.

It is interesting you feel this way. After graduating from a foreign medical school, you trained at Columbia and Harvard and in one of the best medical programs in the country. You became an international hero in the field of public health.

Yes, but my foundational education was in Egypt. That's why when I hear people making judgments about doctors who are foreign graduates, I always think to myself: Just wait and see. You don't know what that person is capable of or what they will accomplish one day, if given the chance.

Exactly. That's the essence of this book about women who came here and really contributed to this country. They became successful despite the skepticism and against all odds. Let's get back to ICAP. As the world celebrated the discovery of the treatment for HIV, the drug went from the laboratory to the clinic at an unusual speed. Then many public health issues arose that prompted you to conceive ICAP. What is the mission of ICAP, and how did you go about accomplishing it?

I established ICAP here at the school of public health in response to the raging global HIV epidemic in the early 2000s. This was motivated by the disparity in access to HIV treatment where persons with HIV in poor countries had no chance of accessing treatment. Working together with a small group of colleagues, we established ICAP and worked very hard to get funding to be able to do work needed and to bring treatment and prevention to many of the poorest parts of the world. From day one, we felt that the mission for ICAP was to enhance the lives of families around the world, with a focus on the poorest areas, the most disadvantaged populations.

Today we are fortunate to work in more than thirty countries in partnership with people on the ground, supporting them to do what they want to do for the wellness of their own people.

Which part of the target population do you concentrate on—in the United States and globally?

At ICAP we work on more than HIV. Over the past fifteen years, we've truly expanded our efforts to respond to a large number of public health challenges. We also work with malaria, tuberculosis, maternal health, and noncommunicable diseases. We support clinics and laboratories and help put in place systems of care. We've expanded our portfolio to respond to whatever the need is in a specific country.

And the populations we serve are the populations affected by whatever that public health threat is. One of our key foundations has been this focus on healthy families, on the family as a unit, to think not just of individuals, but to think of how we can have healthy families, healthy communities. We want to have an impact on the whole population.

In the US, currently our work is focused on the prevention of HIV, and we work with the vulnerable people who are at risk of getting HIV. For example, we focus on men who have sex with men here in New York City, especially African-American men who are at very high risk. We also focus on women of color, who are also at risk of HIV. Overall our focus is whoever is affected or at risk.

Did you face resistance when you came up with the idea of ICAP?

In the early years the main issue we confronted was skepticism that what we hoped to do could be done. There were people who believed that it was impossible to bring treatment to poor people in Africa, that they wouldn't understand about treatments, that they wouldn't come to the clinics because of stigma. That they wouldn't know how to take the pills. That the healthcare workers, the doctors and the nurses, wouldn't know what to do, and that the clinics weren't ready. There were many naysayers. We had to prove them wrong.

This is all from the model in Harlem?

Yes. We learned that if you put in place strong and high-quality programs that are responsive to the needs of the people, guess what? They appreciate it, whether they are in Harlem or in Africa.

Tell me a little bit about ICAP's work in awareness, prevention, testing, and treatment.

When I think about HIV and responding to the HIV epidemic, our goal is to try to get to the people who need to get tested—those who have HIV but do not know that yet. In this day and age, it's really tragic if somebody has HIV and they don't know it. If they knew, they could get treatment and have the opportunity to live a healthy life. They could also prevent transmission of HIV to somebody else. Our goal is to build trust by working with organizations that can reach individuals who are fearful or in denial. Getting tested for HIV is the foundation. For those who are positive, we support their access to treatment. I think it's not easy to stay on treatment for life, so our goal is not only to get them to start, but to stay on it, to get them the support to stay healthy. For those who are negative but at risk for HIV, our goal is to guide them to prevention services so that they can stay negative.

You establish clinics in those places?

We don't establish clinics. Our goal is to support the clinics that exist in those communities. We are there to support the structures that exist in the countries where we work.

Which are?

We are fortunate to have several prevention tools that work. Examples include the use of condoms, medical male circumcision for heterosexual men in Africa, and harm reduction programs for drug users. Now we also support programs for PrEP, which is pre-exposure prophylaxis.

PrEP is for people who are at risk of getting the HIV infection. This involves taking a combination pill once a day, which has been shown to protect someone from getting the HIV infection. But taking PrEP daily is also challenging, and it requires putting in place support systems so that people who are often young and healthy can stay on PrEP as long as they need it.

We've also supported programs for the prevention of transmission of HIV from pregnant HIV-positive women to their babies. ICAP has supported HIV testing for millions of pregnant women. For those who are positive, ICAP has enabled them to get to programs for prevention of mother-to-child transmission so that their babies will be negative at birth, and to ensure that these women continue HIV treatment beyond delivery for their own health.

With HIV treatment and the success of saving lives, you have many people living with HIV, 37 million people who are living with HIV. A lot more people stay alive, right?

Yes, treatment is extremely effective. Somebody who has HIV and who starts treatment early can have almost the same life expectancy as someone without HIV.

Has the death toll decreased tremendously?

Yes.

And the quality of life for people living with the virus increased?

Yes, people living with HIV can lead productive lives thanks to treatment.

Is this also a public health problem, because now they have other diseases they're dying from, like TB, or heart disease, or hepatitis?

Having millions of people living with HIV is not a public health problem. It is only a problem if they cannot access the treatment they need. HIV treatment also helps prevent tuberculosis among persons living with HIV, which is an added bonus. It is not surprising that as people living with HIV live longer and age, they become susceptible to diseases of older age similar to others in the general population. Therefore, we need to put in place the resources they will need to stay healthy.

And you're still in some way responsible for those people that are on this drug?

Yes. We as a society must take care of people living with HIV like anybody else with a chronic disease. We need to acknowledge that HIV is a chronic disease and people will live longer with a chronic disease if they're on treatment. They will become vulnerable with age to the diseases of older age. Obviously, the cost of HIV treatment, the cost of keeping people with HIV healthy is much less than the societal costs of letting people get sick. We must invest in health, in keeping people healthy. That's a huge issue in this country and it's not only for people living with HIV; it's for everyone's sake.

I think our role is to keep making the strong argument that, whether it be in the US or globally, HIV is not a thing of the past. We need to make a commitment to keep investing to keep people healthy because it saves money, and also to invest in prevention. We still have tens of thousands of new HIV infections in the US every year, and there are close to two million new infections a year, globally. We have to continue investing in this epidemic because if we don't, it's going to affect all of us.

Why do you think we haven't been able to eradicate it? The World Health Organization predicts 90/90/90 in 2020. What does that mean?

It is not possible to eradicate an infectious disease without a cure and without a vaccine. The reason we were able to eradicate smallpox is because we had an effective vaccine and those who got smallpox either promptly recovered or died. That's very different from HIV, where you have a chronic infection and most people don't know that they have it. I think the idea of eradicating HIV is not realistic. The goal is to work toward ending HIV as a public health threat. That means that people with HIV are in treatment and stay healthy, and that we decrease the numbers of new infections. I think that's how we're going to control the epidemic.

The phrase 90/90/90 or 95/95/95 refers to trying to expand treatment as much as possible. You get 95 percent of people who have HIV to know it, 95 percent of them are on treatment, and 95 percent of them are virally suppressed. This would have enormous benefits for individuals living with HIV and for prevention of its transmission.

Tell me about your MacArthur honor.

Every year, the MacArthur Foundation announces about twenty people or so as MacArthur Fellows. I was very honored to be selected to be one, and quite surprised by it.

It was certainly so well deserved. You're very humble about this, yet you've been honored many, many times since then. Congratulations!

Thank you.

I have to ask you about immigration. How do you handle this complicated situation in the world when people are coming to the United States from vulnerable places?

I think it's a totally unacceptable situation and so contrary to the ethos of the US I think many of us came to this country because of what this country represents to so many people around the world. It's a place that has been a haven for immigrants for generations. To see that being turned on its head is absolutely horrific. I don't think it bodes well for the country and will come back to haunt our country. I hope that one day people in the US will wake up from this current hysteria and say, "How did this happen?" For now, we must stand strong against all anti-immigrant sentiments.

You are an immigrant who has been very productive in this country with your humanitarian work. You dedicated your life to help the "Others." But from a public health point of view, aren't the immigrants going to be a public health problem? They're coming from Africa, from Mexico, from places where they have health conditions that may affect our country. Are they making us more vulnerable?

Immigration has been going on for eons, right? For decades and decades and decades. Most of the public health threats in the US have not come from outside the country. There's the once-in-a-blue-moon exception, like the handful of cases of Ebola that everybody remembers. But if you look at the HIV epidemic in the United States, it's not driven by people coming from other countries. Actually, immigrants tend to be healthier than the resident population because they tend to be young and in the most productive ages.

Obviously, we need to have strong public health systems in every country including in the US to ensure diagnosis, prevention, and treatment of all people.

You are a role model in the field of medicine. What do you do to get students stimulated to join the field? We need more doctors, more nurses, and more health care personnel to be able to accomplish everything that you're doing.

Certainly, a lot of what we do is to try to attract young people to the field of public health, and medicine, nursing, and so on. One way of accomplishing this is to support programs that give young people the opportunity to learn about these fields. I'm encouraged. Here at the school of public health there are a lot of young people who are very interested in making a difference, whether it be working domestically or globally. I don't think there's a shortage of such people. I think they're there; we just need to guide them and support them to pursue such careers.

There is a silver lining. The example of HIV and the success treating it proves that engaging people can make a difference.

Now more than ever there are opportunities to make a difference and to engage in addressing really important problems that the world faces. HIV has paved the way. It has motivated so many. Today, there are other opportunities to engage in tackling infectious diseases, non-communicable diseases, environmental threats, aging, and so many other worthy causes.

So, education is power?

Yes. That applies here.

Dr. Wafaa El-Sadr was named a John D. and Catherine T. MacArthur Foundation Fellow in 2008, and in 2009, she was appointed to the National Academy of Medicine. In 2013, she was appointed University Professor, Columbia's highest academic honor. She also holds the Dr. Mathilde Krim-amfAR Chair in Global Health.

HAN FENG

CHINESE-AMERICAN FASHION AND INTERIOR DESIGNER

"Everywhere in the world, I feel at home."

I MET HAN FENG ON THE first day of summer, the solstice. Sun flooded her studio and highlighted the warmth of greeting on her face. She guided me through her high-ceilinged loft, and I saw her beautifully designed blown-glass vase resting on the kitchen table. I'd soon learn that Han has many facets to her creative side, with inspiration coming from nature and providing a bridge between the East and West.

We sat in the far corner of the room, where wild cactus plants framed Han's natural beauty and elegant simplicity. She was wearing clothes she designed. Her shining brown eyes expressed wonder as if asking, *What could you possibly want to know about me?* I took a different, more direct route than I usually do during my interviews and said: "I want to know *you*! Who you really are." To my astonishment, Han understood the depth of my question and replied: "Everybody sees the beautiful side of my life and thinks anything I do is great. And oh, my life is fabulous. But I go through a lot. Nobody knows about the struggle."

Han Feng was born in 1962 in Nanjing, China. When she was one year old, her father was assigned work back in his hometown of Hangzhou. Han started taking care of her ailing mother and had daily routines that few children her age are equipped to handle. She discovered that charm and an easy-going manner made it easier to manage new challenges.

Han was eight when the Cultural Revolution ended. Under the leadership of Deng Xiaoping (1978–1992) and his far-reaching market-economy reforms, Han was driven toward education and earned a degree from the China Academy of Art in the field of graphic arts. Still, the repercussions of the Cultural Revolution and Communist strictures influenced her desire to follow her American boyfriend, and later husband, to the United States in 1985. There starts her American-Chinese immigrant story fueled by a limitless desire to fulfill her dreams.

Her art and designs reflect the way she manages her life—independent of anyone else's influence, timeless, and never trendy. Her talents flow smoothly between designing fashion wear, producing opera costumes, sculpting with glass, and creating gourmet cuisine.

Though she has never strayed far from her original concept of scarf-making from bits of fabric, Han now enhances the personality of clothing with her sculptural applications.

Han shared with me the peaks and valleys in her journey to become an internationally acclaimed Chinese designer. Throughout, she expressed a zest for life revealed by the sparkle in her eyes, the joyful tone of her voice, her smile, and her mischievous spiky-blonde haircut. I utterly failed when I tried to extract stories of her immigrant struggles. "Everywhere in the world I feel at home," she told me. And I was happy to hear that.

As our interview drew to a close, and Han reflected on her stories of perseverance, luck, and acceptance in a new country, she let out a sigh of relief. It was clear that for Han Feng, the struggles of today are tomorrow's history, and great adventures are sure to come with every new solstice.

So, let's start. People have a glamourous image of you. I first heard about you in 2005, when you were celebrated for your costume design for Puccini's opera Madame Butterfly. *But we all have a side that is unknown, so I'd like to know about you, who you really are.*

First, I am very thankful to be included in your book. And, secondly, actually, I have been thinking a lot about telling my life story because a publisher wanted to do a book about me. But I hesitate whether I should talk about my life. It is very hard. In so short a time, everybody sees the beautiful life of me—Han Feng did this, Han Feng did that. Anything I do is great, but nobody knows how I struggle.

Yes, people think my life is fabulous, and indeed it is. But I went through a lot. When I think about it, I actually had an unhappy childhood. I was born in Nanjing, in China, at the time of the Cultural Revolution. Because of the system back then, everyone's work was assigned, and my father had to return to his hometown, Hangzhou. I was just a year old. For the following ten years, my mother was very sad, crying constantly, waiting for her husband's letters and money that never came.

At the same time, my mother was a very successful, independent woman, working with both Chinese and Western medicine to develop birth control. We were relatively "wealthy" compared to most people at that time in China because there were only two of us living on my mother's salary. I also grew up in an intellectually "wealthy" household—my parents were both well-educated.

Did you ever reunite with your father?

Yes, when I was eleven years old. He had risen high enough in his organization that he could transfer my mother's work to the same city.

So you understood the importance of being independent early on, correct?

Yes, I decided early on to never depend on anyone in life, to be my own person. When I was a child, I was like a little adult—I needed to be strong. And I came to value what it means to help people, to make others happy, to do my best.

Partly that came from the unhappy marriage of my parents. Though we as a family reunited, my parents were arguing all the time, and I resented the change in my life and disliked my father. Very soon after, my father committed suicide. I was twelve. At the time I was happy that he was gone—a sentiment I feel very sorry about today. I found my mother again as my mother and my friend, but once more, like in my earlier years, I became a mother to my mother.

From my childhood and teens, I learned how to be charming. You can drop me in any country now, and without knowing the language, I can figure out how to live. Even today, every city I visit I fall in love with the place. I even wanted to move to Los Angeles, but I don't know how to drive.

It sounds like you are adventurous.

My mother believed traveling would make me independent, so she sent me out exploring in my early teens. That gave me a love for traveling. When I was in Russia recently, I fell in love with the place and the people because I love seeing new places and meeting new people.

That was why I was not concerned about coming to the United States, even though my husband at the time warned me that life would be difficult. I said that if I can make it in China, I can make it in the US. I love an adventure.

Tell me more about your life in China.

My mother, despite all her own difficulties, worked to help me develop into a rounded person. She also sent me to violin lessons, though I wasn't any good. She knew I was very creative because I used to do small art projects and drawings. In school, I was good in writing and bad in physics.

She even took me to a fortune-teller to consult if I should continue with my education or if I should go to work in a factory, to earn more money. And the fortune-teller said forget it, she has a much better life than you; she has to go to a good school and make sure she studies hard.

I took eight months after high school so I could learn to paint to get into art school. When I went to art school, I regained the childhood that I didn't have. I was free, studying painting and graphic design for four years.

What was college like for you socially?

I used to think art is just drawing and sketching, and I didn't realize there was so much more, such a long history, so I had to study hard. I was one of four women in my year, and the class was small, but at art school there were lots of people that I had never come across before— international students, and teachers and students of different ages and backgrounds.

Did you ever learn fashion design or how to sew?

No, I never studied fashion design or learned how to sew, but people said I looked like a designer, so I thought, *Why not try it out?*

What was it like for you when you got to New York for the first time?

I was amazed at first to see money coming out of the cash machine. I had never seen one in China. I started studying English at Hunter College, and my in-laws received me as their own daughter and exposed me to tennis, golf, opera, and classical music, and we frequently went together to the New York museums. They included me and made me part of their upper-class society. I'm particularly thankful that my father-in-law insisted that I work. He said, "Every immigrant has to find a job in this country."

I wanted to be a bartender and work in a restaurant. But my classmates said it would not have worked for my marriage to be away at nights. I took the advice and worked in a department store. I went first to Macy's, but they didn't even let me apply. Then I went to Bloomingdale's. That was how my career started as a salesperson in 1986. I didn't even know how to fill out the job application. I had to provide job experience, so I made up that I worked in a dry cleaner's store on Park Avenue.

Somehow I was hired, and I remember how I struggled with speaking English. All my communication with customers was smiling and saying, "Oh beautiful! Beautiful!"

How did you advance from being a saleswoman in Bloomingdale's to the fashion industry?

It so happened that I met a couple that owned a fabric company, and they thought I could be a great salesperson and invited me to work with them. I didn't really want to change jobs, but they told me, "You will meet American designers as they come to buy fabric." My job there was to cut fabric swatches, clean the showroom, and look after the sales to young or smaller designers. The more established salespersons weren't interested in working with them because they bought in very small quantities. It was at that time that I asked the people maintaining the fabric store for scraps, collecting basketfuls of them, and I started making scarves.

Even though I was already making scarves, I became a designer by accident. I was browsing in a boutique once and the owner said I looked like a designer—and I told her I designed scarves. She was interested in seeing my work, so I went back in a few weeks with the scarves I had made. That was my first "big" sale. After that, I quit my job and became a designer full-time.

You created your own accessories company in 1989 to sell your scarves, then debuted at New York's Bryant Park in 1993 with your first collection, eventually opening your own store. Your climb to success was a gradual process, a testimony to your artistic creative talent and entrepreneurship.

Soon after I started with the scarves, I began producing matching shirts that could be attached to the scarves through a buttonhole, as well as pleated skirts. I got my first big order for five thousand US dollars. I needed lots of friends to help me. The next step was that I sold accessories, such as gloves and hairbands, to Bergdorf Goodman, Barneys, Brooks Brothers, Henri Bendel, and Neiman Marcus. When the King of Morocco saw his secretary wearing my pleated dramatic scarf, he ordered many of them as Christmas gifts. Soon after, Henri Bendel ordered five hundred shirts.

Since I was not trained in cutting and sewing, I hired pattern experts that were introduced to me. Following that, a friend advised me to meet a PR woman who introduced my fashion. The lady said, "I will make you rich and famous." And I responded, "Just make me rich." And that is how I produced my first fashion show. I drew the style, and the pattern-maker followed my instructions on how to drape the fabric around the mannequin. It's a very similar idea to the way I produce my glass blowing, vases, and sculptures. I exhibited my collection in Bryant Park every season until 2001, when my show was scheduled on September 12. Obviously it was canceled because of 9/11. After that I only did showcases at my space. No more runways. Elsa Klensch from CNN interviewed me.

It sounds like you were on the road to fame and success, and that you were on the way to achieve the American dream. Do you think luck played a part in your life, in addition to the hard work?

I worked hard for many years and was lucky to move forward in the fashion designing world. In 1995, I got a certificate from the US Commerce Department for being a great American designer and was invited to the White House and a breakfast with Hillary Clinton. That made me feel amazing as an immigrant because I hardly spoke English. Something like that isn't likely to happen anywhere else.

But as I put so much energy into fashion design, my marriage fell apart.

Do you think this career could have happened to you if you had stayed in China?

If I stayed in China, I think I'd probably be doing something different but still creative. Whatever it might have been, I think I'd find success.

How did you feel about having to start all over again after your divorce?

Of course, it wasn't easy being back to square one. I had to reestablish everything from scratch by myself, but I didn't have a horribly difficult time because I have great friends who supported me in every sense.

How did you wind up producing opera costumes?

I first met the movie director Anthony Minghella in 1998. He made *The English Patient,* which I watched so many times. He had seen the pants and jacket I designed for his wife and asked her to contact me. When he asked me to lunch in 2002, he approached me to produce the costumes for *Madame Butterfly* for the intended opening in 2005 in London at the English National Opera. I was overwhelmed. When Anthony asked if I had done costumes for the opera before, I said no and he said, "Me either! Let's have fun together!"

In 2004, he looked at the five suitcases I brought filled with costumes and said, "We are not doing a fashion show. This is theater." I walked away crying. He sent me away with his blessing to go to New York and take a month to come up with new designs. That is when I understood the project he was looking for. I knew that he was a great storyteller, but I didn't know whether the costumes should be contemporary or conservative. That's when I realized it's not about that but about telling a story through design. And so I came up with the idea that my clothes are to follow the story, from the climax of the wedding to the suicide.

From the most glamorous appearance of the bride Cio-Cio-san, to the most faded outfit when she reaches the end of her life, it was a story. We chose a white wedding dress rather than the conventional red because in the story the singer plays someone half her age, only sixteen years old, and red just didn't feel right. As the story went on, the clothes faded to green and pink and took a modern look. Cio-Cio-san had no income, so I dressed her with what looked like a skirt and top made out of leftover kimono material.

This makes me want to see Madame Butterfly *again, after having this new perspective about the story through your costume design.*

After Anthony didn't like the initial designs I brought him, I did a lot of research. I was introduced to Tony Walton, an Academy Award-winning costume designer; he was eighty years of age at the time. He showed me paintings, all the designs he ever made for different performances, but he alerted me to the fact that I should find my own way to do it. I walked out having a clear idea of what to do. In my studio I took hold of as many magazines as I could for design and color and made collages. My young assistant and I found the perfect outfit for the main character of Mr. Pinkerton, who wore an American Army outfit from 1910. I did a lot of research and came up with the costumes that I presented to Anthony in London. He said, "Oh my God. Darling one, that's it, you did it."

We had a great success with the opera in London in 2005, and in 2006 the opera came to New York. I worked in the Met for three months, and because the Met is bigger, I had to make the costumes bigger for the wedding.

I was overwhelmed when people who met me asked me to sign my name. Anthony said to me, "I guess I did the right thing, huh?" He continued to say that his Hollywood friends talked about his direction and Han Feng's costumes.

I was at the performance at the Met, and I must say, it was overwhelmingly beautiful. There was not a dry eye. People were pointing you out from the audience. I will never forget the way I felt and the repercussions your work generated in New York.

Later I produced costumes for smaller operas like *The Bonesetter's Daughter*, based on Amy Tan's book. I showed my costume designs to Anthony, and he said to me, "Oh my God, you grew so much! We're going to work together until 2016. All my operas, you're going to design. With some you even can be involved with the set."

Sadly, he passed away in 2008, and still today I can't get over it. When I heard about his death, I was in Shanghai. I couldn't walk or speak for three months, and that's when I decided that I had to start to be independent. So I made costumes for many operas like *Semele* and *Miss Fortune*, and the movie *The Karate Kid*. I feel I owe a lot of my fame to my association with Anthony.

Can you tell me about the artwork you collect and your support of emerging artists?

Through the years I've collected a lot of art, and my art school connection played a part. Some years ago I went to South Africa, and I was impressed by a gallery that presented African art. Then I had the opportunity to take charge of four sunken spaces at the Amanyangyun, the Aman Resort in Shanghai, and I thought, *Why not have a gallery of my own?* So Han Feng Art Space came to be. Now, on the Amanyangyun site, I have my studio where I design my fashion, a gallery where I present my art collection, and three other spaces where I promote young artists' work. I also reside there. And I maintain a studio in New York because I have such strong connections and friendships in the city.

Is it different working in Shanghai and in New York?

For me it is the same. I feel at home equally in Shanghai and in New York. I have a great life in Shanghai, as I've made many friends.

How does it work having an American husband, your second husband, and living in New York?

My husband, Bill Kalush, is a very intellectual and interesting man. He wrote a book on Houdini and is a magician himself. He has the best magician library in New York. Of course, it is never simple having two homes in two parts of the world. We just have to balance between needing each other around and needing our independence. I'm lucky that my work allows it. In fact, being in both cities makes it better.

Let's get back to your designs. Do you feel that your aesthetic has changed significantly over time?

Well, the only thing that has changed is that I don't produce many designs. I change it only a little and make the inside and outside more beautiful. For example, the director of the Neue Galerie loves the cut of my clothes, the sewing, and the small details like the buttonholes. She orders a certain style, of which she buys eight different fabrics. I also do new things now. The difference is that before I had completely new collections, which I no longer do. I believe that my clothes are ageless; both younger and older people can wear them. I like to make the menswear out of cotton. I started making men's clothes for Anthony Minghella. I produce menswear only by order. It is usually the wife that will introduce me to the husband and would like me to design for him.

These have been loyal customers for many years. At times my customers have to wait until I come back from China to place their orders.

So you see, it is working for me to live both in Shanghai and in New York. The only problem is that nothing is ever perfect, and I have to accept it because in the big picture I am a very lucky woman and my dream—not to relive my mother's painful existence—came true.

Han Feng in New York City

Han Feng's clothing design and installations have been featured in major exhibitions at the Victoria and Albert Museum in London and The Neue Galerie and Cooper Hewitt, Smithsonian Design Museum in New York, among others. She has received numerous awards, including the Fashion Group International's Rising Star Award. She has long been a collector of work by contemporary and emerging Chinese artists. Han designed the costumes for the spring 2020 performances of *Buddha Passion* by Tan Dun, who wrote the Academy Award-winning score for *Crouching Tiger, Hidden Dragon*.

EINAV GEFEN

ISRAELI-AMERICAN CHEF AND FOOD SERVICES EXECUTIVE

"We all started with peeling potatoes."

EVEN AS A CHILD, EINAV GEFEN lived in a man's world. She was a small but strong kid who often played with the neighborhood boys in Israel. She was tiny and she was rough, but she played a fair game. "For me, hanging out with the boys wasn't an issue," she said. "I have no problems taking things on; I'm never a victim. I won't start a fight, but I will finish it."

Today, Einav rules a largely man's world in the corporate arena of food. She's got a "big, fat title," as she calls it, as the Head Corporate Chef of the United States at Unilever in charge of innovation, which means that she develops new food products for the North American market. When Einav and her team of chefs create a new product, she has to anticipate the scale of the amount of ingredients that she needs to purchase. For example, to reformulate Ragu pasta sauce, Einav realized that it would require crops from endless fields of tomatoes in California.

Einav's rise to top chef was arduous. At every step of her journey, she paved a path of her own, taking jobs no one wanted and at times creating new ones for herself.

Einav's grandparents were first-generation German immigrants to Israel. She grew up with discipline in the house: clothes were to be ironed in tight folds, and you couldn't be a minute late for dinnertime. As she watched her mother, Ruthie, measuring ingredients accurately, being faithful to her German roots, Einav would come to appreciate the beauty in order and organization. Her father, Gershon, was a pilot for Arkia, a major airline in Israel. Einav enjoyed accompanying him on his travels, and while visiting different countries around the world, she explored local supermarkets to find unique products.

She built her physical strength running track and joining an athletics team in Tel Aviv. She served two years in the Israeli Defense Force, a mandatory conscription for both men and women. In the air force she put her discipline to practice, becoming a valuable team member, a leader, and someone who became comfortable taking risks. Gender was no longer a weakness; Einav was an equal, a soldier.

Einav's toughness inspired people to listen to her. She was smart, well-read, savvy, and on her way to a job in advertising. But her passion for food overwhelmed her. Despite her lack of experience, she found work with one of the few female-run kitchens in Israel, at a time when cooking was done by men, and women worked in pastry. However, Einav grew impatient in the bakery.

She knew she was meant for more.

Einav became the first woman to work the line in one of Israel's finer restaurants. The kitchen was her school and where she fell back in love with food. "I thought, *This is it. This is my life*," Einav recalls. But even Israel's biggest kitchen started to feel too small for her. She wanted more.

This time, she aimed for foreign lands. Einav packed her life into two suitcases, and with her boyfriend, Nir, she moved to America. Einav spent nine months at the Institute of Culinary Education in New York, investing in a formal education and training that she felt she lacked, and she was chosen to intern in the kitchen of the famous French chef Daniel Boulud. New York was hard for Einav, but it was immigrants like her—Israeli cooks, French chefs—who gave her work in their kitchens, and a place in their homes.

Einav walked away from restaurants for a while, shifting temporarily during pregnancy to teaching and running a nonprofit culinary center, but she couldn't stay away from food for long.

When I went to visit Einav in her office in New Jersey, the first sight to welcome me was a large, spotless kitchen, done in sparkling stainless steel. "This is where we cook," said Einav, now forty-five, who, having received me warmly at the entrance of the impressive Unilever building, escorted me to her office. Einav is beautiful, with brown hair pulled back to draw attention to her piercing green eyes. She was dressed not in her chef's jacket, but casually, comfortable in her executive's position. The most striking thing about Einav is her magnetic and infectious energy, which flowed easily into our conversation. By doing voices and impressions she amused and impressed, and by her humility and honesty, Einav filled the interview with color and depth as she talked about being a little immigrant from Israel and never settling for anything less than what she wanted.

As we talked, Einav received a phone call. "This is another job offer," she said with a smile. After years of trying to break into a man's world, Einav is in high demand.

What does it mean to be an executive chef at Unilever?

Unilever is an international company that holds many brands in major sectors. One is personal care, the other is household care, and then there is food. So, obviously I deal with food. People don't know what Unilever is, but when you start saying the names under the brand, like Hellmann's Mayo, Lipton Tea, Ben and Jerry's Ice Cream, Talenti, Good Humor, Breyers, Knorr, they're like, "Oh! Really! My mom uses this; I'm using this." Even when I came upon the job, I had the same reaction. I had to go home and Google it.

Unilever is an Anglo-Dutch company with headquarters in London. Our major shareholders are from the British and the Dutch royal family. We have our North American headquarters in New Jersey with a sister company called Food Solutions, where I work.

An important branch of the company is Unilever retail. This is what we sell in the supermarkets. Under the food service, we have four major channels. One is small-chain restaurants that have anywhere from one to forty-nine units. Then we have major national chains, like Applebee's and Olive Garden, with fifty or more locations. Then we have the noncommercial chains, which are the contracted caterers such as airline companies and cruise companies. Then we have what we call Club, Cash, and Carry, such as Restaurant Depot, which small restaurants use to get their supplies.

So it's a large corporation. Where do you come in?

My main job is leading the creative team and helping in strategic thinking. I report directly to the president of the company. Our marketing team can dream of many things, but it's my job to say, "OK! or "No, no, no," or "Yes, that is new." Most importantly, to provide what is needed and relevant to the operators I serve. I turn ideas into products.

For example, we are trying to create dressings that will meet the culinary trends and be valuable to a chef. We will do it under the Hellmann's brand and try to create a new and exciting flavor for them.

There are some flavors that I feel are outdated. It can't be another balsamic, you know. That's not getting us anywhere. Let's think about flavors that are either hard for chefs to create, or that are versatile enough for them to hold it in the restaurant rather than make it on their own. Those are the flavors I want to create.

So a part of your job is to introduce innovation in food?
Yes. A chef I know once said, "It's not the products that are outdated, it's the way we use them." If you use a white sauce like a Béchamel in a lasagna, that's OK, there's nothing new, but if you think about using a Béchamel-like sauce for a creamy white wine sauce instead, then you're making something new. It's now altered to become a new product and can be used for a base for an oyster clam chowder with a touch of Sriracha or something along those lines. It's changing the flavor of a base product.

Chefs are looking for boom, for flavor. Sometimes they can't afford the ingredients they need, or they can afford them but they'll buy a whole case when they need just a tablespoon. Money-wise it's not worth it. If they'd gotten it in a different format that gives them the same results and does not take their creativity away, then they'd be better off. I help to create this strategy.

I worked on frozen foods and on producing new flavors for gourmet cooking earlier in my career. A part of the thinking behind creating frozen meals to distribute to the supermarkets is to adapt them to today's way of life. I just make life easier and tastier to new mothers who do not know how to cook or have no interest in cooking.

You told me you're also trying to get chefs to network in newer ways.
I think that chefs don't attend conferences the way they used to in the past. They go less and less and less. It's because they don't have the time and because it costs a lot of money. Recently, I was at a Culinary Institute of America conference in Napa Valley. It's unbelievable, it's the crème de la crème, the top of the top, the big trends, the Harvard of cooking schools, but it costs a lot of money to participate, and that is before hotel expenses. It's $1,400 per ticket, and it's three days away. Many chefs who have smaller restaurants cannot afford to walk away from their establishment for three or four days and pay this amount of money.

On the same note, you have a lot of content that you can just source online today. You can go anywhere on YouTube, Instagram, Pinterest, and you can see pep talks by food innovators or hear chefs talk. Why do I need to stand in a crowd and see someone on stage when I can just stream that lecture?

At Unilever, our chefs network in different ways. Facebook is a big networking platform for us. I want to create a sharing space for chefs to build a community. This is where my brain is at these days.

In your opinion, who is a chef today?

I used to get really annoyed when anyone called themselves a chef. You can't just put a white jacket on and say, "Oh, I'm a chef." You need to get experience under your belt, and you need to have some sort of track record behind you. But I find that this logic has become outdated. I think today a chef is anyone who creates good food with other people, is passionate about food and feeding, and just knows the industry.

Earlier you would spend time in a culinary school, then a certain amount of years in a restaurant as a cook before you became a chef. A chef oversees and has a creativity component. For me, that's the difference between a cook and a chef. A cook will execute. You come in; you do the job; you hold the station. A chef is the one that holds the creative reins. He or she makes the decision on what the menu should look like, what dishes it should include. Once you have this creative component in your head, this is where you transfer into being a chef.

So if a housekeeper cooks very well, you cannot say she is a real chef?

But that's my point. What is a real chef? Do you need a restaurant to be a real chef? If you just love cooking and you cook up a storm at home, you create new things and try them on your friends and family, can't you be a home chef? Your kids say, "Oh, my mom is a great chef." I think it becomes very gray.

According to my understanding, there are home chefs and restaurant chefs. So what are celebrity chefs?

A celebrity chef is in the limelight. They are the ones that either have a TV show or are well known. For me, it comes with a different set of skills. There are many celebrity chefs that aren't necessarily great cooks. A celebrity chef is somebody who has some skills of cooking but also many skills of communicating with the crowd, projecting their personality, being able to be on camera or on stage and build a following. However, there are many celebrity chefs today that might not have a famous TV show but are famous for their ability to cook and have many followers on social media.

What people need to understand is that behind everyone who stands before a TV, there's a team of five, seven, or ten people working really hard in the kitchen, preparing everything, making sure that it's done right. Among those, there are great chefs with high skills in addition to having a TV personality.

For example, I think Rachael Ray would be the first one to tell you that she's not a chef. She stumbled upon that opportunity. She is more a TV personality. Throughout her career, she's always loved food and worked with it, but she didn't come from having a traditional path in a restaurant.

Can you give me an example of somebody who is a great chef but doesn't have a public personality?

Gabrielle Hamilton from Prune. She's not part of the glitz and glamor and the limelight. She's a great chef who has made herself known through her food, her restaurant, and her recipes, but she doesn't have a TV show. That's not how she's chosen to be known. On the other hand, Mario Batali is a combination of being a very good chef and having a big TV personality.

What about Emeril Lagasse?

I met him in person; he's an unbelievable guy. If you look at who started the Food Network and brought celebrity status to chefs, it's him. Through people like him, real chefs were brought to the front. He's extremely liked, because he's funny, because he's authentic. When I met him in person, I found that he's just a great guy, very humble. Nothing is beneath him. When I see people who have inflated egos, I want to tell them: "We all started with peeling potatoes, you know."

Did you have female mentors when you were working as a chef?

I did not have the privilege of working with many females in the kitchen. When I started my career, there were hardly any females in the kitchen. In Israel, I worked for a restaurant run by two females, Orna and Ella, where I learned how to make classical French pastry. Even then it was unique. But the dynamic between them was amazing. The fact that you can be business partners and very good friends for such a long time, I think, is phenomenal and very, very rare. Working for women was different because the environment was nurturing. You could feel that the vibe in the kitchen was different.

I loved baking, but I really wanted to work in the high-heat kitchen. Most of the females in the kitchen do pastry, and most of the cooking is done by guys. Even though I was totally inexperienced, with zero pastry knowledge, Orna and Ella knew my work ethic and hired me. I did that for a couple of years. It was nice, but it was not my passion. I love baking every now and again recreationally, but it's not how I get fireworks in my belly.

At the time, we made desserts for Mul Yam, which was the number-one restaurant in Israel serving very high-end, upscale seafood. I approached Orna and Ella and basically told them that I wanted to leave, and I asked them for help in finding a job. That's the environment they created—that your growth was important to them, even if it's not in their establishment.

Looking back, it's crazy. What boss can you really go to and say, "Well, I want to move to another place. Can you help me get in?" I told them I wanted to work in Mul Yam, and I asked if they could talk to the head chef, Yoram Nitzan, for me. He interviewed me, again coming in, zero cooking skills, nothing. I got the job. This is how I became the first female line cook at Mul Yam, and soon its sous chef.

What was the ratio of men to women in the kitchen?
There were only men. Three to four men in the kitchen, and no women.

How did they respond to a woman working in their space?
I grew up a tomboy; I was never a girly girl, and I think my attitude was tough. I might be tiny, but I bring it on. I think that's what I broadcast, so that was basically my ticket in. I always hung with

the guys. My best friends were boys. I had short hair, and I was always playing in the dirt when I was a kid. For me, hanging with the boys wasn't a problem, but if you tried to cross me, then we had an issue. I have no problem taking things on, but I'm never the victim. I don't start a fight, but I will finish it. If someone threatens you, you make sure you finish it. I think that earned me a little bit of respect.

There was somebody at the time who tried to antagonize me and tried to set me up sometimes. It did not go well for him. After that, he left me alone. I didn't need to do anything; he did it all to himself. I don't think it was because I was a female. I think it's natural competition in the kitchen.

My mother, Ruthie, was born in Israel, but my German parents and my grandmother were precise, very disciplined. We always joked, "Even the dust is afraid to come into our house, because it was scared of mom." My mom grew up with strict parents, not cracking-the-whip type, but with a very strict upbringing. Oh, my God, if my mom had even little donkey ears in her notebooks, her mom would unleash on her. When she folded things, she'd straighten them like a soldier would arrange his closet, in military fashion. I'm not that extreme, but I was brought up with the same sense of organization, order, and precision.

Did you follow her example as a child?

Oh, my God, at one point I was the messiest. But my mom just let me be. She just closed my bedroom door behind her and said, "Whatever." But when I grew up and went to college, I thought about it all. I don't know if it was the rebel in me as a kid, or I was doing it out of spite, but I got over it as an adult. Everything that I had observed started to sink in. All my notebooks were very organized. I was a note taker for many of my colleagues.

Did you grow up watching someone cook? Where did your "overwhelming passion for cooking" stem from?

My father was a pilot who traveled a lot. Thanks to my father's profession, I got to travel the world at an early age and experience many new cuisines. But it was my mom who took care of all the day-to-day cooking and housework. I remember we ate home-cooked meals. I would tag along with her to market when she shopped fresh—seasonal fruits and vegetable, fresh roasted coffee. I would then help her out in the kitchen. My dad was a more extravagant cook—throwing crepe parties or Chinese dinners for their friends every once in a while.

How did your time in the Israeli Defense Force shape who you are today?

I did my army service far from home and only came home on weekends. Not only did I want to break free from home, I wanted to try and make the most out of the mandatory two years. My father had been in the Air Force before becoming a commercial pilot. It just so happened that I served in the army (Air Force) during the first Gulf War—which gave my service even a stronger meaning. Being in a strict environment, following orders, living with people you never met before forces you to grow up—I think I matured a lot during my two years of service. It shaped me by making me think more clearly about who I am and who I want to be. I was part of a command chain where I was far away from calling the shots. It made me learn respect.

In the kitchen, this discipline was very handy. My genes decided to pop up at a later age, when I was doing pastry and stove cooking. So in the kitchen, I was very organized and very precise. I think that's what Yoram saw in me.

How was it cooking at such a fine-dining restaurant?

A lot of what I learned about food is through Yoram. He was my mentor. He taught me a lot about the kitchen environment, about respecting high-end ingredients, and about my work ethics. He really gave me a chance.

Earlier, I was in "cold preparation." It's a lot of work. For example, when somebody orders the fish, you fillet it, make the sauces, you reduce the stock, etc. However, when our line cook, who was a big muscular man, quit, Yoram asked me if I would take over his job. Line cooking requires a lot of physical strength. You have to carry big pots of stock, and drain them, and oversee the cooking. I answered, "I'm able to handle it. Bring it on."

But that must need a lot of stamina?

I was a track-and-fielder and an athlete all my life. I knew I was a strong person, and I liked challenges. I was the first female to hold the line cooking position.

How many years did you work for him?

I worked with Yoram for close to five years. While I was working for him, I realized that this is what I wanted for my life. I loved working in restaurants. I didn't see myself doing anything else. But later I felt like I needed to take a step back and go to school to learn the basics. I wanted to understand the theory beyond cooking to take it to the next level. I took all my life savings and packed all I needed into two suitcases. I did a lot of research about where I wanted to go: Paris, Sydney, New York. I didn't speak French fluently, and Sydney seemed too far away. So New York it was.

So how did you pursue your career in the States?

I joined the Institute of Culinary Education (ICE). It was a new facility on Twenty-Third Street. They were hungrier because they were just up and coming. I felt comfortable there. I signed up and paid them everything I had.

And you were single then.

Yes, but I came to the States with my boyfriend. I met him when he was the general manager of Mul Yam. When I decided to go to the States, I pretty much said, "I'm going. Are you coming with me or not?" Now that I knew what I wanted to do, I wasn't going to give up the dream for anyone. I wasn't going to wait for anyone.

How old were you then?

Twenty-six. I had my eyes on the prize.

You went to college in Israel?

I went to the College of Business *(Ha'Michlala Le'Minhal)* Tel Aviv. I studied social behavior and communication because all through my childhood life I wanted to be a copy writer. It's funny because now I do commercials, too, so I do advertising from a whole different angle. I never saw that coming. But it's interesting how life throws opportunities your way. You either grab them or not. My knowledge of advertising comes in handy in my present work.

However, I don't think I would've been able to do advertising. For instance, now we work with some creative agencies. We go to their creative team and say, "OK, we want a campaign for soup or side dishes, or we want to highlight the ingredients and the quick cooking time, the fact that you can have dinner within twenty minutes." We give them the framework, and they need to think about how the commercial would look, its slogan, and the face of the product. The team puts together a campaign. But if it doesn't feel right, someone will look at it and say, "Nah, I don't like this; go back to the drawing board"—I don't think that I could've handled advertising. I'd rather do the cooking.

So back to your culinary education.

What I liked about ICE was their philosophy. They prepared us for a career, and so the methodology of teaching was very hands-on and not a lot of fluff. We did internships, too, because as I like to say, cooking is like driving. You're not really a good driver until you've skidded a few times on ice or have been in an accident. It is only then that you develop your instincts and know how to read your environment. It's the same with cooking. The fact that you have the skills doesn't make you a good cook or a chef. Along the road, you need to start living in the real world, under pressure. You will have stressful days—like when your chef is having a bad day and takes it out on you—and only then you learn how to grow a thicker skin and hone your skills.

I really loved that ICE had a very intense program that was all about covering the basics and then going out into the industry and learning on the job. After nine months of school, I interned with Daniel Boulud.

First of all, he's very accepting of foreign talent starting in his kitchen, being French himself and a foreigner. You imagine a French chef yelling or being old-school aggressive, but Daniel is not aggressive at all. If he yells, it's with a reason and in a constructive way. That was good, because if I get yelled at for no reason, I know I shut down. Then you just won't get the best out of me.

The kitchen gets really intense, though. I remember an episode with a guy named Matthew, who was the sweetest and had just moved from the soup station to the pasta station. One of the lunch menu items was a soup with a ravioli. Matthew puts the soup together and the ravioli was falling apart. The soup is not clear; something's wrong. Daniel runs to the station, checks the ravioli, and figures out that the dough is not right, but he comes up with a way to do it right.

Another soup is prepared, still wrong, and Daniel goes back and fixes it again. The third time, he loses it.

He starts screaming and yelling. Let me do my best French impression for you. "What this is? Do you think you can work here like this? This is Daniel; this is my food." You see a kitchen of twenty-five people who froze. All of a sudden, everyone found a reason to look in the refrigerator or fix something on their counter. The whole kitchen was just ducking down. I'm standing in the corner, not part of the soup thing, and I was cracking up because the whole thing just felt unreal, like in a movie. The chef yelling, the cook looking miserable, the kitchen silent. That was Daniel. It took this guy three times to mess up before Daniel started yelling.

But Daniel is a genius. He has a great perception for flavor. He respects people who are humble and work hard, no matter where you came from. And I think it's one of the reasons he took me as an intern. That, and the fact that I didn't come out of school but already had six years of experience.

I interned for three or four months. It was before 9/11, so it was open for lunch at the time and it was twelve-hour shifts: 6:00 a.m. to 6:00 p.m. and noon to midnight, six days a week. You had no life basically. Later, I was working with Alex Lee, the sous chef, on the specials, downstairs in the freezing kitchen. It was so cold that we had to keep a big pot of hot water so we could warm our hands. Imagine, I had my long fleece under my chef jacket. At Daniel's, the way the kitchen works is that every station is like a mini-kitchen, so you have somebody who's doing the sauce, somebody who's cooking the fish, somebody's doing the vegetables. Daniel oversees everything, makes sure everything looks great, and pushes it to the waiter to take it out. Everything funnels through him.

His apartment was upstairs, so he came usually when we prepared in the morning. He would speak French with his chef buddies. I remember once Julia Child walked into our prep kitchen, and we all got to meet her. Once he asked me something in French without thinking, and I replied in French. He was taken aback. "You speak French?" he asked.

Do you?

I understand it better than I speak it. He was very careful about it afterward. He no longer had his secret weapon that he wielded when he didn't want the Americans to understand him.

Now you are really a certified chef with an education. And you're the Corporate Executive Chef at Unilever.

It's funny that you say *certified,* because I never felt certified. I don't know if it's good enough; you always feel like there's so much more to learn—even with my role with its big fat title. Sometimes I feel like I'm wearing my mom's clothes. I cannot believe I have this title sitting next to my name. I cannot believe it happened. Little immigrant from Israel, you know.

Tell me how you settled into life in America.

We came here with nothing, nothing. I spent all my savings on cooking school. I came here with seven thousand dollars; that's it. Nir, my husband, who was then my boyfriend, followed me, with a couple thousand dollars. So all we had for America was nine thousand dollars.

Nir came on a tourist visa; I was on a student visa. We weren't married, but we were very lucky. That's why I say someone is really watching over me. I have no doubt that there is a bigger power looking over me.

When I came here, I stayed with a friend of a friend that I had never met. I crashed with her for a couple weeks until I found a studio in Hell's Kitchen through an Israeli guy. Some friends I knew arranged for Nir to take the tests needed to work in the consulate. But it was just us; we knew no one. We had no "Vitamin P" as we say in Israel, meaning P for protection or help. We had no cousins or uncles or neighbors or friends who were connected. But just when we thought that we were going to get sent back to Israel, which wouldn't have been the worst, things started falling into place. He started working for the consulate, and we got married right after I was done with school.

Another thing happened, almost by a stroke of luck. When I was sixteen, my parents and I had visited my relatives in Miami. My father decided that I needed to get my driver's license in Miami. It was such a different reality back then. We went to the Social Security office and they issued a Social Security number for me, a sixteen-year-old tourist. I still have it. It says "Not Applicable for Work," but I had a Social Security number, which is a big deal. I could open a bank account. If you can open a bank account, you're a person in the United States. If you come to the States and you don't have credit history, you're doomed. But things lined up. Having a consulate visa, a Social Security number, and a bank account, Nir and I were able to rent an apartment. We started living our lives. Down the road, we became American citizens. It's been a long and hard journey.

What was happening to your career then?

Daniel offered me a job to stay, but I had already done high-end cooking in Israel. I wanted to do something that was more accessible to people. I took a job with a restaurant called Danal, a French restaurant near Union Square. It's since closed. Then I worked with an amazing woman called Nelly, another Israeli who moved back to Israel. When she left, I took over as the head chef of the restaurant, a Middle Eastern Mediterranean bistro.

You were in charge?

Yes, it was a very male-centric, male-dominant culture. But I believe that you become respected by giving respect. I don't believe in yelling at people. I think I'm a very soft-spoken person, relatively speaking. If I'm not happy, you'll sense it. My kids say I don't have to yell; just one look is enough. They know exactly what's going on. For me, it takes a matter of respect in working my way up. You know the most important people in the restaurant are your dishwashing and prep guys. You can be a chef and leader by title, but nothing will get done if your hardest workers are not working. If they're not, then you're stuck. Either you call somebody else or you have to do it yourself. The fact that I hold the chef title doesn't mean anything. If my dishwasher is overwhelmed, then I'll roll up my sleeves and get into the dish room and wash dishes. And that's how it should be. That's how I gain respect.

I loved my work. I worked there for two-and-a-half years, until I was very much pregnant with my first son. When my husband saw me running up and down the stairs, carrying pots and pans all day while I had a huge belly, he asked me to resign. I wanted a family, and I could see that this was not going to work. I made a decision and walked away from restaurants for a while. I think I held a grudge for quite a few years against my husband for forcing me to walk that intersection. In my head, I do my diligence and work hard, until one day I open my own space. That was the plan.

Your vision was to eventually open your own restaurant?

Absolutely. I did not see any other way. It was a given path for me.

What is your favorite food?

I'm in a ramen craze, and I have been for a while. I can be stuffed full in my tummy with a bowl of hot ramen. When I don't know if I'm tired or hungry and when those lines start blurring, all I feel like having is Japanese soupy noodles. It's also associated with my childhood. When I was growing up, my mother always made me soup. It could be ninety-five degrees outside, but when I went home from school, my mother would make me a hot bowl, either vegetable, tomato, chicken soup, or beef and barley soup. I think brothy food is my comfort food.

After the birth of your first child, how did you manage to become a housewife and a mother? Did you miss your professional life?

I grew quite frustrated at home. I wasn't out of work for long. Through the ICE alumni network, I saw a job of being the director of the culinary center under the JCC in Manhattan. The job description was very intriguing; it asked for someone who could build a center, create a curriculum, create classes for the community. I created a culinary center/school.

I designed the culinary center in the JCC Manhattan. It became a cooking studio. I created a culinary community, invited chefs to teach classes. I became creative in the kitchen, and not just with food. I had no problem picking up the phone, calling big chefs and inviting them to teach in the school. Sarah Beth Levin at the time was the "It" chef. Her place was the place for brunch and jams. I picked up the phone and called her up. My boss said, "Oh my God, you are crazy. The balls you have on you!"

But working for a nonprofit turned out to be a pain in the neck. I'm a doer; I need to get things done. Tell me what to do; I get it done. It wasn't exactly working for me, having meeting after meeting and accomplishing little. It's bureaucracy. Whoever donates money has a say in the working of the nonprofit, and if you have different people donating money, they all need to have a say. It's very hard to get work done. I was there for three years. But after the excitement of building the kitchen and creating a space, I lost the spark. So when I got pregnant with my second child, I left. For my next stint, I taught at ICE, teaching professional chefs everything from simple knife skills to cooking complicated cuisines. In 2008, and after another child, my daughter, I found my way into Unilever, working as a Corporate Chef for Research and Development, and then last year I got bumped up to my current title of Executive Corporate Chef.

What was your most challenging interview?

It was part of a Unilever interview, where I was given ninety minutes to create three meals with whatever I could find in the research kitchen. I made three dishes: one representative of the food eaten in Israel, one relating to cuisines of the United States, and the third revealing my perception of food of the future.

You struggled a lot when you came to America, and since then you have achieved so much. What do you feel about other immigrants, outsiders who are struggling in today's political climate?

I think we are living in tough times. I am an immigrant who was given the opportunity—I followed the rules and did the right things to allow me to root in this great country. I believe everyone deserves a chance, and I think diversity should be the route to a more accepting, non-judging society. It might be provocative, but I also think that one needs to be a part of the culture they choose. It is a two-way street.

Einav Gefen delivers a TED Talk

Einav Gefen is the executive corporate chef for Unilever Food Solutions, North America (UFS NA). In addition to her recognition as a global cuisine expert and under her current role, she launched a social mission to enable cultural change in the food industry and create a more sustainable, healthy work environment. Beyond her passion for food and the industry, Einav works to empower women, in the food industry and beyond, by mentoring and sharing her experiences as a way to inspire and motivate women as they pave their professional paths. Her career as a chef began twenty years ago in Israel, when she worked as a pastry chef at Orna and Ella and as a sous chef at Mul Yam, Gault et Millau, the top restaurant in Tel Aviv and one of Les Grandes Tables du Monde's 114 best restaurants. A graduate of the Institute of Culinary Education (ICE), Einav interned at Daniel and was the executive chef of Danal in the East Village. In 2001, she founded and became the director of the culinary arts program at the Jewish Community Center in Manhattan. Between 2003 and 2008 she was a chef-instructor at ICE in the professional division, before joining Unilever as the corporate head chef for North America. In that role, Einav led a team of chefs in charge of innovation development, product rejuvenation, activation with customers and consumers, and deployment of global projects. She was a speaker at TED@Unilever and competed on the Food Network show *Chopped.*

ILANA GOOR

ISRAELI-AMERICAN ARTIST AND MUSEUM CURATOR

"It takes forever to know oneself and to understand what you are doing and what you want to become. Nobody can tell you; it has to come from you."

Photo Credit: Ben Lam

I TOOK MY FAMILY TO VISIT the Ilana Goor Museum on a hot summer day. This gem of a stone structure on the top of a hill in Jaffa, Israel, was built in 1742 by a Jewish-Turkish family who used it as an inn for their pilgrimages to Jerusalem. Looking for relief from the heat, tired and sweaty, my family and I climbed four flights up to the roof terrace of the museum.

From here, the Mediterranean Sea over Jaffa's port revealed its entire glory. The blue sky merged into the horizon. Glistening waves carried fishermen's boats. We saw the peaks of the ancient mosques and the towering palm trees that transported us to biblical days and the story of Jonah and the whale.

Ilana's husband, Leonard, came to check on the invaders who wanted to meet his wife, the artist and curator of this precious museum. You could not find a more romantic place to be introduced to the love story that united the couple and the history of the museum. "She was the most beautiful girl I'd ever seen," Leonard said. "Long ago, I promised to come back in one year to marry her, and I did."

We passed through corridors lined with photographs of Ilana with many celebrities and found ourselves in the living room facing the legendary sculptor. Comfortably dressed in baggy trousers and an oversized shirt, with long silver hair and a face that has attracted many painters, Ilana Goor projected a warm look through her round glasses and made us feel at home. We spent a few hours with her as our guide through the museum, and an instant friendship developed. I wanted to know more about the life of this incredible Israeli-American immigrant, an artist who conceived, built, and filled a museum in Jaffa with international treasures, her own sculptures, and the works of promising young artists that she promotes.

Ilana has exhibited her work in museums throughout Israel and Europe. She creates art in many disciplines such as sculpture, jewelry, installations, and furniture, for which she has received numerous awards. She is especially proud of her solo exhibitions in the Israel Museum in Jerusalem and the Tel Aviv Museum. Two years ago her museum was chosen as one of the five most beautiful privately owned museums in the world.

After our initial visit, I traveled to the Israeli towns where Ilana's monumental statues are installed. A few weeks later, I met Ilana again at her brownstone in Manhattan. Not surprisingly it was reminiscent of her museum. Here is where I learned about Ilana's life in the United States and how she became an accomplished sculptor. What I found endearing is that she remains humble and, like her art, never tries to seduce or please. She remains rooted in life.

You conceived the idea of the museum, you built it up, and you singly maintain it. How did this idea of a privately owned museum in Israel come about? After all, you've lived in America as an immigrant for many years.

Actually, I never thought about it. People think that it was my life's dream. And to think about a thing like this, you really must be out of your mind, and I'm not, so it just evolved. It started in Jaffa. I love Jaffa very much because it always reminds me of Tiberias, my hometown where I was born. There, I was always sitting on the porch and seeing the Sea of Galilee. At that place I spent the best times of my life. In Tiberias I was a little girl, fully protected by my parents, by the surroundings.

We bought the house in Jaffa that eventually became the museum. It was built in 1742. A very close friend of mine bought it; he rented it for himself to make a gallery. He was American. His name was Horace Richter. When he couldn't afford the rent any longer, he called me and said, "Ilana, you must buy the place." That's how it started.

So you bought the house with the idea to live there. You didn't have the idea of making it a museum right away.

First I bought the part of the building that had the view. Then I learned its history—that it was built by four Jewish-Turkish families in 1742. They built it so they could come from Turkey a few times a year as a pilgrimage to Jerusalem. In 1860 the Arabs threw them out. They destroyed the whole house, cut it to pieces, and built a soap factory. So I first bought the part of the building with a view. Two years later, my dear friend Horace suggested that I buy the entire place and call it the "Ilana Goor House." He explained, "You are an artist. You collect. You love to help young artists."

I renovated the entire building. I was afraid to take on an architect, because every architect builds a house as if it is for himself, and I wanted to show the original as much as I could. And so I hired a young Israeli architect who promised, "Ilana, it's going to be the way you want it." The place required a lot of cleaning and effort to restore it as much as possible to maintain its original character. Horace helped me a lot, and I couldn't have done it without his encouragement. He was a very special gay man. He was an artist, and he loved life. With him, I started traveling to different shows, like the Basel Art Fair. He used to be informed of what was happening in the art world and took me along. My husband, Lenny, was always there for me, supportive and protective. Lenny is very smart, and his business talent was and is still necessary for me to embark on this extraordinary journey.

Horace gave you the first art pieces to put in the museum?

Yes. He had a great collection of paintings. He had very, very good art. When he came to Israel in 1968, he came as a very rich man. He died so poor that he couldn't pay his bills; everything was stolen and taken from him. He was such a great guy. And I was the person that he wanted to be. I had the talent; I had the openness. And he really loved me in a way I cannot explain. The saddest part is that finally when the Tel Aviv Museum gave me a show, Horace was sick and unconscious. His dream was that I would get to have recognition because although I was born in Israel, I was considered an outsider for having lived in America by now for about sixty years. So I wasn't one of the group. I was one of myself. All I wanted was for people to leave me to do whatever I wanted, do it when I wanted to do it, and be by myself.

You almost felt in Israel like the way immigrants feel when they come to a new country, despite the fact that you were born in Israel. You were the "other."

Exactly. My friend Horace could not write as well as I do. He was dyslexic, and so was I. But whenever he had to go someplace and meet somebody, I always took him to the exhibition. I owe him so much. Before him, I was nothing. I was busy with my own little drawings. I had a lot of ceramic, awful pieces of junk. But one day a friend invited the director of the California Museum of Science and Industry in Los Angeles to my house, and he said, "Who did all this?" I wasn't proud when I said I did it. But he felt differently and invited me to exhibit my work in his museum.

You don't think much of yourself, do you?
At that time, no. Not at all. I had no direction.

But you loved sculpting with clay.
That's the only thing that I loved to do. I always called them my toys. I made the garage into a studio in Los Angeles.

I believe that often your sculptures express and were motivated by experiences that you endured growing up in Tiberias, Israel, and that influenced your artistic expression. Tell me about Tiberias.
The best time of my life was when I was growing up in this tiny town. People from all over the world used to come to Tiberias for natural mud baths. That's why Tiberias had so many doctors. It was a real cultural little city, run like a European city. I grew up in a home that had a lot of Persian rugs, walls full of books, classical music. My mother had us listen to the philharmonic orchestra. My mother was a known and respected doctor, the head of gynecology, delivering babies. She also had a very good sense of humor, and people adored her. She was a very elegant, fashion-conscious woman.
I always used to run around in my underwear; I never wanted to wear clothes. I used to climb everything I saw. I was so wild, a real tomboy. I was referred to as the daughter of Dr. Sapir, although truthfully, my brother, Danny, and I did not have much contact with our mother. She was often sick and frequently went to Switzerland for cures. It was so hot in Tiberias; there was no air conditioning. My father used to wet sheets and place a fan behind them to cool the air. Between 1:00 and 4:00 in the afternoon, you could not hear a fly in Tiberias. It was like a closed town till the sun went down. [Ilana paused and teared up.] This is so hard because it reminds me of memories of my brother, Danny, who I love. The only things that moved were my brother and I, when we stole my father's car and drove up and down the street, the

only main street in Tiberias, avoiding the English police that ruled the town. The main street started at the sea and continued all the way up to Nazareth.

How old were you?

We were very young. Danny was only a few years older than me, but he always was very jealous about my relationship with my parents. For some reason, they loved me much more. I was fun, I was laughing a lot, and he was always mad and sick. I was never sick, even if I ate out of the garbage. And he was always negative. My brother was extremely handsome, extremely talented. He could play the piano, but my parents never bought him a piano. When he was fifteen years old, he could play the flute and the harmonica. I don't know why he wasn't welcome. And even though he was older than me, I was the one that got a bike.

He taught me how to ride a two-wheel bicycle. I'd say, "OK, if you wash the dishes, I'll let you ride my bike." I was already making business. When the maid left in the afternoon, somebody had to do the dishes. One day it was him, and one day me. So I would say, "If you take my turn at dishes, I'll let you ride the bicycle." And that's how it went.

It sounds like you had a very strict mother who had things in order all the time.

She was born in Odessa and went to Bern, Switzerland, to study medicine. Her father was a doctor, and so was her grandfather whose name was Dr. Paries. He wrote the first medical book in Russia, after the Rambam. My grandfather was a doctor, sculptor, and artist, and I exhibit his work in my museum today.

It looks like artistic talent ran in the family.

They all had talent; they all were scholars. They all went to school. I was the exception, a wild person. For me, school didn't exist. It was boring as hell, and I can say that I really grew up in the streets. After my mother died, everything fell apart. It was 1948, the birth of the state of Israel. The Arabs fled, and new immigrants took their place. The city ran down and fires destroyed the trees. That was when we left Tiberias and moved to the outskirts of Haifa, and my father bought a house. In Tiberias we lived in a rented house because my mother was against buying things. She was a very elegant and sophisticated woman. And never in her life would she want to own a house. In her mind, showbusiness people owned houses, those who carry a watch around their waist.

When my mother was alive, she traveled abroad for treatment for her failing lungs from tuberculosis. Danny and I were sent to foster homes in a kibbutz. The foster family was proud to host the children of Dr. Sapir. We stayed with a family called Chadash; Ita and Motke Chadash had a son I had a crush on. He was beautiful and a great swimmer, able to cross the Kineret lake. I hated living in a kibbutz with them. I spent the entire first grade there. My mother used to come and go. Although Danny and I really adored her and loved her, she shouldn't have had children. She lived for herself with her "back to the kitchen," meaning not very involved in the house or her family. She never bought me dolls, and maybe that's the reason why later I had a collection of dolls, which resides in my museum.

I was fourteen when she died. But the last two years of her life she was in hospital and she would not allow us to see her. She was a very proud woman. We missed her but respected her wishes. None of my parents' friends asked what happened to Dr. Sapir's orphans. Nobody showed any interest. That impacted the way I faced life; I am independent, and I've learned to expect difficult times and endure them.

That's when Danny, my father, and I moved to a village near Haifa call Kiryat Motzkin. My father was an engineer. Their marriage was a very strange story. He was ten years younger than my mother. They met in a little coffee house in Tiberias where everybody gathered to drink Turkish coffee. My father was an extremely good-looking man. She looked at him and said, "I'm going to marry him because I want to have good-looking children." But it wasn't really a marriage. She was busy with herself and her medical doctor friends that she studied with in Switzerland. And my father felt like an outsider.

My father's story was very interesting. He didn't know that he was Jewish until later in life. His mother was Jewish, but she died when he was four years old. His father was Hungarian, and he committed suicide soon after, so my father grew up as an orphan since the age of four. He grew up with his paternal grandfather. He didn't know until the family tried to get passports to travel in Europe and he was the only one denied a visa because he was a Jew. He didn't know the significance of that word. They told him that he was a Jew and that he could not get a visa. So he said, "What is a Jew?" And they said, "You." He walked by foot from Hungary to Turkey, and from there he traveled to Israel. He knew nothing about Judaism. It reminds me that I knew nothing about the Holocaust. And so, later, when I was asked to sculpt a memorial for the Holocaust, I had to learn all about it. You have to understand that we were isolated, rooted in Israel for many generations. Anyhow, my father served in the British army in Israel and only later became an engineer. He was a brilliant guy, and there was nothing he didn't know. He was interested in everything.

Was he interested in you and in Danny?

In me, very much. With Danny, he had problems. Danny wished that my parents could have been present when he became chief of the Department of Cardiac Surgery in Israel. He wanted so much for them to be proud of him because they never believed in him. Danny was thinking about this all his life, and I never knew. [Ilana tears up.] My father really loved me. He came to visit me when I was about to get married in Jerusalem. Actually, he came to warn me, saying, "This guy is not for you, and you will never adjust to life in America." My father was acquainted with life in America because he studied at Johns Hopkins in Baltimore, where he later became a professor and then was sent by the United Nations to Manila, which he loved. But I spent many years alone as a result of my father traveling and my mother passing.

I followed my brother to Jerusalem where he studied medicine. And I joined the Bezalel School of Art, where I was very bored; I never felt a part of the school. I simply went to follow Danny and to avoid going into the army. I knew I couldn't survive in the army because I am not one to follow orders. So I enrolled in Bezalel, the only art school in Israel at the time. I really loved my brother, and I used to wait in the house for him to come home. But he had a girlfriend, and so I was very lonely. Especially because I wasn't one to belong to youth groups. But people always used to come to me. I don't know why because I really wasn't an interesting person. I was bored, and I was very athletic and a great swimmer, so I became a student in a prestigious athletic school called Wingate. I knew it was a temporary solution because it was a time that I was not sure how to deal with my life. In that vulnerable period, I met Lenny by chance. You have to understand the feeling in Israel, which was a new country and very patriotic, what it meant to choose a foreigner as a boyfriend. It was a real no-no. Especially in my family. It was as if you went with a British soldier. We were supposed to stay away from those people. Lenny fell in love with me in a place in Jerusalem that was a restaurant in the daytime and on Wednesday evenings became a meeting place for Israeli folk dance students. That's where I met Lenny. I never understood what he saw in me, but unknown to me, I was considered beautiful.

Lenny wore a striped, wrinkled cotton suit and looked different than any Israelis I was used to. I'm a very detail-oriented person. There is nothing I don't see even though I pretend that I don't. Sometimes I scare myself that I see too much. It makes life much harder when you see all the details that other people don't see. It bothers me. And I am very critical, so I was not sure about dating Lenny.

Lenny and I made a date to meet in the YMCA, where I was competing in swimming. I regretted having made the date and tried to escape an hour earlier, but he caught me leaving. He was annoyed with me not being honest with him. I guess I inherited from my mother a dislike of foreigners. But I don't feel this way about the Arabs I live among in Jaffa. They work in my foundry. They're the best people you can ever meet. I support a few of the Arab families in Jaffa.

So how did you wind up marrying Lenny?

He was a sweet guy, and he kept his word. I don't know why he was attracted to me. There was nothing there.

But you were beautiful.

That was something else. I was not able to express myself intelligently. Danny, my brother, didn't like Lenny. "My sister is not going to marry this stranger. Never." He did not come to the wedding. Actually no family came. My mother was dead, and my father was in Manila.

Lenny kept his word. After we met, he left for a year and promised to come back to marry me, and he did. His word was good, and I respected it. After our marriage, I followed him to the United States. I experienced difficulties. My father was right. It was hard for me to adjust. But Lenny stayed beside me and made my life somewhat easier.

What a change, coming from your background of living in a small town and on kibbutz, being very protected, and with specific values, and now you find yourself in the midst of a capitalistic culture.

Meeting Lenny's parents made it even more difficult for me to adjust. His mother died when he was young. His father emigrated from Romania and was an accountant. And his father and stepmother, who was one of the richest women in New Jersey, didn't receive me very well. They couldn't understand why their son, who was so brilliant, who graduated from Georgetown, and who was celebrated in the book *Who's Who*, wound up marrying me. I realized a lot about him having met his family.

You couldn't speak English. You were not well received by the family. And you were in a foreign country where you felt like you didn't belong.

My father predicted it all. "Ilana, Israel is for you," he said. "You're going to be the best in everything you do because you are talented, and you know who you are. You may have to fight for it, but you're going to get far."

So how did you survive in New York?

Lenny was working for Paramount Pictures, but the theaters were doing very badly. So we tried to find another way to improve the movie business. He was selected with a couple of guys to think about how to bring more money to the theater. That's when they started selling Coca-Cola in theaters. And he progressed with the idea to establish concession stores in movie theaters all over America. He made a lot of money for the company. He had a very high salary. For Lenny, it was enough. He's not a showy person and doesn't need a lot. Give him a good television, books, and he's happy.

Maybe I cannot read and write well, but I'm a thinker. So I encouraged Lenny to get out and start his own business. He said, "What are you talking about?" I said, "I'm talking about life. I know about life. I happen to know about life because I learn from life. You learn from books. I learn from confronting and tackling life's obstacles and finding solutions."

For forty-five years he's been with the same company he owns. He's satisfied, has no interest to explore other opportunities. I'm different; I live for excitement.

When I met Lenny recently while visiting your museum, he told me two things. He said that you were the most beautiful girl he ever met and that you gave him an interesting life. Tell me about your life in New York.

Lenny was traveling around, establishing the stands at all the movie theaters. He developed the company and made a lot of money for them. I was traveling with him, and he told me, "Don't look at New York. That's not America. We're going to go on a trip. Omaha, Nebraska, all those small towns with one main street." We just traveled in a car all through the United States.

We stopped in New Orleans and rented a house. He was gone for a week and came back. In the meantime, I met some friends. I remember one of them was special. Her name was Frieda—a Jewish woman married to an extremely rich guy who didn't give her a dime. She lived in a nice home. And Grace, her girlfriend, had no money at all. In the morning I used to get up and go to Frieda's or to Grace's, or I'd go walking. There was jazz in New Orleans. But Lenny wasn't there.

My mind wondered, *What am I going to do with my life?* I knew this wasn't my life; it was Lenny's life. I'm sure if I had had family in Israel, I would've left. But in retrospect it's actually good that I stayed in the USA, knowing how I was able to grow and become who I am today. And I had my boys, my family.

But the beginnings were not easy. We stayed in New Orleans for three years. And since I was very unhappy, we came back to New York, and then Lenny got an offer to go to Los Angeles. We left our small apartment in Forest Hills, where my son was born. When they brought him to me, it was the first time I experienced happiness in America. We didn't have any money. I never went to a department store. Everything was secondhand. The washing machine, everything. I didn't mind, but I didn't see anything new. All I knew was how to make a nice home. The days with nothing were the best. Whatever I did was the most beautiful, even if it was small. It was charming. This is my better talent—to put things together.

We moved to Los Angeles, and Lenny became the boss of the company. In the meantime, I took a course in clay sculpting. Vito, the instructor, set us up in a circle and gave each one of us a bushel of clay. Each one was allowed to do whatever they wanted, while he was teaching. This was a night that I used to wait all week for. Vito asked me, "Did you ever study sculpture?" I said, "No, I went to art school, but to tell you the truth, I didn't study anything." He said, "But you really have a great talent." I didn't know what he was talking about, but I loved the clay.

I was unhappy in Los Angeles. It's not a city. It's like a big village. Most of the time you spend in the car, going from one place to another.

But that's where things started to happen for you. You mentioned you were invited to present your clay work at the Museum of Science and Industry.

The director was a very nice man, and he invited me to exhibit my work. My first thought at the time was I wish my mother were alive to hear that. He recognized a talent in my work. I used to come every day to the museum, to sit and listen to the comments that visiting students said when they looked at my work. It astonished me that they liked it, but maybe because they didn't know anything. The director wasn't savvy about art. He was a manager of the business side of the museum. If he knew what art was, he wouldn't have let me have a show at the museum.

It takes forever to know who one is. What you're doing and what you really want to do. Nobody can tell you; it has to come from you. I didn't know what I had, but I knew that I saw details in everybody wherever I went. People look, but they don't see. I always saw details and grew up for myself. I took a long time, and I was concerned all the time about how I was going to make a living. It was very difficult for me to ask for help, and I never did.

What was your first big break?

It was in Los Angeles. When the twenty-five-year celebration for

Jerusalem happened, I was friendly with the consul's wife. The consul was a prince of a man whose name was Hezi Carmel. His wife was an elegant woman. She said to me that she believed that I should be the one to sculpt a memorial to commemorate the twenty-fifth anniversary of Jerusalem. She thought that since I was a talented sculptor and I was Israeli and Jewish, I must have an emotional connection to the Holocaust. But I didn't know much about the Holocaust because we lived forever in Israel. My grandfather came to Israel in 1920. He believed in the importance of building a Jewish state, a real Zionist. I have a picture of him in Odessa leaving for Israel.

So in 1973 I accepted the commission, and because I knew so little about the subject, I went to Germany to learn, and I saw things that I wish for nobody to see. In order to start the project, I went downtown to Venice, Los Angeles, to a studio that was owned by a friendly guy who liked to drink beer and watch a ball game, a true happy American. I asked for his advice on how to start the project, and I bought chicken wire that I found in his foundry. I was thinking a lot and decided that I would not repeat the images of imprisoned Jews hanging over a camp fence begging for food and blankets. I would have my own idea, and I knew what I was going to do.

I created a monumentally powerful woman with a hollow face, representing a chimney. She has huge arms, carrying the remains of her son and a pair of shoes. The shoes indicate that it was not a normal "death," because a person who dies a "natural death" in bed dies barefoot. The statue kept growing and growing, and I had to continue work outside of the garage. It didn't fit, as it reached ten feet in height. And finally, I sprayed it with bronze.

Teddy Kollek, the mayor of Jerusalem, came to the memorial and liked the statue. He said the memorial had to go to Yad Vashem, the Holocaust museum in Jerusalem. We became very close friends, Teddy and I. When the committee from Yad Vashem came and approved it to go, we named it *Never Again*. And I was in heaven. Since then I have built many large sculptures that are located in museums in different cities in Israel.

Today I know who I am. I'm confident and know what I'm good at.

Tell me about your outdoor sculptures.

When I was commissioned to do a sculpture for University of Haifa, I was wondering, Why does Haifa have to be decorated since it is such a beautiful town with a beautiful view? I was very surprised. But I did a very large statue of a Bedouin woman holding a child and named it *Mother and Child*. She is wearing a large gown. You can see, from under the gown, the toes of mother and child touching. I thought it was appropriate for Haifa, where a mixed Jewish and Arab population live in peace together. I wanted to unify the love.

When I was in LA, I did another statue called *Morning*. It is in remembrance of the murder of an Israeli family—mother, father, and children—in the morning by Arabs. The grandmother asked me to do the statue so the town would remember. And so it is now standing in Naharia. At the time I was actually building furniture, and I hesitated doing this sculpture because I thought I would not be able to express the life that was lost. You know, it is very difficult to put life into plaster. Very few sculptors can do that. Henry Moore I admire, because he's the only one who wasn't afraid to go through the material. He built a statue, and then you could see through it. He was the first one to do it. He was brilliant. Sometimes when I travel, I can see completely unknown statues in different yards that I admire. And there are no names attached to them. It's an inherent quality within the artist to be able to give life to a material. So I named the statue *Morning*, fulfilling the grandmother's request.

What do you think is your best work?

The one that I made in tribute to my mother in Tiberius, the *Mother Ship*. It was installed in 2003, and it is positioned where my mother and I used to meet every day for lunch on the beach promenade close to the shore. Many people in Tiberius still remember my mother. They were so happy that they had tears in their eyes, and they said, "The doctor is happy." It is the best I ever did. My mother, Dr. Raya Sapir, was the head of the maternity ward in the Schweitzer Hospital in Tiberius. The ship is made of a wooden deck with sails made of a sheet of galvanized steel extending on either side of the mast. It is a metaphor for wandering and migration. The height and the strength exhibited by the ship is a metaphor for my mother's free spirit and strength. Like many immigrants who come to a new country, my mother, like the ship, was anchored and dedicated to thriving in Israel.

The memorial that you did for the fallen soldiers, for the town of Ra'anana, is very powerful. It was erected in 1988, and it is very different from the rest of your sculptures. The red column growing as a vein in the middle is a metaphor for life continuing in an upward stream.

I got a phone call from somebody who said, "Ilana, why don't you compete for Ra'anana?" I said, "What is in Ra'anana?" It was explained to me that they wanted to beautify a town that is filled with drug addicts. So I came up with a statue that stood erect, unlike the other competing artists who had suggested statues that were lying down. And I won the competition. It is a twelve-meter high rise using vertical plates made of rusting COR-TEN steel. It symbolizes the hard material from which we people are made and the scratches and bruises we absorb through life. It is topped with four plates that form the Star of David, visible from a bird's-eye view. In its lowest part, it is interrupted with a red plexiglass pipe that represents bereavement and courage. I named it *Beit Yad Lebanim*.

So Lenny, as usual, was aware of your unhappiness, and you moved to New York.

In Los Angeles we lived in a wonderful house, with a swimming pool and a tennis court and our two children. Lenny was driving a Rolls Royce and felt like a movie star. But I found this life empty. I wasn't living. Every year I was looking forward to visit Israel, but I had no family. I had some friends; these friends are good, simple people—they work hard, and they're poor. They worked for me forty years in my foundry. I brought them to the US to visit, otherwise they couldn't afford it. They stayed with me because we love each other. So we moved to New York, and we bought an old brownstone on East Seventy-Fifth Street that we renovated.

When happened in New York that changed your life?

One day we went to shop in Bloomingdale's to buy shoes. Lenny was in the men's department. He was wearing a belt with a buckle I sculpted. A person from Bloomingdale's stopped him and asked about the belt.

So Lenny said, "My wife does it." And the man asked if I sold them. Lenny said that I made them as gifts for my girlfriends. He said he wanted to meet Lenny's wife. And he came to meet Lenny's wife, and his wife was me! He asked me to make them for the next week. I said sure, and I flew to Israel to have them made in my foundry, and I brought them back a week later.

He bought all of them and asked Lenny if I would be a representative of those belts in the United States. Lenny saw that if a professional guy wanted to manage me, why not do it himself? So Lenny took over the project. He took pictures of my belts, presented them to Bloomingdale's, and a museum and many department stores bought them. I made millions.

Lenny in the beginning was excited, but he lost interest. We opened a store in Midtown. I flew all over the United States. People bought the belts online, and it went on for three years until people started to produce less expensive versions of my belts. Then we stopped selling them.

You were honored with the Roscoe award for the most beautiful line of residential furniture. How did you get interested in furniture making?

That was after I exhibited my furniture at an art expo in the Jacob Javits Center. Building furniture started in my very small apartment in Jaffa with a beautiful view, and Prime Minister Yitzhak Rabin asked me to host a group of friends for a small party on my terrace. The museum did not yet exist. He said, "I want to bring twenty-five very important politicians. Can you host them, please?" I loved Yitzhak Rabin, and I said yes, but I was wondering how I would do it. I got the idea to use rebar. It's a regular building material that reinforces cement, and there's a beautiful decorative line on it. I decided to use it as the legs for the table. Then I found a small store in Jaffa, and I bought heavy glass that was used during the 1948 war to protect tanks from bullets. I used the panels as tabletops. I decorated the tables with bronze birds I sculpted. Those birds always stay on my table, unlike the ones that fly to my terrace in the morning and then disappear. Yitzhak loved my tables. We used to spend a lot of time together.

That's how I started to make furniture. One day my friend Horace said, "Ilana, why don't you participate in a show in the Javits Center? And since then, I've been asked to present my furniture in design buildings in many cities in the United States.

Following the show in the Javits Center, I got the Roscoe Design prize for the most beautiful residential furniture. It was in 1986, and that's when I met Andy Warhol there. He said to me, "You're really going to succeed. Your material is all leftovers that nobody paid attention to. You made it elegant." He was right. I succeeded. In 1987, the furniture was presented in the Israeli Design Museum wing. The furniture featured clear-cut designs made by cutting, bending, and hybridization of simple materials. Today I fabricate them with iron, leather, glass, and authentic fabrics.

Tell me about your museum and your collections in Jaffa. It's very eclectic and filled with hybrid art and sculptures you have made, right? You have collectibles from all over the world. You find stuff in nature, and you make something out of it, and you promote young talent. What is your fascination with stuff that you find outside in nature?

I make them to be fascinating. When I meet them, I see them, and I know that I can do something with them. Something that will be beautiful. I have a vision, an eye for detail.

I don't plan ahead. Just like I never plan a day. When people say, "Ilana, what are you doing today?" I say, "I don't know. I didn't open the door yet." People say, "Ilana, where do you find all those things?" I say, "I don't find them. They find me."

One of my favorite sculptures of yours is the famous bronze pots series.

I love them too. Each carries the head of a different nation. The head wishes to get out, and yet it is enclosed in the pot just the way immigrants live their lives in their adopted countries. They stay with their own kind. We try to merge and make one nation, but we like to stay with each other. It's hard to get out. Just like me. "I stayed in the pot." I looked at myself. I lived here all my life, and I was lonely. I never tried to change my way of speaking. I speak American as if I speak Hebrew. But I have to say that America was my school. What I learned in America I could never learn anywhere else. You live here, you feel here, and you learn here.

For a long time, I was very unhappy here in the United States. It takes several generations to know who you are, to learn your identity in an adopted country. Look at the Holocaust survivors and their children. They are still feeling the horrors, living in their parents' past.

But I say to myself, "Maybe it's a good thing that I don't have a family in Israel. If I had one, I probably would have gone back, and maybe nothing great would have happened to me."

You've often tried to make social statements with your work. For example, the box full of dolls. You kept one out of the box. And with the benches in the park in Hulon—you arranged them in a flower garden, but you kept one bench out of the circle. Why do you leave things on their own?

With the dolls, I originally collected them as decoration for my kitchen in Los Angeles. But then they bored me. The poor dolls from Peru needed companions. When I went to Morocco, I found rich dolls with fancy clothing, eyes, and hair. I mixed rich ones with the poor ones, and that made it for me. By themselves, they were boring. I placed them all in a box, and I kept one out of the box—that was me. I always was, and always will be, "the other."

In 2007, I created the benches in Hulon Park. All the artists were assigned to do work inspired by children's stories. I had the story *Two Cats on One Bench*. I installed five benches and eleven bronze cats. They were stretching on the benches that were in a circle, but I kept one bench out. That was a metaphor for me.

I liked that project for the same reason I like to produce furniture. They are artistic, but they also serve a functional purpose.

What about The Golden Plow?

It's about how far we got from "working the earth" to "worshipping the golden calf," or becoming materialistic. Did you also notice the big table I named *The Day After*? [Note: shown on page 107.]

I sure did. It's scary. It's set up like one is invited to have dinner in hell. You set up the chairs and the bronze plates around the table. However, on top of the table you arranged skulls and bones of human and animal bodies, an imaginary spider, and plants, all in a surrealistic state of a nightmare, like the end of the world. By the way, I like the beautiful candlesticks and the chandelier above, lighting the table, that you sculpted. What were you thinking when you made this display?

I was thinking that the world is imperfect. Truly I was thinking about many things, especially when I see the richness of food in supermarkets and restaurants. Then I think of the disaster going on in Syria and the rest of the world. It is hard. I think about myself, from the age of fourteen when I lost my mother. I could have become somebody else. I could have grown up poor. It's amazing that I became who I am, growing up alone. When people cry to me and ask for help, I give to some, and others I don't. I know that if I would have taken the wrong step, I would have figured how to change it to the right one. It is a learning process that started at the age of four. People don't have to teach you; you learn by watching. I am a watcher. I was watching my family, and I remember the very good things. I say it's amazing what I have become. It's not luck. You bring your own luck. I was unhappy for many years, but I said I'm stronger and I'm going to win. Now I know myself, and I am confident in who I am.

Ilana Goor has exhibited her work around the world, including solo exhibitions at the Israel Museum in Jerusalem and the Tel Aviv Museum. She has received many awards and honors, including the Peres Roscoe Design Prize for Best Design in Residential Furniture (1986); a Life Achievement Award from the Israel

Ilana Goor and her preliminary Eagle sculpture for Herzliya, Ilana Goor Museum

Construction Center (2011); and being named an honorary citizen of Tel Aviv and Jaffa (2016). In 2016, the Ilana Goor Museum was honored as one of the five most beautiful, privately owned museums in the world.

MI JONG LEE

KOREAN-AMERICAN CLOTHING DESIGNER AND BUSINESSWOMAN

"When one collection ends, I can't wait to start design for the next season. That is a time to dream. It is time to put things together, and I can't wait to see what I find out about myself as I'm going through this process."

LIKE MOST ARTISTS, MI JONG LEE struggles to find the concept that will grow into next season's fashion line. But once the moments of despair subside and she lands on her inspiration, she knows she will never stop designing womenswear.

The dresses, blouses, soft jackets, and other components of the Mi Jong Lee brand express a sensibility inspired by Mi Jong's Korean heritage and a childhood spent living in diverse places. And though every season she reinvents herself, Mi Jong's look is consistently geared for strong women who communicate their personalities via their clothes. Her work is an expression of power, elegance, and flexibility.

In Spring 2017, I head to Thirty-Seventh Street and Seventh Avenue to meet Mi Jong Lee at her studio. She greets me with a warm embrace. I'm struck immediately by the intimate environment she has created at EMMELLE—the name is based on her initials M and L. Her salon is awash with sunlight, brightening a mannequin dressed in a silk blue-and-raspberry gown. In another corner I see an off-the-shoulder white dress decorated with black-and-gold calligraphy, and Asian-style wide-bottom pants with a coordinated brilliant gold silk top.

I'm in for a treat as I'm led to where the action takes place. About thirty busy workers rush to complete their personal assignments for the Fall 2018 collection. The summer line is finished and ready for sale in the store on the west side of Madison Avenue. These women are mainly from Mexico, Ecuador, India, and Guyana. The only sounds I hear are those of the cutting and sewing through a cloud of ironing-water vapors. "Do you have any American employees working for you?" I ask. Mi Jong proudly responds, "These are all American citizens. They are first-generation immigrants like me." There is no outsourcing at Emmelle. All the work is done right here.

As I head back to the studio's salon, I pass a young woman working on a computer, changing the colors of an Italian lace from white to turquoise and then raspberry. Chosen for garments in the Summer 2018 line, the colors were inspired by the Mexican artist Frida Kahlo. Many rolls of different materials and hues are aligned along the wall, ready to go "under the scissors" to make Mi Jong's latest visions come true. Kahlo, along with artists Toko Shinoda, Zaha Hadad, and Henry Matisse, have recently inspired Mi Jong's fashions, which emerge with hints of calligraphy, bold lines, and additional influences that mesh with the designer's internal compass.

Mi Jong's heritage traces back to Korea's Buddhism of the Goryeo Dynasty (918–1392), Confucianism and neo Confucianism of the Joseon Dynasty (1392–1910), and the Christianity that gained popularity during the Imperialistic time of the oppressive Japanese regime (1940–45).

Afterward, Korea was divided into North and South.

Mi Jong was born 1959 in Seoul, South Korea, where she spent her early youth and eventually returned as a young adult. She embraces some of the Buddhist Confucian values she grew up with, such as simplicity, humility, reverence, obedience, social generosity, and respect for her elders. But other characteristics of the ancient Korean traditions, such as social hierarchy, a gender-defined society, and suppression of individual growth, would hinder her personal life.

Her travels with her diplomatic family to Mexico, Spain, and Costa Rica, as well as graduating from an Ivy League college, westernized Mi Jong. She chose the road "less traveled," from an ambitious girl from South Korea who wanted to be a teacher to becoming an independent and successful designer in New York City.

Mi Jong is not only one of the most sought-after designers for women in New York, or one of the city's best-kept secrets. She gives women a voice. Mi Jong doesn't just design clothes; she designs confidence for women. "I don't think my clothes are for everybody," she says. "I think my clothes speak to women who have their own philosophy, who have their own personality." She brings in elements from around the world and integrates them into her clothes. By owning her own culture and heritage and by bringing it into her American life, Mi Jong has truly become an American treasure.

Tell me how a young South Korean woman managed to make a statement in the competitive world of fashion in New York.

I was born in Korea to parents who were the first generation to rebuild their society after the Second World War. Dad was sponsored to study in Australia international foreign affairs, and when we came back, his career and diplomacy started.

When I was seven years old, we followed my father to his first post as a diplomat in Mexico. There my brother and I attended a Canadian international school. Korean is my first language. Spanish is my second language, and English is my third. We stayed in Mexico for three years, and then we went back to Korea for two years. When I was twelve, we moved to Spain for three years, and after that we proceeded to Costa Rica for the next two years. My dad was a common ambassador in the area. At the age of seventeen, I came to the United States, to New York, and I graduated from Cornell University after majoring in sociology. I saw my future in academics. But since my father was a very fervent nationalist and a patriot, I went back to Korea thinking that I would be able to fit in and be a part of the teaching establishment in a prominent university. I was so looking forward to living in Korea.

Unfortunately, it was not meant to be. It was the first time that I encountered rejection for being a woman and the person that I had become. The empowerment path I had taken, which gave me self-confidence, now stood in my way. The professor who interviewed me shocked me when he dismissed my thesis for which I was honored at Cornell University, and without looking at me, he said: "I will not spend my time investing in a girl, especially a young, pretty one from a good family. I won't do it; it's a waste of time." For the young girl that I was, coming with all the bright emotion and possibility, it was shocking. Soon after that I was set in an arranged marriage that lasted six months. I divorced and left, and unfortunately, I was disowned by my family for doing so. I was very close to my family, and that broke my heart.

Obviously, the Confucianism and Buddhist traditions guided your parents' decisions. To them, you betrayed their belief that the individual's well-being is secondary to honoring the family and the tradition.

Yes. It's interesting that my mother, who was the daughter of Buddhist parents, converted to Christianity. My mother is a very strong woman; she read the Koran, the Bible, and the New Testament, and she found that all religions are similar and decided to convert to Christianity, which was the trend after the war.

Why is it that Christianity attracted so many in Korea, especially after the Japanese War?

Well, I believe that the Protestant missionaries provided education to theimpoverished Koreans after the war, and they were able to convert them more successfully to Protestantism than to Catholicism.

Going back to our discussion, at that time it was unheard of that a girl would leave her husband. The other way around was accepted. I explained to no avail that my country had rejected me, and therefore I was now driven to follow my passion, so I left for New York, arriving alone with two suitcases. I was scared. I stayed in a small hotel for two full days, and finally I got the courage to get out on the third day. I came out of my room as a result of a scare I had after a drunken man knocked on the door of my room—at which point I thought, *Oh my God, this could have been the end of me without having even tried.* So the first thing I did was to wander around the fashion district and register as a student in the Parsons School of Design. I needed to find a job, so I walked on Madison Avenue and knocked on a few doors, and I actually was offered two jobs at the time, and I chose one. I presented myself as a twenty-two-year-old, announcing that I graduated with honor from Cornell and was attending Parsons and needed a job. Do you believe it?

Yes, I do believe it. You are the product of two strong-willed parents.

I took the job on Seventy-Seventh Street and Madison Avenue, a company that made their own clothes and employed six Eastern European women. They did everything by hand, including smocking, and I learned from them how to sew. Within eight months, I became the manager of the store. Not knowing any better, I announced to Mr. Beth, the owner, that I was going to be there for two years until I finished my associate degree in Parsons and then I would leave and open my own business. Now, how many twenty-one-year-olds would say something like this? Mr. Beth was my first angel.

You took a chance; he could have let you go, but obviously you must have been very important to his business.

Well, he was a very interesting man. His response was, "Well, meantime you are here to help me." He used to make beautiful cotton shirts from Switzerland. I learned from him about quality and how to create a piece from thread to seam. Two years later when I graduated from Parsons, I also reconciled with my parents—after all, I was their little jewel, the one girl that did everything perfectly, and my mother forgave me.

At the age of twenty-three, I tried to rent a four-hundred-square-foot store. The owner was Mr. Harris, and his manager looked me up and down and said, "Do you have any real estate agent?" "No," I said. "Are you a national brand?" "No," I said. "We don't speak to anyone who doesn't have a real estate agent." So I walked out of the store and went to Douglas Elliman— their office was around the corner—and I asked for a real estate agent. I returned with a young, inexperienced agent. I said to the manager, "Can we talk now?" And this little man who was the general manager was horrendous to me; he had absolute power. He looked at me, this young Korean girl, and answered, "No, you have no credentials." My real estate companion disappeared. I was disappointed, and on my way out I mumbled, "This is not fair. You said you needed a real estate agent to talk to, and I brought you one. Thank you very much." But at that moment I heard a voice from the back of the room say, "Could you bring in this young lady, please?" That was Mr. Harris, and he asked, "Do you think you can manage four months' security deposit?" I said, "Yes, I think so." He said, "Young lady, I'm going to take a chance on you; I think you will be successful." Isn't that amazing? So he was my second angel.

Was that your big break, the one that enabled you to start your own business?
Yes, I got the store. I started my business with four-hundred square feet on Madison Avenue in the Upper East Side of New York. The first year was a failure because I did not know what I was doing. I refused to have a gate to protect the store because it was not attractive. Shortly after, somebody threw a cinder block at my glass wall, and the entire merchandise was stolen. It was 1984. The first thought that came into my mind was what I was going to tell my parents, who gave me the seed money for the business.

But my mom is a very strong woman, and I remember when I consulted with her whether I should start my business on Madison

Avenue, since rent is pretty expensive there, or whether I should start it in a less-desirable place like Third Avenue, she responded, "No, start on Madison and stay on Madison, because if you start on Third Avenue, you may never get to Madison." So now at the time of need, my mother came through and said: "This is the money you requested for the tuition to go to Harvard, and we denied it from you. You can now use it to restart and build your store again."

By the way, the reason they denied me the opportunity to continue my studies at Harvard after I graduated from Cornell is because they felt that I would be overqualified for marriage. But now, at this point my mom said, "Go for it; reopen your store." And I promised her that I had learned my lesson.

I lived at 1040 Park Avenue, in a little apartment, and I set up a sewing machine in my bedroom, and I had one man who worked for me, cutting and sewing. That's how I started.

By the fifth year, I was very successful in creating and manufacturing my own designs. I directed my merchandise to the consumers only. I did not do any advertising; it was all word of mouth, and I still have customers who have been with me for thirty years.

My company is called EMMELLE, and it is successful by word of mouth. It is said that I am the best-kept secret in New York. Now I own a large store on Madison Avenue as well as one on Lexington, but I also have a wholesale business that sells to sixty-five stores around the United States.

I remember another immigrant story when I felt disadvantaged because I was young, female, and of a different race. I was twenty-four, and I found a store I wanted to rent and eventually extend up to the second floor. One of the owners took a liking to me. He gave me advice that when his brother came, I should ask for a twenty-one-year lease with no rental for the second floor because I'd be adding value to the property by doing so, and that's exactly what I did. The deal was signed. Shortly after, they changed their mind and called me back, after I already had a permit for construction in six months. They sat me in the middle of the room surrounded by eight men, some lawyers, and some other members of their family, and they tried to have me pay the rent for the second floor. I was shocked and furious, and my response was: "Gentlemen, I've already negotiated my lease, so I'm not here to negotiate another lease. Let's battle this out." I was scared, but I was angry. I said, "If you think that I don't have the legal resources to battle it out, you're wrong. In the end, it is your loss, not mine. Please let me know your decision." And I walked out. I don't think this would have happened if I had been a man and not a minority.

I guess they underestimated your strength and your intelligence. How many people do you employ now?

I employ thirty people, mostly women, mostly immigrants. Most of my staff have been with me for a very long time. My bookkeeper who is from Guyana has been with me over twenty-two years. My head sewer who is from Colombia has been with me nineteen years. My presser from Ecuador has been with me sixteen years. It is a very tight team. We fight, we butt heads, but at this point we have grown together to become a close family. It is a small organic family. It is mostly Latin, it is warm, it's loud, but everybody is invested in it.

But when I visited there, it was silent. Maybe they're afraid of the boss?

No, actually nobody's afraid of me. In the production area, they have Latin music. We just didn't go up there. That is one of the things that they requested of me, so they always have Latin music, salsa, etc. However, in the design area where you were, it is very quiet. We are a small company, so we are always multitasking, and everybody is wrapped up in their own thing.

I saw an area where a high-tech young woman was sitting in front of a computer and changing the color of lace on the screen.

These days, the young design graduates are incredibly skilled. Even me, in each phase there are certain things I haven't mastered, but the world is changing and fascinating. This lace that she was working on is from Italy, and my design for this season is very bright, very vibrant.

It is raspberry and turquoise. I'm inspired by Frida Kahlo. In the old days, what you had to do was call the mill, send them a Pantone color, they would send it back to me for approval, and back and forth. Nowadays, immediately I can approve it on the computer. We then send the computer-generated file to the mill where they produce a little swatch, what they call a "strike- off." They send it back to me. The whole process has been shortened by about three to four weeks.

Your production is very manually intense, and yet you do not replace it by machine.

Agreed. That is a very strong core of my philosophy. I've been in this business for thirty years. I've done everything literally my own way. I work directly with clients, consumers. I'm doing my own take on fashion, and I'm very grateful for this because I think those things get translated out. I'm still really trying to preserve that; it is important to me.

Explain to me how this philosophy of not taking any shortcuts translates to being alive financially?

Very, very difficult. I'm one of the first companies that a long time ago decided to have a vertical structure. What I mean by that is that I have my own retail outlet, my own wholesale, and my own manufacturing. I'm not relying on anybody else. And by having a vertical structure my profit margin stays within the company. I'm not going to say it is easy.

You don't have a middleman?

I don't have a middleman; that's very important. Except for my wholesale business that grows on the side, and it continues to grow because it has wider outreach. My wholesale business is also very different; the production is all year long. What I mean is that if you are a store that buys a garment from a company that manufactures in China or even in Italy, that store can only buy once, receive the merchandise, and sell it once. From me you can buy all year-round because when the sizes of the clothes have been sold, the store can order more, and I can supply it within two weeks. Actually, I double my volume of wholesale business in a season because by the end of the season, the initial order that I get from the store doubles because it is continuous. It is not a structure that will make me into a hundred-million-dollar brand, but it is a structure that keeps me tight, organic, and financially viable.

Brilliant. When I came to your atelier, I saw garments that were being prepared for the next year. I'm just wondering, how do you know what would be sellable so far in advance?

It is crazy about this industry.

I would think that a designer needs to sense the customer demand at the time, and customer demand is volatile and influenced by the change of weather, politics, and economics.

Right now, I'm working on the spring season. I can tell you that the fabric mills and the trend forecasting is already coming out with the fall season. What they do is they look at social changes, they look at the global flow, they look at many factors to predict where they are going. When I started the business organically, outside of this industry, they used a lot of flowery words to describe the trend. I would go to trend seminars and they were declaring things like, "We are going for transparent opacity." Now what does that mean?

Sounds like an oxymoron to me.

Exactly. Beyond the flowery words, beyond the transparent opacity, or luminosity, beyond all that there is a social emotionality that is guiding my design.

I'm influenced by nature, by architecture, by change in evolution, and by happenings. Does this predict all the time? No. If the industry could predict, then the coat industry wouldn't have suffered two years ago so badly. We have global warming, so what went on with the fur industry and the heavy outerwear industry could not be predicted. This industry suffered deeply.

But women love the feel of fur, so it is coming back in a different manner because we have less severe weather. Also, buildings are air-conditioned or heated, and clothes have to be adaptive.

I would think that with many women taking high positions, their clothes have to look good from the morning to evening as they proceed through meetings. The requirements are to design clothes that won't wrinkle and are fluid so that they can stay elegant throughout their entire day. I cannot be too trendy because clothes should not label the woman.

I believe that because you are a multicultural person having lived in Asia, Mexico, Spain, Costa Rica, and America, you have integrated those condiments into new flavors that stamp your design.

Thank you. I think this is tied to the business of the immigrant experience. I think it is so important that I bring something different to the American culture. I bring my heritage. I bring my life experience. Both my grandmothers were Buddhist, and they were co-heritage traditional Korean, and I still have that in me. All those memories, spices, smells, I bring with me. I was raised in Latin America. I love that culture. I speak Spanish better than Korean at this point. I work with Hispanics. I love the warmth, exuberance, the directness, and the emotionality in contrast with the calmness of my Korean background. I love it, and that does come through in my design. Whether it is the Asian flavor or the Latin one that comes out in my interpretation, my collection presents a point of view that makes it different and unique.

So every season I get bonded, connected, to an artist, to a culture, to a place, and my collection gets inspired from that. A couple of seasons ago it was Zaha Hadid, the amazing architect from Iraq who passed away. She was amazing. It seems that I am really drawn to very, very strong women. The next season I did the colors of Matisse. I fell in love with his vibrant colors. This fall season I was inspired by a Japanese artist, Toko Shinoda. I saw her calligraphy and prints. I love calligraphy. My grandmother used to sit me down, and we used the calligraphy brush. It looks simple, but it is not. It is the strength of your spirit, your core, coming through your hand to the brush stroke. The simple brush stroke really conveys all of that. I always have had such a cool feeling about that, and there it was. So I said, "OK, this is my inspiration this season." What a joy to be able to do that each season!

This season coming up I am going back to Mexico. It's where I was raised. Their culture is so artistic. I'm touching base with Frida Kahlo, not just her art or her painting, but really who she is. The woman is amazing; she's defiant.

It took so much strength to overcome what happened in her life.

Her defiance manifested in the cultural traditional garments she wore and the decision to dress like a man if she wanted to do so. Her defiance showed when she looked into the camera, and that's inspiring to me.

I can see the refined line and the precision of the subtle changes of black in the art of Hadid and of Shinoda. It is so opposite to Frida Kahlo's vibrant colors. How do you find balance to convey both?

I love the fact that I can jump from one culture to another, from one perspective to another. When I went to Paris to research Zaha Hadid, I realized that there is a lot of calligraphy in an Arabic form. Yes, there is an absolute tie into that and what Toko Shinoda does with her art. So it is a human commonality that happens no matter where.

I can't wait to see your creation jumping into the world of Mexico, but maybe you see a common thread there as well.

I do. Right now I am in the process of selecting fabrics and collecting colors. I'm curious about how these things are going to come out. My challenge is to bring in that exuberance but make it modern and elegant. This is exciting to me. You are getting me thinking while I'm talking to you. Yes, I am so tied into that exuberance, but I guarantee you that my process will bring in the control of Oriental culture. I think that in the end it will be an amalgam of the two. I really want to express the power of Frida. The individualism of Frida. You know, our conversation really is helping me.

Well, you know I love art, and I love fashion, so I'm totally mesmerized by the process of the way you think and create. Women have to understand your philosophy, and certainly it takes a specific personality to wear your clothes. Not everybody can wear them.

Agreed.

There was an article in the New York Times *describing fashion adapted to the woman of today who needs to assert her importance and equality in the present political mood. They showed ridiculous fashion—combinations of things that make a woman look like a clown. You are staying away from that.*

Yes, I've always done that. There is a fashion, and there is style. There is the fashion industry mechanism where they have to reinvent the trends right now with street wear. Women who are going to board meetings are not going to wear an oversized parka. It is just not going to happen. Fashion to me is in the long spectrum of art and functionality. Fashion has to be an incorporation of both. I really do believe that I can express my own creativity without pushing women to different trends. At the end of the day, I am hoping that my clothes speak to the woman who is actually living, functioning, and leading the world with her own personality, intelligence, and individualism. And not by wearing an oversized parka.

It's my belief of not wanting to be so immersed in the trend of the moment. My clothing is not for department stores because, like you said, it does not appeal to everyone. You have to feel empowered by my design, and you have to be able to absorb and digest what I am proposing.

The combination of the modern and classic lines is attractive to me.

Yes, the deep blue and raspberry fabric that you are referring to is very technologically at the forefront. I'm classic. I do believe that, at the end of the day, the canvas is the female body. For me, making that as flattering as possible is a core fashion. That is where classic things last through decades, through tradition, and through everything. My point that season was Matisse *Blue Nude*, deconstructed and recolored. When I saw the Matisse *Blue Nude (Nu Bleu)* sitting figure, I said, "Oh my God, the feminine form with the long leg raised sitting on the floor is just the way my grandmother used to sit." There is that clean Oriental aesthetic in that. There is that commonality coming right back in. So yes, my lines are always very clean, yet I cannot call my collection minimal because where I find exuberance is on the fabric, the print, and the color.

How do you keep relevant after thirty years in this profession? Statistics show that after five years, 50 percent of designers disappear.

I keep reinventing myself.

Reinventing yourself to be relevant demands that you will produce a design that is dictated by the social environment. Now, for example, there is a fear of the unknown—especially regarding women's rights, health care, and the ban on immigration. That affects freedom. In order for you to design, you have to be relevant to those facts.

It is in my subconscious. Picking Mexico and picking Frida is not unrelated to the defiance and the strength of Frida. She's not a woman who would accept being silenced, even though she was married to a huge talent. She stood on her own merit. I've quite a few people in my crew who come from Mexican heritage. The pain they felt through the process of the immigration then, it is so unfair what is happening now with the immigration ban. In fact, a young English producer, who wore my Toko Shinoda print, told me: "There is something about your clothes that speaks to empowerment, that speaks to strength, and that speaks to the force of minority, and that is why I wanted to wear your clothes." To me that was the most important compliment anybody can get in this industry.

You have a beautiful store in one of the most expensive rental streets in the United States and you don't do any advertisement. How do you survive?

I don't think my clothes are for everybody. I think my clothes speak to this young filmmaker, speak to women who have their own philosophy, who have their own personality. It is not about wearing so-and-so's design. It is about, wow, that fabric is amazing, or that cut looks so good, and that little detail speaks to them. This cannot be readily found. I'm OK without advertising. We're not everywhere. I couldn't produce to satisfy department stores this organic way. I'm very happy dancing to my own drumbeat.

Was there a specific moment in your life that you felt that you wanted to be a fashion designer?

There are two points that really tied me to fashion. One, when I was thirteen and there was the period between Mexico and Spain when we went back to Korea for two years. One of my mother's best friends was the premiere designer in Korea, and my dad was working at the Blue House, which is like the White House in the United States. I saw my mother transform from field attire, which she wore when she helped construction workers in the morning, to an elegant woman accompanying my father in the Blue House at night. I have been inspired by this multifaceted woman who is a force of nature. Defying the Korean hierarchical tradition, she ate with the field workers and cleaned their dishes, and then proceeded to wear a gorgeous dress to a diplomatic meeting with my dad. This is the base of my philosophy. It is the base of my design for professional women. So this was the point where my mission as a designer took off.

The other pivotal moment was the artist inspiration on my work. That happened when my business grew and I was contacted by a photographer who told me, "I see something in your design that really speaks to me." She wanted me to collaborate with her photography for an exhibition at the Museum of Photography in Paris. This was about five years ago, and that is where the artist inspiration all started. She gave me her portfolio and said, "Look through this and pick five photographs that speak to you." I picked five photographs which inspired my design. We did five outfits that I was so proud of. That exhibition stayed in that museum for two months, and a germination of the new way of designing happened right there and then.

When one collection ends, I can't wait to start designing for the next season. That is a time to dream. It is time to put things together, and I can't wait to see what I find out about myself as I'm going through this process. Believe me, there are moments of despair where I'm going to my husband for emotional support, complaining to him, "Nothing is coming out." But when an idea happens, I foresee that I will never stop doing this. It's so exciting and fulfilling. I'm in my atelier seven days a week. I go there on the weekend to be alone. I can then sit for hours and dream; I'm touching and feeling the fabrics, and I'm sketching. I am very blessed to be able to have the tools and have the arena to be able to express my creativity.

So you're transmitting a feeling—a feeling that is imaginative and serene. Now, if Melania Trump walks into your atelier, what approach would you take?

That's a very interesting question. I dressed Mrs. Clinton for a while, so I know that side. I've dressed Madeleine Albright. So if Melania Trump walks in . . . she is an absolutely stunning woman. She used to be a model. But Melania is not the president, so I don't feel like I—or anybody—should be in the position of judging her. I like her sense of fashion. She's a classic with a little twist. And I can see her wearing my clothes. I have empathy for her, and maybe subjectively I feel that she has been put in a position that is not of her choosing. And as an immigrant, I would like her to express her voice as an advocate for women and newcomers to America.

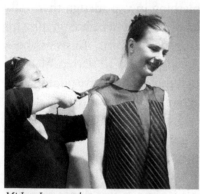

Mi Jong Lee at work

Mi Jong Lee's privately owned atelier in Manhattan offers her eponymous designer collection unmistakably inspired by her Korean culture and years spent in Spain, Mexico, and Costa Rica. Her close work with leading women in the entrepreneurial world has led to her involvement with the C200 community of women business leaders. She is also a member of the Women's President Organization and the Women's Forum of New York. Mi Jong is a thirty-year design veteran whose credentials include Cornell University and Parsons, The New School for Design. She founded her Mi Jong Lee collection in 2014 after establishing success in the retail world with her first brand EMMELLE. The collection's pillars include classic foundations with a distinct influence from the world of fine arts, a refined embrace of color, original custom print design, and high ethics-sustainability standards. In 2019 she received the "export achievement certificate" from Gilbert Kaplan, former undersecretary of the US Commerce Department, as she explores global outreach.

HUNG LIU

CHINESE-AMERICAN PAINTER

"Even when I grew up, I experienced oppression, placed into the box of being a woman who is supposed to act and be a certain way. You're expected to be a mother, wife, and grandma, and you're kept in your place. Although it is nice to be taken care of, I didn't want to just be rescued. I don't want to be a victim. I want to be a soldier and fight for my own rights and for women's freedom and dignity."

I MET HUNG LIU YEARS AGO in a gallery in New York's Greenwich Village. My eyes were fixed on her painting of the last child emperor of China, Pu Yi, whose gaze went through me as he posed innocently for the royal portrait. The large-scale canvas referenced the details of an original, small black-and-white photograph, yet Hung Liu created an expressive and atmospheric background through colorful paint washes and ominous birds to explore the story of his life.

The little emperor was a child born in the wrong era who lived in exile. He was powerless and considered no more than a Japanese puppet.

Today, I own this painting. And I have followed Hung Liu's life and career closely.

Hung was born a year before the establishment of the People's Republic of China by Mao Zedong. Her father, a member of the Nationalist Party, was imprisoned soon after she was born. Hung experienced continuous civil unrest between the Nationalist and Communist parties and, as a young adult, was sent to a labor farm where she worked for several years in the rice and corn fields. These formative years left an impact but never erased the strength Hung still draws from her ancestors.

At the age of five, Hung's grandfather, Liu Weihua, first appreciated and praised her early painting attempts, including her observation that water refracts and distorts images. Her grandfather's support fueled her self-confidence and sense of intelligence. Her simple drawing of people holding a portrait of Mao Zedong, saved by her mother, is a fitting legacy for one of the greatest Chinese painters in the United States.

Hung's painting technique integrates the Soviet Realistic training she learned at the Central Academy of Fine Arts in Beijing with the freer approaches taught at the University of California San Diego. She immortalizes important moments to prevent history from being forgotten, "because if you do," she said, "then emotionally and psychologically you become thin and hollow."

She focuses on facial expressions that reveal common men's and women's dreams that were suppressed during China's imperial reign and oppressive Communist regime. She lost some of her beloved teachers to suicide during the Cultural Revolution, and her exile and work in the labor fields would provide fertile ground for her more recent paintings of photographs by Dorothea Lange. "Dorothea photographed poor peasants trying to migrate to find a better land in America, just like the Chinese peasants I saw when I was sent to the countryside during the Cultural Revolution in China. They had the same desperate faces of trying to find a way to feed their families. The connection was profound."

Similarly, Hung's paintings express the bravery and resilience of Korean women who were made to bring comfort to Japanese soldiers in World War II and the Chinese women soldiers who sacrificed their lives to defend their country.

What's next for Hung? "With the zero-tolerance policy, I feel more American than ever . . . ," she said, leaving open the possibility of addressing American immigration, children separated from their mothers at the US border, and the unknown future of the Deferred Action for Childhood Arrivals (DACA). There's no lack of inspiration.

Tell me about your life as a child and your family's adaptation to the enormous political and cultural changes in China.

I was born in February 1948, a year prior to the establishment of People's Republic of China in Changchun, in Manchuria in Northeast Asia, which was previously ruled by Chinese. It was really under Japanese power, considered as the Japanese puppet state of Manchukuo. After the Americans dropped the atomic bombs in 1945, Japan surrendered, and Chinese armies from different parts of the country started to fight. The Communist and Nationalist parties of China were fighting, and after my father joined the army to defend the country from Japanese invasion and the Communists took over China, my father joined the Nationalist Party. The Communists surrounded our town. I was six months old. My family, including my mother, grandparents, and my uncle and aunt, put on civilian clothes to try to get out of the city. But it was completely surrounded by Communists.

A lot of people were fleeing. When I look at the graphic images of Syria today, I imagine that the destruction was similar in China then. I was told that we tried to leave the city, but the Communists blocked the exits. My father was asked to which political party he was connected.

He told the truth: "I am with the Nationalist Army." They took the two things he had: his watch and his fountain pen. And then he was arrested, while they let us go. So, from the age of six months, I didn't see my father until I was forty-eight years old in America.

Initially, he was put in jail, and my mother was forced to divorce him, threatened that if she didn't, she and her daughter would have a hard time in the future. Since she knew that she would not be able to see him anyhow, she signed the paper.

When I was in the US, one day I got a phone call saying, "We found your father." It was pretty shocking news. I located him through a friend who was a police chief in the city of Changchun. In an old rusty car, I made my way to the labor camp. It was quite a journey. My father was out of jail because Mao's regime was over and Deng was running the country, and he had been placed in a labor camp. It's a type of a prison where you have to work the field. I reunited with him and found him old and living with a roommate in a dirty place. Of course, he didn't recognize me, but he remembered my existence. I told him that I was a professor teaching art in the United States, and so on. We spent the night talking. I told him, "I'm your daughter, your only child. Your wife didn't forget you." I found closure to something I had cared about my entire life. And according to the Chinese belief, when we die, our eyes will not be closed and we won't find peace until we find closure. That was 1995, I believe.

I learned that he loved to paint and play the guitar. In his civil life, before he was arrested, he worked in a college teaching young people. Being an intellectual and a professor was not favored by the Communist Party, and he was considered one that brainwashes and pollutes young people and their minds, and a capitalist. So, therefore, he found himself in jail.

To tell you the truth, I felt embarrassed and ashamed to see the condition in which he lived. They had to wash their clothes by hand, and I wondered about their basic needs, questioning what they did with the leftovers without a refrigerator. Here I was living comfortably and safe in the United States while my father had been living in poverty with a roommate sleeping in bunk beds, closed up and away from his family, waiting to die.

I tried to convince him to come to the United States to visit his daughter and maybe he'd live a free life in his last days. Since my mother had never remarried, I thought maybe they could reunite after almost half a century. I was imagining a wedding with family members being bridesmaids.

I even bought him a ticket. Since he was not a criminal anymore, he was free but just had no place to go. We got him out of the camp, and he stayed with his nephew as we arranged a visa to US. But shortly after he got sick, and my mom and I went to the hospital. And that was the second time I saw both parents in the same room. Later he died—he never made it to the US. I believe he was seventy-four when he died.

So you finally made peace with yourself.

I expressed this feeling of closure through a painting on a canvas of me holding him. I was crying; you can see my red eyes. I named it *Father's Day.* This is because a few days before I saw him, it was Father's Day, and so when I met him, I gave him a watch to commemorate the watch that was confiscated from him when he told the truth. He could not lie. My father was a dignified man, and he preferred to be arrested rather than to lie. Giving him the watch was also an indication of the time that had passed.

I found that a lot of your work is autobiographical. You paint your mom, grandparents, and your aunts, everyone in your family. Tell me about your mother.

Her dream was to be a doctor in Manchuria. But at that time, women could only become nurses or midwives. My mother got her license as a midwife. But after the revolution, she preferred to become a schoolteacher. She taught biology and mathematics. She graduated from high school and had a good college degree. She is a very strong woman with a self-identity. She supported me through my studies in China and in the United States. She encouraged me to fly away so I would also become an independent woman. I regret that we did not get to spend that much time together. She visited the US about seven to eight times and would come to my show openings. In fact, I have a historical picture with her in front of the White House.

At what age did you start painting, and was there a particular person who inspired you?

There is a drawing of mine that my mom saved from when I was five years old. I drew a group of people holding Mao's portrait. I was inspired by the Chinese national day of October 1, 1949.

My supporter was my grandfather. He collected art, calligraphy, and he was a sculptor. For many years he researched a religious mountain in Manchuria. He was a schoolteacher who during recess visited the nuns, monks, and priests in that mountain where he photographed landscapes, donkeys, trees, and rocks. Although my mother always supported me, my grandfather inspired me as an artist as I watched him at home always writing his book, editing something, or looking at his photographs. Fortunately, because the mountain was far away, the Red Guards of the Cultural Revolution that happened from 1966 to 1976 never destroyed the temple.

My grandfather even hired a photographer from the city to document all the important landmarks as well as all the people there. Men, women, priests, and monks—they're all different, with different attire. My grandfather also had photographs of himself, so I put together a whole show in New York dedicated to him in 1993, called "Grandfather's Mountain." My mother, her sister, and her aunt donated my grandfather's manuscript with all his research of the Mountain Qianshan, which was his work—a total of thirteen volumes and thousands of photographs of the mountain. The donation was to a local history bureau.

My grandfather always had encouraging words for me. When I painted a chopstick dipped in water and it looked disconnected, I remember him observing that I painted the way they would look in a reflection, as disjointed pieces where they meet the water, as if they were broken, and he always said, "She's so smart. It is just amazing." I felt encouraged to believe that I'm smart. I remember painting portraits of neighbors and friends, sometimes on the floor, sometimes on a wall, and my grandfather telling me how good of an observer I am, and I remember telling myself, "Oh, I'm good." So he was my positive reinforcement and encouragement.

I've always painted. I always took classes to learn how to become an artist, but never as a career. It wasn't my major in elementary school, junior high, high school, or middle school. In China you cannot just make it your career unless you belong to a famous artist's family or attend a famous art academy. That was not a serious endeavor to follow as far as the government was concerned. In fact, I remember my mother, whose dream was to be a doctor, could not achieve it. So I wanted to fulfill her dream and become a doctor. I wanted to be a surgeon so that I could save people. I felt that I had faith. But then when I was eighteen, the Cultural Revolution happened, and I couldn't go to medical school, so I applied for art school. At that time, the Red Guards closed the schools and sent all students to the countryside to work in the fields where we were educated through hard labor. We worked in the corn, rice, and wheat fields. We never had a day or a weekend off. And in fact, if we did not rise to the expectation doing enough work, we owed money to the community. I spent four years doing hard labor. I hitchhiked home, because I did not have money, four times a year to see my mother. So, I guess ironically, I have to thank the revolution for throwing me to the mud, which made me become an artist.

At the age of twenty-two, after finishing my labor duties, I joined the Teacher's College in Beijing. The Art Department was named the Revolution Entertainment Department. We served the country through art. We learned art and music with the idea that we would become future art teachers of elementary and middle school. We were still a part of the Cultural Revolution, but we were super politicized. The subject of our paintings was imposed by the politics of the Cultural Revolution, so the subjects were that of workers, peasants, soldiers, and always the face of Mao Zedong in the background. Always painting our leader and the working-class people. I went on to teach students from elementary school to high school. While doing so, I was invited to teach how to draw through the Chinese Central TV station. So I became recognized, being exposed through TV to the country. I then applied in 1979 to a mural painting program at the Central Academy of Fine Arts in Beijing.

At that time I was thirty years old, and I was considered an old student. But the idea of doing a mural excited me. And so I became a graduate student from 1979 to 1981. The mural I made was a set of Chinese musical instruments, two thousand years old, from the Han dynasty. By doing that, I avoided participating in political paintings. The painting was called *Music of a Great Land*. My wish was to eternalize our heritage, culture, and glory because of our great tradition and civilization. This painting took me a year to complete and turned out to be almost seventy feet long.

At that time, it was displayed in the dining hall of the Central Academy of Fine Arts. The mural is now gone, but I redid it, and it turned out a completely different thing. Because it was in the dining hall, my new painting related to food, displaying thirty-four containers filled with local food from different parts of the country. For example, some had rice, some had chili peppers, etc. Together, it was the map of China.

You developed a specific style of painting.

Since my grandfather's encouragement made me feel special as an artist, I loved to paint human faces, faces that are real—not artificial or superficial. Regardless of their age or gender, I feel that faces have content and tell stories.

How do you reconcile the strict Soviet Realist style of painting that you were taught with the way you paint today?

In the academy, because of the Russian force over the union, our teaching was very strict, and there were days upon days that we would paint the same model or statue, painting the same position for many, many hours. In 1984, I was accepted by UC San Diego as a graduate student. From 1981 to 1984, I was just waiting for a passport.

Why did you want to go to the United States?

Because I felt that to study art, I needed to see the world. I wanted to visit all the big museums there. I felt that in China, we only had Socialist, Realist paintings exhibited.

Expressionism was too avant-garde and was never taught in any school. I just knew that there was a lot in the whole world to explore. It was crucial to see it. And that's why I wanted to go to the US. I wanted to be there as a student, not as a tourist.

When you came to the States, did you speak English?

At my middle school I studied English as a subject. When I came to America, it was almost like I had to learn over again. Everything was different. Even the way Americans greet you: "Hello, hi." We learned "How do you do?" and "I beg your pardon." Nobody says that in America.

Was it an artistic cultural shock for you when you came to America? Art was taught differently here. You were taught by Allan Kaprow with his style of "Happening."

In China, I was prepared for anything. I wasn't afraid of difficulties. It's almost like I was too new to be scared. Then I realized that the organization in America is so different. To support myself, I became a TA for some classes, such as drawing or introduction to art. So teaching was a learning process for me at the same time, and I was learning the language, new concepts, and opening up to other possibilities—not only to paint on canvas or rice paper but also to do sculpture, installation, and performance art.

All this stuff was new. It took me many years to learn and understand it better. It was a great opportunity because, although I was thirty-six, I was still young. Nobody said I was too old. In my class, there were people older and younger than me. I realized that it was all about working hard. Observing and working hard was the way to follow. I tried to absorb all the possible things I could learn.

What was emphasized was learning how to think and the story we're telling through art. We were no longer trying to imitate what the camera saw, but rather display our thoughts. I remember going to a dumpster, and Allan Kaprow, our professor, asking us to pour paint. He didn't tell us how to do it. Since there wasn't one way to do it, you had to be a good thinker first and find your own way of expression. I always try to figure out what the impact of that style had on me.

Your paintings are a combination of Soviet Realism and abstract freestyle, taking the basis from a small black-and-white photograph. What is your train of thought and the style of your painting when you peel away the layers of the photo to create a monumental expressionist painting? Describe the significance of the drips and the paint washes and large birds and flowers providing an atmospheric background to the historic small photograph you draw the ideas from.

In the '90s, I did several shows based on the photographs of young Chinese prostitutes at the turn of the century. It's a black-white photograph, so easy. They were nobodies. Nobody will remember their names, their stories. They are forgotten. I made them big and special, I forced people to notice them. That's why they are large paintings.

Secondly, I gave them color. The birds and the flowers are like offerings. When somebody dies, we offer flowers. It's a memorial site. The washes and the drips are thought of as sweat and tears. To me, the background is Socialism and Realism combined. I portray the person accurately, but I do not lock it tightly. I loosen up the picture like the paint, and I create a visual feel. I interrupt your look. I create a moving vibration, which ends with the observer's interpretation. I bring back stories that a lot of people forgot. I create a dynamic between preserving the past which interacts with the present.

At the same time, through your paintings you preserve a history; you send a message by representing the exploitation of women prostitutes, refugees, and street performers as well as displaying the bravery of women soldiers, a series that is presented under the title Daughters of China *at the Kala Art Institute. You show us the courage of armed Chinese women soldiers at the events of 1938 where women joined the Chinese Communist party to fight the Japanese and die rather than surrender. Exploitation of women and their bravery is relevant today as we witness the #MeToo movement confronting male sexual and physical assault.*

I do not have to go far into history. Even when I grew up, I experienced oppression, placed into the box of being a woman who is supposed to act and be a certain way. You're expected to be a mother, wife, and grandma, and you're kept in your place. Although it is nice to be taken care of, I didn't want to just be rescued. I don't want to be a victim. I want to be a soldier and fight for my own rights and for women's freedom and dignity.

I feel like this is still a very big problem today in China. The #MeToo movement in America exposes powerful men who take advantage of women who just want to have a career. I believe that women should help each other, forming a Band of Sisters, similar to the movie, *Band of Brothers*, signifying gender unity. So I do have a message. Even though I paint what happened a long time ago, it is relevant to today's situation. I show how women would rather die than being exploited. I show that women are ready to fight. I show how women are not little timid creatures but strong.

The immigrant issues seem to have bothered you. Your painting of a green card uses the title Resident Alien, *a contradictory term. And for the name on the card, you used* Fortune Cookie, *a Chinese-American invention.*

In fact, I used two-hundred thousand fortune cookies to make a fake gold mountain installation. It was a tribute to the Chinese workers who played an important role in building the railroad, Union Pacific West, to connect America from the east to the west. Quite a few of them died.

The immigrant issue that is so relevant today is expressed by your work in the past.

Sure. For almost three years, I have been doing the American Great Depression. Many are based on Dorothea Lange's photographs. She is one of very few female photographers who in the front line documented the hardship of American people's life. Also in photographs with some Mexicans, we see Filipinos, whites and blacks—everyone had problems at that time. Everyone here, that's the core of the country.

Some of your works express your duality as a Chinese-American immigrant. For example, the tapestry you named September, *regarding the tragedy of 9/11 in New York, shows a massive duck wrapped around the head of a Chinese bride which also signifies gender superiority. The painting* Strange Fruit *is inspired by listening to Billie Holiday's poetry where you find similarity in the oppression of African Americans to Korean women pleasing Japanese soldiers in World War II. Besides depicting human cruelty, it also indicates your own integration into American culture. Do you feel American in your adopted country while you obviously maintain your loyalty to China, exposing Chinese tradition and integrating it with American occurrences?*

Presently, I feel more American than ever after Trump took office.

By voting, by acting, I feel like a true American immigrant. Some will say, "It's not my generation," or "I was born here; I am a true American." The whole thing about this country is that everybody is an immigrant.

Without new blood and new immigrants, it is not America. I feel that both what happens in China and what is happening in America unites us by emphasizing humanity and dignity. As women globally, representing strengths and intelligence whether Chinese or American, we fight for Billie Holiday's song—for freedom and dignity.

Hung Liu, Mu Nu (Mother and Daughter), 1997, Collection of Kemper Museum of Contemporary Art

Hung Liu is among the amazing individuals featured in *Great Women Artists* (Phaidon, 2019), and *Women in Art: 50 Fearless Creatives Who Inspired the World* (Ten Speed Press, 2019). A *Wall Street Journal* review of "Summoning Ghosts: The Art of Hung Liu," a 2013 exhibition at the Oakland Museum of California, called her "the greatest Chinese painter in the US." She has been the recipient of two painting fellowships from the National Endowment for the Arts. She has also received the Joan Mitchell Fellowship, and in 2011 she received an SGC International Award for Lifetime Achievement in Printmaking from the Southern Graphics Council. Other awards include a Society for the Encouragement of Contemporary Art Award and a Eureka Fellowship. Her work has been exhibited extensively and collected by institutions including the San Francisco Museum of Modern Art; the Whitney Museum of American Art, New York; the Metropolitan Museum of Art, New York; the National Gallery of Art, Washington, D.C.; the Asian Art Museum, San Francisco; and the Los Angeles County Museum of Art. She is the recipient of the 2016 Fresno Art Museum's Distinguished Woman Artist Award. She is represented by Nancy Hoffman Gallery, New York City.

NERGIS MAVALVALA

PAKISTANI-AMERICAN ASTROPHYSICIST

*"Some people get uprooted by being seen as outsiders.
For me, it gave me freedom."*

I MEET PROFESSOR NERGIS MAVALVALA in her office at MIT, a very prestigious institution in Cambridge, Massachusetts, and I'm struck by her casual appearance. She's as relaxed as a college student, dressed in a button-down shirt over a printed T-shirt. I'm so caught up in the excitement of meeting this world-renowned scientist and explorer of the universe that I'm surprised by her initial interrogation.

"How did you find me," she asks, which I quickly discover is a testimony to Nergis' greatness—and curiosity—hidden underneath layers of humility. Her achievements are well documented and well known in the world of academic science. "It was not hard to find you," I answer. She had recently been selected as one of the 2017 Great Immigrant Honorees: Pride of America by the Carnegie Corporation of New York.

It takes ten minutes to convince Nergis that she would be an asset to my book. I make my case by pointing out that she has successfully challenged many stereotypes: being a woman astrophysicist in a predominantly man's world; an immigrant academician; a self-described "out, queer, person of color"; and to top it all, a working mother of two children. But once she is persuaded, her exuberant personality takes over and reveals to me the infinite vastness of her own life as well as the mysterious skies she studies.

Nergis was born in Karachi, Pakistan, to a family that encouraged and supported curiosity, knowledge, and education. She believed that the best learning occurred outside of the classroom, and hers began at the neighborhood bike shop and local electrician where she first discovered and explored the ways gears and circuits work.

She continued to develop her interests and practical skills, exploring machinery and electronic circuitry and building a laser, which eventually led her to join Dr. Rainer Weiss' team at MIT in 1991, working on the Laser Interferometer Gravitational-Wave Observatory (LIGO). (Weiss won the Nobel Prize in physics in 2017 for his and his team's work on the LIGO.) LIGO detects the effects of gravitational waves on precisely aligned mirrors that reflect laser beams, a new method to discover events that happened millions to billions of light years away in space. In the hopes of building a more sensitive LIGO to detect fainter and farther gravitational waves, Nergis has explored the fields of quantum optics and optomechanics. Her work could lead to solving the mystery of the Big Bang, thus combining her lifelong love of construction and physics, a love that flowered and was nurtured back in that bike shop in Karachi.

Nergis' relaxed philosophy about being an outsider culturally and professionally—a Pakistani immigrant and one of very few female physicists—in some ways also made it comfortable to reveal her sexual identity. When she fell in love, she says it was an organic process of coming out. And in retrospect, she sees her tomboyish behavior during childhood as a gender-bending process in the making. By being herself, she has become a role model, a fact she learned when her students sent congratulatory messages for receiving the MacArthur "Genius" Award in 2010.

Through Nergis, we learn that a scientist is more than just a robot analyzing physical events of the universe, but a human being with imagination, feelings, and dreams. While she peers into the skies to gaze at the stars, happy to go unnoticed, little does she realize that they're shining down on one of their own.

Our childhood years have enormous effect on how we evolve to become adults. There's no doubt that curiosity is in your genes. However, the environment you grew up in, your parents, and your education have had a significant impact as well.

Neither of my parents went to college. However, they were lifelong supporters of education, and I feel like they got their education vicariously through my older sister and me. Through my entire childhood, my sister and I attended an expensive private school in Karachi where we grew up. But we were not a family that could readily afford that, so my parents made certain compromises. I think about this now for my own children, too; the greatest gift we can give them is education. So that's where it started.

Then curiosity's an interesting thing, right, because all children are curious. But how do you keep the curiosity going through the rest of your life? My parents more or less did that by getting out of our way. I was the kind of kid who took apart toasters and things like that. My sort of mechanical passions started probably when I was ten or eleven, and it came with a bicycle. And this is a story that I've told before.

I inherited a thirty-year-old bicycle from my older cousin. It needed a lot of repairs. Of course, as a kid, I had no money for fancy repairs, so I would go to the bike shop that was very close to our house. The man who ran the bike shop was kind enough to guide me through the repair of the bicycle. He got involved in instructing me. He would allow me to use the tools, and he corrected me along the way. The bicycle became road worthy, which is really nice. But in time, as I wanted more repairs or parts for the bicycle, I actually would repair other bicycles in the shop, and he would give me a new inner tube or a new patch kit or something like that.

And then it turns out that right next door to the bicycle shop was an electrician. I remember finding in the pile of junk an old bicycle lamp that was run by a dynamo. Most kids, and certainly my own kids, have no idea what a dynamo is. But back in those days, in the 1970s and '80s, you could actually power a bicycle lamp by the friction against your wheel with a little motor. That's called a dynamo. But it was a little electrical device and it didn't work, and so I had to take it apart, and the electrician showed me what it was, and then we put in a new brush and we got it working.

So that was my first foray into what I would call my interest in science. My science today is lofty and out in the universe, but my everyday work is building experiments. And that was the starting point.

I'm always reminded of something else when I think about this. I went to a school where I got a good education, but so much of our education comes outside of school, right? Just by being allowed to mess with things. And I think that's an important piece of it. My parents would have been horrified to know their kid was spending her afternoons in the bike shop. But if they knew, they chose to look the other way. So it worked out.

You said, "There is a scientist in every child, and what we have to do is cultivate the sense of wonder."

Wow, I said that? That sounds so profound.

It is very profound. And generally, the belief is that for girls in the Middle East and South Asia, exploration of science is not supported. Is this true for Pakistan, and do you think it is changing?

That's a great question. I don't know if it's true or if it's changing because I have not lived in Pakistan for almost thirty-five years. When I was a kid there, I think it could have been true. It wasn't true in my family. My family, and my mother in particular, was just completely convinced that girls can and should do anything and everything that boys do. So that was a message I grew up around. A more typical sort of thing, which was true for girls and boys, was that in much of South Asia, the only worthy professions are to be a doctor or a lawyer or an engineer, to be a professional. So this notion of being a scientist, to actually being able to make a living and support yourself as a researcher, scholar, or educator, was not prevalent. I had to overcome this notion. I didn't want to be an engineer. To my parents' credit, they were clear that if that's what I wanted to do, that's what I should do.

So interacting with other girls, did you find that the majority were not encouraged to continue education?

I saw it a lot around me, of course, but I think that in the people I hung out with, that was not the case. People I hung out with were all going to go to college. It was that sort of crowd. And I think most of them did.

Here's another one of your quotes that may surprise you: "It doesn't matter what you learn; what matters is that you learn how to think."

I'm surprised at the profound things that I was wise enough to know or say. But I completely agree. I think about that a lot even as an educator today, as a professor teaching college-age students, that my job is not just to teach students how to do something, but it's to be kind of excited to try. I think that's really important. I even do that in our family; my partner and I do that with our kids. Our younger one is only one, but our older one is nine. And when we read something, we try to think it through and think what's behind it. You read a newspaper article—what's behind this, what's the history and context?

And that's how you cultivate their thinking.

Absolutely. Thinking is really about providing a framework or scaffolding and then constructing a building upon it.

Albert Einstein always searched to understand why, to explore the reason why things are the way they are. As a child, he was curious about the simplest things in nature. Like, why is the leaf green? And you were blessed with similar curiosity which leads to innovation. Therefore, hard work is not enough.

I agree with you. You're doing a book on achievers, and I think there are a lot of things that go into achieving. Some small piece of it is what nature gave us as our innate talents. But an enormous piece of it is the environment we got plopped into, the people who then supported us or didn't. And there's also just plain dumb luck. Being at the right place at the right time, or being at the wrong place at the wrong time.

Totally. I thought that I would be a pediatrician, but the opportunity came to change my specialty to radiology, having been in the time of enormous technological advances in imaging. How old were you when you came to the United States?

I finished high school in Pakistan, and I came to the US to go to college. Right here in Boston at Wellesley College. I was eighteen when I started college. My sister had come to the US to college two years earlier. I can't really remember a time in our growing-up years when it wasn't clear that we would go to college. At some point that turned into going to college overseas. That point came as it became more evident that both of us were going to be scientists. And I wasn't clear that you could have a career in science in Pakistan. I never even thought about it that way. I was like, "Oh, there's so much cool science going on out there; I must go be part of that." In my high school, it was common for kids to go overseas for higher education. So it wasn't some anomaly or something completely unusual.

And you spoke English very well.

It's actually my first language. This is not uncommon in South Asia. My parents' generation was the first post-colonial one. English was the language of the household. English was the language in school. The accent was different, but the language was the same.

Were your parents part of the division of Pakistan and India in 1948?

I don't know their history incredibly well, but I think my father's family was always on the Pakistan side. There's a number of families that had to move during partition. But my family didn't have to move. This is where they were when the division was done. Since they were neither Hindus nor Muslim, they didn't feel any need to go in any one direction. They just stayed put.

So being Parsi, you are a minority in Pakistan.

A fairly small one.

Was that any problem?

No, I actually think quite the opposite. I think it allowed me to be freer because as an outsider, you didn't have to conform to any particular norms. Some people get uprooted by being seen as outsiders. I think it just gave me freedom.

You graduated from Wellesley College, and you got your PhD at MIT. Now you're a professor in physics, researching and teaching as part of the faculty at MIT. You're a part of the team that detected gravitation waves, which result from explosions in space. That led to an explosion of science, as it changed the direction of exploring space. You have evidence of occurrences that happened billions of years ago, so that you substantiated Albert Einstein's theory of relativity regarding how gravity affects the fabric of space, forming gravitational waves. Tell me how it works and what this discovery leads to.

The first discovery was of two black holes that collided with each other. And these are not black holes that randomly collided; these are black holes that have been orbiting each other for billions of years before they collided. So what's special about these things? The first question is, what's special about black holes? Well, the thing that's special about black holes is they're like dead stars. They're stars like our own sun, but bigger, usually more massive. The sun shines because it has a nuclear generator in the center. Stars are basically little nuclear reactors. And so the sun shines, but eventually it'll run out of nuclear fuel.

And so the sun will, like all stars, lose its shine and stop generating light. Normally the light that shines outward is holding the star up against its own gravity, which wants to pull the whole star in. So now if light shuts off, gravity causes the star to collapse inward. And as this star kind of implodes and crunches in, it can become a black hole. So basically if you could just take our sun and scrunch it into a ball a few centimeters big, it would turn into a black hole. Stars are doing it all the time. That's what black holes are. In fact, interestingly, black holes themselves were predicted from Einstein's theory of gravity, but Einstein himself did not like them. They came out of the math, but he didn't think nature could do that.

We've known that these black holes could exist, and since about the 1970s we've even seen some evidence that black holes are out there in the sky. The way we've known about black holes in the sky is by observing that there are certain stars that are orbiting something very, very massive but very compact and of small volume. We've never directly seen black holes before, and the reason they're called black holes is because they don't give off light. Their gravity is so strong that even light cannot escape them. When you point your telescope at a black hole, you see black; you see nothing.

Einstein gave us a new way of thinking about gravity. We learn in high school that gravity is a force between two objects, according to Newton's theory. Einstein told us that gravity is not a force—it is the curvature of space-time. And then he added one other piece that didn't exist in Newton's picture at all, which was the idea that when a star or a massive object shakes or moves, not only does it create a dimple or funnel in space-time, in fact it creates waves. He called them gravitational waves—ripples in the very fabric of space-time itself. He predicted those in 1916, and it's taken us a hundred years to detect them. And the reason for that is that they're extremely faint, really, really weak. And in fact, if you look at his original paper, Einstein dismisses them as having no practical use whatsoever. Very early on, he understood that they're very weak.

There was a lot of debate about whether it could be true, whether gravitational waves existed and if so, what could emit them. Einstein himself, in 1936, wrote a paper claiming they don't exist. Later he retracted that claim. He was ambivalent, and the scientific community was not convinced that gravitational waves were real.

Then in the 1950s, people started to think about whether one could actually measure these gravitational waves, weak as they were. And some ideas were put forward that looked like they had some chance at it. In 1960, the laser was invented. In the late 1960s and early 1970s, the first of these black holes, and a lighter cousin of theirs called neutron stars, were discovered. So the scientific world is kind of starting to warm up to this idea that you could maybe measure gravitational waves using lasers and new technologies.

My PhD advisor, Professor Rainer Weiss, was one of the most instrumental scientists in advancing the detection of gravitational waves. He's an amazing individual with an incredible story. He was one of the inventors of the idea that you should be able to use lasers in a very precise way to make a measurement that proves the existence of gravitational waves.

Let me just add one more thing. I keep saying that gravitational waves are faint and weak. To put a scale on it, let's ask what a gravitational wave does when it passes between us. It basically pushes us ever so slightly farther apart and then pulls us in. So it pushes, pulls, pushes, pulls. That's what it's doing between you and me as we sit in this room. And on this scale, we're about a meter apart, it's changing our distance by ten to the minus twenty-one meters. OK, so even if you're not a scientist, all you have to know is that that's an incredibly small number. I'll put a scale on that. That number ten to the minus twenty-one meters is a million times smaller than the nucleus of an atom. The nucleus of an atom is ten thousand times smaller than the atom. The atom is another ten thousand times smaller than a microscopic object that we can barely see. You can just see that the scale is crazy.

Rai Weiss came up with this idea of using laser beams and doing a precision optical measurement called interferometry to detect gravitational waves. He's been working on it for nearly five decades. I joined the effort in 1990 when I started graduate school. This is another one of those beautiful accidents of life, because I didn't come to graduate school thinking I was going to go searching for gravitational waves. I was just looking for something interesting.

When I met him and he told me what he was working on, I actually thought he was insane. I really did. I was like, *This is crazy; no one can do that.* But then the more I thought about it, the more I felt like it's really, really hard, but if we succeed, it's a game changer. It's a game changer for reasons that I've alluded to already, which is that it allows us, for the first time, to see objects through their gravity rather than through light. Black holes are just one example of what might be out in our universe that is dark but has gravity, and we should be able to detect such objects.

That's how that all got going. I'm happiest building, and my part in LIGO has always been to come up with the ideas and technologies for making the instrument more sensitive so that you can actually measure these tiny, tiny motions. When you think about measuring motions of mirrors one thousand times smaller than an atomic nucleus, as LIGO must do, it sounds really impossible.

It's been a long journey in part because so many technologies had to be developed. But actually for me personally, it's also what's made it the most interesting because there's nothing that you can go to the store and buy. Nothing. Everything you have to build and invent yourself, and that's been fun. And as we invented new technologies to make more sensitive gravitational wave detectors, it became more real, more palpable that it just might be possible to detect these elusive waves.

So your team uses principles of physics and mathematics?

Yes, that's right. But we also use a lot of ideas from engineering, because in the end we have to build things, and they have to work at the precision that we need. So our labs are filled with glass and metal and lasers and electronics, and we're just always trying to think about better ways to make a measurement of something that's already the most precise measurement ever made.

What we do is measure using a complex instrument made of mirrors with a very simple principle. The principle is that you shine a laser beam at a mirror, and it reflects back. The laser splits itself in two beams that are ninety degrees apart. One goes out down one arm of the laser (4 km in length), and the other in its perpendicular arm. At each end, there is a mirror that reflects the laser beam back. We simply measure the time difference that it took for the two beams to come back. Therefore, a lot of effort is put into keeping the mirrors protected from any other force that would cause movement. If the mirrors move because of a gravitational wave, then one beam will take a little bit longer to come back, one beam will take a little bit shorter to come back, and we can measure that difference in time. That's how we make the measurement. In principle we just measure the difference in the travel time of the two laser beams. In practice, the system is of course much more complex.

I'll add one thing. We shouldn't lose sight of the bigger picture, which is that this measurement that we've done, of observing gravitational waves, will be remembered a hundred years from now, not because we discovered colliding black holes, but because we opened a completely new lens through which to look at the universe. It's the first time we can use gravity instead of light to look at dark objects, which may give off no light but emit gravitational waves. And these gravitational waves bring inherently very different information than light does because they come from different physical processes in stars. I think what's really big and important is not this one discovery of colliding black holes, but a new method of looking at the universe.

It's a little bit like four hundred years ago when we believe Galileo was the first person to point a telescope at the sky. Most people don't remember what it was he saw with his modest little telescope. Since then we've built much more powerful telescopes that have allowed us to see to the edge of the universe. What Galileo is really remembered for is the paradigm shift he brought about—that humans can use an instrument to see things better than with their naked eye. So we're going to be remembered as the first people who had an instrument that could see these gravitational waves. And from here on, who knows where it will go?

So we owe it all to the LIGO, and to Professor Weiss and his team, who influenced you and included you in the process.
Tremendously.

He's your mentor?
Yes.

You said things happen in life that you don't predict. In your case, the opportunity came about after having met Professor Weiss.
Yes. It's been decades in the making. My love and admiration and respect for him has just kept on growing. When I first started to work with him, I didn't work directly with him; I worked with other people in

his group. He was a busy man, so at that time I kind of appreciated him for his vision and his leadership. But when I did work with him on a real technical problem, I was completely blown away by the cleverness of the man. He's been revealed to me in layers. At first it was sort of this leader and visionary, then it was this incredibly clever and technically just deep and smart person. Then, in more recent years, I've seen humility and ability to draw everyone into this enterprise that he's doing and make everyone feel like they're part of it.

He's not someone who ever says, "I did this; I own this; I started this." He genuinely believes that this was the effort of an enormous group. He's an incredibly admirable man. He's also very generous with ideas. He's someone who thinks carefully about an idea before he'll bother you with it.

There are some scientists who are competitive. They're not as open and transparent and don't want help from other institutions.

Exactly. And that's part of why he was able to pull this whole LIGO thing off, because in the end it wasn't just something he could do alone. It was a CalTech/MIT joint project when it started, and then eventually as it grew, it became a large community of users. It grew to almost a hundred institutions. And he was always sort of at the lead of being both inspiring and exciting, because he really believed in the science, but he also believed in the people. I've learned a lot from him, not just about science and how to do science, but also about how to run a group, how to behave with students, and how to put value in your co-workers.

He seems like an exceptional man, especially since he claims he failed college.

Yeah, he likes to say that he flunked college. And I'm sure he did. But it was not because he wasn't brilliant; it was because he was distracted by other things.

I think that this indicates that he is a little bit like Einstein, because he's not interested so much in learning but in exploring.

That's right. He's deeply engaged by nature's puzzles. Why does nature do what she does? Einstein was similar. I think Einstein really liked to think outside the box.

I think you definitely follow in his footsteps.

Me personally? Oh my goodness, no. These guys are total giants. I'm just a doer.

You've got several honors. What does it mean to be a MacArthur Fellow?

It's from the MacArthur Foundation; they go all over the world looking for people they think are creative or have done something unusual or special in a creative way. Look, I'm humbled and grateful to be honored in these ways—it means people outside of myself think I've done good work. But really you do it for the excitement of the work. You don't do it for the honors and awards.

But I think it's nice when you are being appreciated.

Oh, I agree, I agree. And the lesson for me is that I have the advantage of paying it forward with my students. So I try to make sure they get a solid education and are set up to achieve great things too.

Your students benefit, and they get recognized for their work.

The support I get allows me to support my students in a way that I wouldn't be able to do otherwise.

Let's go back to your discoveries. I forgot to ask you something that intrigues me. How do you figure out the times that an event occurred?

How far away the source is. That's a complicated technical answer, but it's basically to do with how bright the source appears when you see it. So the best analogy I can give you is to imagine that I have a light bulb, and if I shine the light bulb right here in this room, it's nice and bright. If I take the light bulb and I put it across the river you'll see a tiny, tiny little dot of light. And that's more or less how we can tell how far it is, by how bright the source appears.

So the gravitational waves that happened to hit your observatory . . .

1.4 billion years ago. That calculation is a big, messy calculation that involves many other properties. From looking at the signal that we've detected, we can tell how heavy the black holes were, we can tell how far they were, we can tell whether they were spinning about their own axis, and we can tell how fast they were going. That's all embedded in the signal that we saw. The gravitational wave is a wave that carries information, just like a light wave carries information. So when we look at a star and we look at the light from the star, we can tell a lot about the stars by looking at the colors of the light, by looking at what colors are missing, and by looking at the intensity of the light.

So you have the height of the wave, the frequency of the wave, and the width of the wave to give you the information.

Yes, the many frequencies and heights. It's not a single frequency; the frequency changes with time. It tells us that the two black holes are getting closer to each other because they're going faster around each other. That's why the frequency increases. And then as they get closer to each other, the height of the wave also increases. There's a lot of information encoded in that because the frequency is changing with time; the height is changing with time. And from those things you can tease out all these properties of the wave.

So how did you and your colleagues feel when you first discovered the gravitational waves that were predicted a century ago by Einstein?

The first time I saw the signal, I, like most of my colleagues, didn't believe it. We simply thought that either it was some glitch in the instrument, or that more likely it had been injected into the data by someone. We do that periodically to ourselves—we inject fake data into the system to make sure that our analytical systems can pick up signals. So we thought that these were blind injections. Then it took a process of hours to days to eliminate that it wasn't a blind injection; it wasn't malicious; it wasn't a mistake. Eventually after about two weeks, our excitement was growing. Everything we checked was working out. So for me, the final confirmation came in early October 2015 when we completed a more detailed analysis of the signal, and it was there. The signal itself was detected September 14, 2015; two weeks later we confirmed it, and we announced it in February 2016.

Since then we've seen several others. We made another announcement in October 2017 of a new object we haven't talked about, which is about two neutron stars colliding. So we've seen a lot of things since then.

You get a lot of signals of gravitational waves lately?
Yeah, I think we have about six or seven now.

There are a lot of things happening up there.
Exactly, and as we make the instrument more sensitive, we'll get even more. What we're seeing at the moment is about within the range of what we might expect.

The fact that the signal came consecutively in both the locations of the LIGO is exciting.
Yeah. That's very important. Without that, we wouldn't believe it. It should come in both places if it's real. If it doesn't do that, then we know it was something local from the environment of that detector and not something coming from the sky.

In a way, I'm glad those waves are not strong, because otherwise we would shrink.
(laughs) No, a little stronger wouldn't be bad. We still wouldn't care if they were a thousand times stronger. I wish nature was a little more generous.

What is the closest event you have detected?
The closest is something that happened a couple of hundred million light years away. These things are far and rare.

You think that the collision of black holes or neutron stars is rare?
Yes, they're very rare. What we see are the last moments as they collide. They orbit each other for billions of years, but it is only when they collide that we get to see them. So most of the time, they're just orbiting around each other.

So you only get the gravitational waves when they collide? Not even when they're closer to each other?

When they're close enough, we see them. We see them only in the last seconds to milliseconds before they collide in a lifetime of billions of years.

Do you have an idea when the sun is going to become a black hole?

Certainly. There's a prediction that about five billion years from now, the sun will run out of nuclear fuel. If the prediction is that the sun will get dimmer, it will swell up into a giant red star, and it will be bigger than the solar system. At some point it will envelop all the planets. It will not become a black hole, though; it's not heavy enough. It will probably end up as a white dwarf star.

How would your work in quantum science measurement, for which you received the Joseph F. Keithley Award in 2013, improve the detection of gravitational waves?

Here's a way to think about the quantum measurement world. Quantum is simply the world that's microscopic, compared to when we look at the world around ourselves at a human scale. If I throw a ball, I can describe the motion of that ball just using ordinary Newton's laws. On the other hand, when you get to the size of atoms, if I throw an electron, I can no longer describe it by using Newton's laws because it's microscopic enough that the rules of quantum mechanics must dictate.

So you'd think that our detectors at LIGO, which are kilometers long, should have nothing quantum about them. But it turns out that the motion of the mirrors, even though the mirrors themselves are huge, is so small that quantum mechanics starts to matter. So here's the place where my work has been useful. We're measuring the distance between two mirrors using laser beams. The laser beams are jittery because of quantum mechanics. Some of my work has been trying to reduce that jitter in the laser light, which is something that is quite difficult to do and hadn't been done very effectively before.

Is it because of the thermal properties of objects?

Some of it is. But even if there was no heat in the system, quantum mechanics is difficult to wrap our heads around because of the idea of quantum uncertainty. For example, let's take an electron as a nice, small light particle. You cannot measure its position and its speed with infinite precision. If you know exactly where it is, you can't know how fast it's going. Or if you know how fast it's going, you can't know exactly where it is. That is quantum uncertainty. The same thing happens for our laser light. If we know exactly when photons arrive at our detectors, we can't know how much energy they carry. So we try to get around some of that by using these specially engineered quantum states of light that don't occur in nature. You have to make them in a lab, and that's what we've done to get around it.

I have a question that you probably don't have an answer for, but you may have a feeling. Do you believe that life exists somewhere else in space?

I think almost inevitably it must. Whether it's life that we would ever recognize or that looks anything like ours, I have no idea. But I don't see any reason why we should be so unique in this vast universe, or multiverse even.

Exactly. It's quite a pretentious idea to think that we're the only ones. There's got to be a physical reason that explains our existence. Do you believe that your research will lead to detecting the faintest gravitational waves that have been created by the Big Bang?

Ah, yes. That would be something. I don't think that will happen in my lifetime. I think it's possible to do, and it will be done in the generations to come, but such faint waves require more sensitive instruments. Going back to Galileo, his first telescope was such a small thing that even some toy telescopes today are better. But it's been four hundred years since then, and we have built incredibly bigger and more powerful telescopes. And that has allowed us to see farther and farther. What Galileo saw was in our own solar system. He saw craters on the moon, he saw Venus, he saw Saturn. Our light telescopes are looking out to the edge of the observable universe. And so that's the next thing that has to happen in this field in gravitational waves. You have to make more and more sensitive instruments. At times it means bigger, at times it just means cleverer, and sometimes it means both.

Would it require longer laser paths and observatories in space?

Yeah, there is the idea of putting them in space, so it's within human reach to observe gravitational waves from the very early universe.

Well, that would be amazing because it might cause a controversy with religious beliefs.

Will it cause any more than there already is? Just because we saw gravitational waves that take us back to literally the very beginning doesn't mean we'll have an explanation for how the very beginning happened. Well, I don't think it will help the controversy if there is any. It will just give us more information that the Big Bang either happened the way we thought, or maybe there will be a surprise and it didn't happen the way we thought. And what caused the Big Bang?

Which means that you needed both creation and evolution to get to where we are.

I think that would be nothing new added to that debate.

There's some important social issues that I would like to talk about. Did you face difficulties trying to achieve in science in a man's world?

Personally, no. Do I think or observe that there is systemic bias out there? Yes, it's out there. My own personal experience has been very positive, and I think it's in part because I've had amazing mentors who don't mentor me because I'm a woman—they mentor me because I'm a scientist. But that doesn't for a moment mean that I'm not aware that there are structural factors and bias out there that keep certain demographic groups out. But it hasn't been my experience.

What about being an immigrant? Did you find yourself different? Did you have difficulty adjusting? Think about when you came to this country. Because once you became famous and appreciated, the world was yours.

That's a good question. When I came to college, I came to an environment that was pretty welcoming. Certainly I've had experiences of the same kind that others have had of being exoticized: "Oh, you're from Pakistan, you must be somehow an exotic creature." I think if anything, it made me more determined. I wouldn't even say they were negative experiences; they were more experiences where I encountered people who just didn't know much about the rest of the world. So they had funny questions or funny expectations. I, on the other hand, even growing up in Pakistan, had much more awareness of what the rest of the world was like.

I'm the kind of person who just blows through all of that stuff. I don't notice it; I just keep going. I also did not have any culture shock, because I grew up reading English and American books and watching English and American television. I certainly didn't find anything unexpected.

What about being openly gay? Was it easier to deal with in the United States?
Yes, I think it's part of the milieu that I moved in. I first recognized for myself and acknowledged to the world that I was gay when I was a graduate student at MIT, and it kind of came pretty naturally, being in the US and not one to feel too bound by existing social norms.

I was in my early- to mid-twenties when I came out. No one seemed to care or notice. I think the hardest part of it might have been working through it with my family, but certainly not in the workplace. If people thought anything of it, they had the good sense to not say anything.

In one way I believe that discovering you're gay later in life saved you from the heartache of confronting this knowledge as a child.
Yes and no. When I look at young people today coming out as queer, for many, especially in the cities where I live, it's often a very natural, very supported process. I know that's not true all over the country, though.

You're strong and confident—knowing who you are, what you're all about. And that translates to the ability to adjust.
I think strength and confidence are correct because that's what you need to just glide through it.

What's your opinion about the political atmosphere regarding immigrants?
Everyone has opinions. But I don't believe that dwelling on this moment in time is valuable.
Well, there is a silver lining in that the US Constitution protects freedom of

speech. And a lot of crises that occurred in the history of the United States actually improved life here. For instance, we had a black president. And today with the #MeToo movement, women are starting to speak up for their rights. So I think controversy is important for change. But instead of dwelling on the present, let's be futuristic. In billions of years, we may not even exist.

That's so far into the future. I think we should be worrying about protecting our own environment and our planet and climate and pollution now, today.

So in the end, the universe will go back to what it was?

It's the cycle of life. Stars die, and new stars are born. We're just in one part of the cycle of life. The only difference is that for stars, the cycle of life is billions of years.

Nergis Mavalvala performs tests in her lab

Nergis Mavalvala is the Curtis and Kathleen Marble Professor of Astrophysics and the Associate Department Head of Physics at MIT. She received a MacArthur Fellowship in 2010 and was recognized as LGBTQ Scientist of the Year by the National Organization of Gay and Lesbian Scientists and Technical Professionals in 2014. In 2015, she was honored, along with the rest of the LIGO team at MIT, with the Special Breakthrough Prize in Fundamental Physics and the Gruber Prize in Cosmology. She was elected to the National Academy of Sciences in 2017 and, in the same year, received the Carnegie Corporation's Great Immigrants award, which recognizes naturalized US citizens who have made notable contributions to the progress of American society. Prior to joining the physics faculty at MIT in 2002, Nergis was a postdoctoral scholar and research scientist at the California Institute of Technology. At MIT, she was appointed associate department head of physics in 2015. An author of more than 120 scientific papers, Nergis earned her bachelor's degrees in physics and astronomy from Wellesley College and her doctorate in physics from MIT.

JACQUELINE MUREKATETE

RWANDAN-AMERICAN ATTORNEY AND HUMAN RIGHTS LEADER

"It's one of the reasons I feel like I survived, to be able to tell the story about what happened to my family and the more than a million other people who were murdered in the 1994 Genocide against the Tutsi in Rwanda. I survived so that I can share that story and hopefully inspire people to start doing more to prevent genocide."

ON APRIL 7, 1994, WHEN Jacqueline Murekatete was nine years old, she awoke to a living nightmare. Years of mounting tension and violence between the two main ethnic groups in Rwanda had erupted into a genocide.

When the killings began in her parents' village, Jacqueline was in her maternal grandmother's village a few hours away and couldn't reach her parents and six siblings. There were roadblocks everywhere in Rwanda where Tutsis were stopped and killed. When the killings began in her grandmother's house, Jacqueline, her grandmother, and other Tutsis fled to find safety. For several months she was smuggled into safe houses and hidden in orphanages as Hutus began a barbaric sweep of the country and hunted down and ultimately killed between eight hundred thousand and one million Tutsi men, women, and children as well as Hutus who were opposed to the extermination.

Although the Rwandan Genocide was the swiftest slaughter in history at just one hundred days, it had been brewing for decades. The kingdom of Rwanda was occupied by three main ethnic groups: Hutus, Tutsis, and Twas led by Tutsi kings. In 1916, during World War I, Belgium colonized Rwanda and, in order to "divide and control," introduced an ethnic ID card system that separated the Hutus and Tutsis based on how they looked. In 1962 the country became independent, and a new government was formed under the Hutus. In fear for their lives, almost three hundred thousand Tutsis fled the country. Hutu children were taught to hate Tutsis and told that Tutsis were foreigners who had come from other parts of Africa like Ethiopia and did not deserve the same rights as Hutus. Radios broadcast racist propaganda inciting the Hutus to violence. Tutsis were dehumanized, called cockroaches and snakes, and considered second-class citizens and foreigners who invaded the country.

This social discord led to further political unrest in Rwanda, and the suppression of the Tutsis led to the formation of the Rwandan Patriotic Front (RPF) by Tutsi refugees with an agenda to return to Rwanda and reclaim their homeland. A Rwandan civil war broke out in the 1990s between the RPF and the Rwandan government. A plane crash on April 6, 1994, that killed the Rwandan president, a Hutu, sparked the genocide.

Overnight, Jacqueline's happy childhood was shattered. Instead of life on a peaceful farm with a large extended family of aunts, uncles, and cousins, she was forced to run, hide, and witness horrors that continue to haunt her. She fled with her grandmother and a cousin, was taken in by a Hutu man and then Italian priests who ran an orphanage. After finding out that she had survived, Jacqueline's uncle brought her to live with him in the United States in 1995.

Jacqueline eventually made a new life for herself with her uncle in New York. The first few years, it was extremely difficult for her to adjust—not knowing the English language, haunted by nightmares, being an orphan, and adopted by a relative she didn't know well because he had left Rwanda when she was just a small child. Often she'd ask herself why she had survived when her entire family perished.

In 2001 Jacqueline found an answer to her question. A Holocaust survivor visited her school, and she found a commonality with him and his mission. The two of them continued on a voyage whose purpose was to prevent future genocides. It was terrifying to recount the worst moments of her life, and it still is, but by sharing her story, Jacqueline found the power to heal.

Jacqueline is the president of Genocide Survivors Foundation, a New York-based nonprofit she founded in 2015 that helps survivors in Rwanda, in particular, as well as around the world. The foundation focuses on the importance of prevention as a way to avoid the need for intervention. She has spoken to students and adults in the US, Germany, Israel, Ireland, Bosnia, and Belgium, and has addressed the UN General Assembly.

Through the foundation, by working to prevent further atrocities, and by building a family of her own, Jacqueline finds the happiness and strength to lift her above a life that is often painful to remember.

In 1994 the Rwandan Genocide killed more than eight hundred thousand Tutsis, moderate Hutus, and Twas within a hundred days. You were nine years old when that happened. Tell me what it was like growing up in Rwanda with Tutsi parents and living around Hutu kids.

Before the genocide, I lived a relatively happy childhood. I was brought up in a large family—four brothers and two sisters and me. I was the second oldest. I had goals and dreams like any other nine-year-old, and so did my siblings and my friends. Tutsi children were aware that we lived in a country that had discriminatory measures against Tutsis. For example, we had an ID system that the government used to discriminate against Tutsi children in high school, in college, and certainly in the workforce.

Even at that young age, we were aware that we lived in a country and under a government that considered us second-class citizens, where we did not have the same opportunities as our Hutu friends and classmates. We were aware of that, but I think that when you're a child, as long as you have your parents loving you and encouraging you, you believe that if you work hard in school, you will be one of those few Tutsis that would be allowed to go to high school and college. So I was aware of the injustices facing my ethnic group, but nevertheless I would say that I had a happy childhood.

Growing up in Rwanda back then, and even now, there was no physical segregation between Hutus and Tutsis. We lived in the same villages. We went to the same school and church, and we did all kinds of activities together. But the extremist Hutu-led government at that time always had an interest in dividing people along the ethnic lines in order to monopolize power. They always emphasized ethnicity by using formal ID cards and by spreading propaganda that the Tutsis were foreigners from Ethiopia and not true Rwandan citizens.

Therefore, when the genocide began, those friends alienated themselves from us. And it was very difficult for me as a child to absorb this.

So your own little friends suddenly did not talk to you?

The genocide did not just happen overnight. From a very young age, Hutu children were indoctrinated in anti-Tutsi propaganda. There were many years of discrimination against Tutsis in every aspect of the Rwandan society. And when the genocide began, that hate that had brewed for many years made our Hutu neighbors turn against us. They didn't want to speak to us. People we thought we could trust, we no longer could. They were the ones that chased us from our homes and attacked us with machetes.

How did the ID system start?

The ethnic-based ID system was introduced by the Belgians in 1916. Because when the Belgians came, the theory behind colonialism was divide and conquer. At that time, we had a Tutsi king. After World War I, many African countries started asking for independence, and the then-Tutsi king started asking for Rwanda's independence. But the Belgians didn't want to lose control of Rwanda, and in 1959 they helped the Hutu majority to overthrow the Tutsi monarch. This was the first massacre of Tutsis in 1959. Before the Belgians came, Hutus and Tutsis had lived in the same country. There were some differences in the way of life in that Tutsis were nomadic people, mainly cowherds. Hutus were mainly involved in agriculture, and the Twas, the 1 percent, were mostly involved in making pottery. But we shared many things. We spoke the same language, and most people at that time were Christians due to conversion by the Belgians. Before the Belgians came to Rwanda, the three ethnic groups had lived together for years in relative peace, exchanging goods and services.

But when the Belgians came, they started measuring people's noses and height, and they came up with what was supposed to be a stereotypical image of the Tutsi, the Hutu, and the Twa. They issued ID cards based on that. From a very young age, when you were born in Rwanda, you were soon taught that you were not just a human being, or a girl or boy, but you were either a Hutu, Tutsi, or Twa. And that type of education was put into us very early on.

So yes, unfortunately the ID system was introduced by the Belgians and ended up having very negative consequences. During the genocide, the ID card became your death warrant. If it said Tutsi on it, you were immediately separated, and most of the times you were shot or killed by machetes.

What sparked the hatred between the Hutus and the Tutsis? Was there something special about them that incited this hatred? Were they of a higher social or economic status? (The estimate is that the Tutsi comprised more like 20 percent and some people say even 30 percent, but definitely no less than 15 percent.)

The Belgians were the ones who introduced the narrative that Tutsis were Ethiopians who had come to Rwanda and took Rwanda from Hutus; they were foreigners. The Belgians taught the Hutus that as the majority and the "true Rwandans," they had a reason to get rid of the Tutsi monarchy.

Of course, the whole narrative of Tutsis coming from Ethiopia is debatable because it is believed by many that the Tutsis have always lived in Rwanda on the basis that, for example, century-old cow skeletons were found, and the Tutsis, being cow herders, were the ones to own them. So the Tutsis were looked upon as a minority of invaders that were ruling an oppressed majority Hutus, but this narrative was made up by the Belgians in order to keep their control over Rwanda.

The Belgians who wished to exert monopolized power were successful in dividing the population—a population that has the same religion and traditions—on the basis of looks. That prompted discrimination restricting the number of Tutsis permitted to higher education.

Were you discriminated in any other way?

The restriction of education prevents one from getting good jobs. That leads to discrimination in the workforce and in the government. So really at that time, there was discrimination against Tutsis in every aspect of the Rwandan society. Many Tutsis were forced to become farmers rather than doctors and teachers. It was so unfair because I was born in Rwanda, and so were my parents, grandparents, and great-grandparents. It's the only country that we knew, so saying that we were foreigners did not make sense to me. My parents were prevented from getting a high school education simply because their ID said Tutsi on it.

It appears that the straw that broke the camel's back was the plane crash that killed Rwandan President Juvénal Habyarimana, a Hutu, and Cyprien Ntaryamira, the president of Burundi. And this was attributed to the Tutsis.

Yes. The death of the president, the plane crash, was indeed what sparked the genocide. But it wasn't the cause of it. The genocide had been planned much before the plane crash, as evidence now shows. In 1990, the RPF was formed. It was a group mostly of Tutsis who had fled Rwanda during the earlier massacres of Tutsis, in '59, in the '60s, in the '70s.

I had heard my parents and my grandparents talking about how, after previous massacres, many Tutsis escaped to Uganda and other neighboring countries like Burundi and DRC (Democratic Republic of Congo). The RPF was made up of refugees who were mostly Tutsis but also some moderate Hutus who were opposed to the then-extremist Hutu-led government. These refugees wanted to come back to their own country. They had been living in exile for decades.

When the RPF started attacking Rwanda, the lives of Tutsis living in Rwanda became even more unbearable. The government scared the Hutus by saying the Tutsis were coming back to take over the government and kill them. Between 1990 and 1994, hatred against the Tutsis escalated as the Tutsis were portrayed as cockroaches, snakes, and a disease. The Hutus organized themselves through those years with imported arms such as machetes as early as 1992 and began planning the genocide. Hutu men and boys were also trained to prepare for the genocide, and lists of prominent Tutsis had been drafted as they were the first targets of the genocide.

The day after the plane crashed, the Hutus, who had been organizing for a long time, were able to systemically, within a hundred days, kill more than a million people. The killings were very efficient because of the planning and importation of machetes. The killings were also efficient because neighbors were killing neighbors, and Hutus knew exactly who among their neighbors were Tutsis. So when the genocide began they went straight to the Tutsi homes and began killing.

To this day, it hasn't been proven who shot the plane down, but the Hutu-led government blamed the Tutsis for it and saw it as a spark to start a genocide against Tutsis. The killing began in the capital city of Kigali and spread throughout the country. It was neighbors killing neighbors. My family was killed not by some strangers, but by their neighbors.

In 1996, Professor Gregory Stanton, an expert in genocide studies, came up with a theory about the stages of the evolution of a genocide. He describes the stages as: classification (division), symbolization, dehumanization, organization, polarization, preparation, extermination, and denial. Apparently, if there is awareness at any of the first six stages, genocide can be prevented.

Yes.

Do you agree with that? And how do you think those stages relate to what happened in Rwanda? Where do you see the Rwandan genocide fitting into this system?

Yes, this is exactly what happened in Rwanda. As I mentioned, we were divided, discriminated upon, and dehumanized, as was illustrated in a book written by Philip Gourevitch, *We Wish to Inform You That Tomorrow We Will Be Killed with Our Families.* The book has cartoons which portray Tutsis as snakes, cockroaches, and as a disease. The genocide planning which took place for a long time was when the world could have acted and interfered. In fact, the UN has a peacekeeping mission in Rwanda. The head of that peacekeeping mission is a Canadian general named General Roméo Dallaire, and he has been traveling the world for the past few years, talking about how before the genocide he sent many cables, faxes to the UN Security Council saying that a genocide is being planned. He spread the word that the Hutu government was importing large numbers of machetes and had already drafted a list of how many Tutsis to kill. He was telling the UN they had to do something. He called the attention of the world to this.

So there's no question that to this day there was ample time for the security consulate and the international community to have done something. But instead of sending more troops, they began cutting down the UN peacekeepers, and in fact they tied the hands of General Dallaire, keeping him from intervention and limited his action only to self-defense.

That the genocide could have been prevented is something that I myself and many others believe. But unfortunately, there was just no political or economic interest in our country. It's hard for me and for people who lost their families to accept this reality, to think that our families' lives did not deserve this kind of intervention. But from what was seen and what was heard from survivors and people who have testified about the warnings sent to the UN Security Council, we know that they already knew. But as they did in the Holocaust and previous genocides, they decided to not take action. And because of that, more than a million people were murdered.

So that is why I do the work that I do. I run the nonprofit organization called Genocide Survivors Foundation. Part of our goal and our strong belief is that genocide can be prevented.

Genocide is not a crime that happens overnight. People don't get up wishing to kill their neighbors. It happens in a process. There are many steps in the process when the international community can see the signs and say, "OK, we need to stop this before it gets to the actual killing."

And I really believe that if people can get educated about the dangers of discrimination, hatred, racism, and anti-Semitism, then we can create a culture where the right to exist for all people is recognized.

How did you survive?

I was staying with my grandmother in a nearby village when the genocide happened. That's what saved me. My uncle who was a doctor heard that the genocide was spreading. He managed to find a Hutu man who agreed to come and try to take my grandmother, myself, and a young cousin from where the killings were happening to a different area of Rwanda where my uncle was hiding at that time.

And long story short, we then found ourselves in a Hutu man's home—a Hutu man who my uncle paid and who agreed to hide us. He hid my grandmother and myself and my cousin for about a week or so until we were discovered. And once again, we came face-to-face with people who were armed with machetes and ready to kill us.

But we were lucky once again because the Hutu man who was hiding us kept saying, "This is an old woman, and these are little children. They are not the enemies of the country." So the men who had come to kill us, for one reason or another, had mercy on us, and they left. But the Hutu man was no longer willing to take the risk of hiding us. The Hutu man told my grandmother that there was an orphanage nearby that was owned and managed by two Italian priests. These two Italian priests had come to Rwanda prior to the genocide to help take in children whose parents had died of malaria and other diseases. And when the genocide began, these two priests were among the few foreigners who decided to stay in Rwanda and try to save as many children as they could.

My grandmother begged the Hutu man to take my cousin and me there. My grandmother, knowing that we had more chances of surviving in the orphanage, sent us there. She told us not to worry, that she would find somebody to hide her. She told us that everything would be OK, and she would come back to get us in a few days.

That was the last time that I saw my beloved grandmother. After the genocide, I learned that she had been killed very soon after she sent us to the orphanage. To this day we don't know exactly where she was killed. We never found her remains. And it's been a search that's been ongoing, as not knowing has been really painful for me.

While I was in the orphanage, I had no idea what was going on with my parents and my six siblings. Throughout the genocide I used to pray that one of our Hutu neighbors was kind enough and was hiding them. And I convinced myself that once the killings ended, I would go back to my parents' village, and they would be there. I really believed that, and I think that's one of the things that kept me hopeful during the genocide. I believed that I would see them. I believed that I would see my grandmother.

In that orphanage, about three hundred other children survived because the priests had made the decision to stay there. There came times when the orphanage was under attack, when the Hutus came and threatened to kill the Tutsi children. Each time those attacks happened, we thought we were going to be killed. And the Italian priests would bribe them, first with money and then with food, and beg them to leave. One day after another, we survived.

The RPF won the civil war, and that's how the genocide stopped. That's when I found out that my grandmother and my parents, all my siblings, and many of my uncles, aunts, cousins all had been killed in a little more than three months.

This is beyond comprehension. Are you in contact with any kids from the orphanage?

Two of my relatives survived with me in the orphanage. The cousin that I mentioned and another that I met while in the orphanage. In 2010, I went back to the orphanage and found out that the kids who were with me had left because after the age of eighteen they could no longer stay there. But I recently learned that there's an association of children who survived and who honor the Italian priests who saved our lives.

Where are those kids today? Are they in Rwanda?

It's mixed. Some of them managed to be adopted by relatives, so they are all over the world. But many of them are still in Rwanda. I've heard that plenty of the kids who still live in Rwanda came to the ceremony that honored the priests in Rwanda. Today, they are in their thirties, like me.

I wonder how they got organized.

They worked with the local government. One of the good things that the Rwandan government has been trying to do is to try to award people, including Hutus, who stood up against the genocide in order to encourage more people to stand up for the right thing. Those two priests were recognized by the local government who worked with these children. Since then, those two priests have retired and gone back to Italy. But the orphanage is still being managed by somebody else.

Similarly, the government honored foreigners that decided to stay in Rwanda to save lives during the genocide. This is how we know that the world knew about the genocide, as most of the foreigners— ambassadors and other foreigners—were asked back by their embassies.

Tell me about the procedures that took place to punish the perpetrators.

Two things were done in an attempt to punish the perpetrators. The ICTR, the International Community Tribunal for Rwanda, was established by the UN Security Council. This in a way recognized that they had failed to prevent the genocide. They set up this tribunal to "prosecute" the masterminds of the genocide. These were people in the government who put out the propaganda, who imported the machetes, who organized and incited the killings.

The tribunal was not set up to prosecute ordinary civilians who participated. That tribunal went on for years, and a number of people were prosecuted. Some of them got life sentences; some of them got ten or fifteen years. The tribunal has since closed, but it left in place something called the residual Mechanism for International Criminal Tribunal to wrap up some of the work that remains. There are still a number of genocide perpetrators on the ICTR Wanted List that have not been apprehended, and many of them are living outside Rwanda.

Many of them changed their names after fleeing Rwanda and got status in different countries in Europe, the USA, etc., because they lied on their immigration papers, claiming they were victims instead of perpetrators. Once in a while you will hear of someone being caught in Europe, the US, or different parts of Africa.

Another justice system is the Gacaca system put in place by the post-genocide Rwandan government. Since so many Hutus had participated in the genocide and the new Rwandan government did not have the resources to give all of them formal trials, they set up a traditional system called Gacaca trials.

In these so-called trials, the perpetrators, survivors, and bystanders were brought together in different villages, and they would talk about what had happened. Many survivors learned about what happened to their parents. This helped the victims' families find their remains and bury them in dignity. At Gacaca trials there was a high incentive to confess because those who confessed would get acquitted or would have less jail time. I believe some of them confessed because they believed that what they had done was wrong, while others confessed simply to get out of jail. Thousands of people went to these trials, with the idea of bringing some kind of truth and justice to what happened.

For many survivors, Gacaca wasn't really a form of justice, as it sent many perpetrators back to living in the same villages with survivors. But many survivors saw it as something that had to be done given that the government really didn't have the capacity or the funds to try everyone in the formal sense.

How did you adjust to the United States as a ten-year-old black girl, having lost your parents, your siblings, and now residing with an uncle you didn't know?

It was difficult. At that time my uncle was living in Virginia, doing his residency. We lived in Virginia for about six months, and then we moved to New York. So New York is where I've been really for most of my life now.

Was your uncle married with children?

When I came, he was unfortunately in the process of divorce. So he was going through his own personal things. He had kids who were more or less my age. But after the divorce, the kids stayed with their mom in Texas, and they would come and visit us during summer break. But they didn't speak Kinyarwanda, so one of the biggest challenges that I had obviously, was the language barrier; the culture was different. I was placed in fifth grade at that time, where I was fortunate to have volunteer teachers who used to come and teach me English. You know, beginning with the ABCs and picture books and things.

I had a lot of nightmares. I remember the first few years, as you can imagine, being very much traumatized. I used to spend most of the days crying. I had nightmares of running, people chasing me with machetes, and remembering my family. It was a very difficult period up until high school. My uncle tried his best to encourage me. But he was also dealing with personal things, so it was difficult. And then as I grew up, I started learning that the genocide could have been prevented. And there were just a lot of feelings—sadness, anger, this lack of understanding. Years before, there was a child with parents, with siblings, with goals and dreams. And now I was an orphan, and my family had been killed by my neighbors, for no other reason than their identity. Something they didn't have a choice about, killed simply because of the way that they were born.

I remember that even at that young age, I had a sense of the injustice—that people were killed not because of a crime they had committed but because of the way they were born. I knew at a young age that genocide prevention was certainly going to be one of the things that I would dedicate my life to. And that became more of a reality when I had the opportunity to meet with a Holocaust survivor when I was a sophomore in high school. He's the one that inspired me to actually start sharing my story. His name was David Gewirtzman, and he was on the board of the Holocaust Museum and Tolerance Center in Glen Cove.

I was sixteen. We read the book *Night* by Elie Wiesel about experiencing the Holocaust. Then the teacher invited David to talk about his experience and talk to us about the importance of tolerance. I remember listening to his story, although the Holocaust and Rwanda had happened obviously decades apart and involved different continents, different people. I imagined—David and I—the way we were as children, going to school with goals and dreams, and how that life for both of us had ended. Not because of anything we had done, but simply because of who we are and because of our identity.

So I wrote him a letter, and he ended up inviting my uncle and me to his home. He's the one who inspired me to start publicly sharing my story. This was in 2001. Between 2001 and 2012 (when David passed away), we went to many schools, synagogues, and churches in this country and abroad to share our stories.

Until now.

We believed in the power of education. The power of teaching tolerance, the power of teaching the dangers of hatred and racism and anti-Semitism. I really do believe that human beings have more in common than their differences. As David used to say, "Diversity is not adversity." We should see human diversity as something we should embrace. I really believe in this teaching, because as I said at the beginning, I believe that the best way to prevent genocide is by reaching people before they become incited and armed to commit this crime.

So that has been a big part of my life. And recently I started my nonprofit organization as a way to continue the educational and advocacy work and to support people that weren't as lucky as I was. I know that having been able to come to this country, I really do consider myself one of the lucky genocide orphans. Because when I think back, if I had remained there after the genocide, I don't even know where my life would be now.

I was given the opportunity to go to school and go to university and law school. I live in a country where I don't have to watch my back and worry that somebody's going to kill me because I'm a Tutsi. Obviously in this country we have our own problems of intolerance and racism and extremism. But living here, I was given the privilege and responsibility to continue my advocacy and vocational work. I can raise awareness about some of the challenges that survivors face in Rwanda and all over the world. I'm trying to have the world participate in preventing these types of crimes and supporting the people who survived.

When did you find the courage to go back?

I didn't want to go back to Rwanda for a long time after the genocide. I came to this country when I was ten in 1995, but I didn't go back until fifteen years later, in 2010. It was a difficult journey when I went back to my home village. I went back to where I used to stay, and there's nothing there at all. It was a psychologically difficult trip. But now I go back to Rwanda as often as I can to support the survivors who are still living there.

So what do you think about the division in our country?

We're talking about the anti-immigrant rhetoric that's so common—the whole thing that has been happening now with the administration saying that people from certain countries can't come here and barring entire groups of people. Having been privileged with the First Amendment, I've raised my voice. You can't say that people from an entire country or an entire race or an entire religion can't come here. In every country and every race, there are good people as well as criminals.

Yes, I understand that we're living in the age of terrorism and extremism. When people come here, they disguise themselves as students, as good people, and they develop bombs and they kill people. This is a real danger that we are facing. And I think that a big way that we can face it is by working to make our immigration system more transparent. It would mean raising our screening measures and making sure the people who are coming here are not dangerous people.

But what is not OK, and what is not a good way to deal with this or fight terrorism, is by casting off whole groups of people, whether it's by nationality or racism. Because I do think that kind of engagement with other countries and with the world is dangerous.

America is the country that has always been proud to be a country of immigrants. All of us, you and I, and many people came here, and we built our lives and have made positive contributions to this country. Now every time I speak to students in high schools and colleges, I talk about the genocide, but I also talk about the rise of extremism in this country and the need to speak out against it.

We have to do the screening, and we have to improve the ways that people are able to come here to make sure that people wishing to do harm are kept out. But many good people from every country want to come here and contribute to the country and put their kids in school and be a part of the American ideals and dreams.

Can you tell me about your work?

The work I do today with Genocide Survivors Foundation is twofold. Part of it is educational in nature—for example, participating in human rights conferences. We also sponsor programs that raise awareness about genocide and other forms of mass atrocity crimes. We teach that genocide is not history, but is something that has happened and keeps happening over and over again today.

The second part of our work is raising funds to support survivors in Rwanda. We are a fairly new organization, but we have a lot of goals about raising awareness and funds to address problems facing survivors. Although the genocide happened about twenty-four years ago now, in Rwanda survivors are still struggling with basic needs, such as proper housing and money for education. There are also people who suffered physical wounds and psychological wounds that are untreated to date. Some people in Rwanda have money; however, the majority is poor. But the survivors' challenges are unique because while it is one thing to not have money, it is another thing to be poor without a mother, without a father, with a machete wound, with psychological and emotional problems as a result of the genocide.

Our focus is to get the survivors to more or less the same level as the other Rwandans. We have a very broad mission. One of the big problems now is aging survivors who are aging without a family support system. We don't have nursing homes to care for the ones who are left alone.

In Rwanda, your social security is your family. So now the question is, what happens to a widow who lost her husband and all her children? They're now sixty, seventy years old, and they live in the villages where everything requires physical strength. You have to farm, you have to go get water from a nearby well, you have to go get firewood. And they're not in a physical condition to do this.

So we are trying to find a solution where we can build old-age homes where survivors without family members can age with dignity and have access to health services and other services they need. So that's the kind of project we're trying to raise funds for.

Who's helping you?

Individual donors. I'm now hoping to start looking into foundations and grant writing. So far, we've been able to help a few individuals. But when you compare the need to the little resources we have, we're not anywhere near addressing those issues. I'm starting to have a little bit more time with my baby being a little older, and I am now trying to work with my board members and other people who want to help us to address the many problems facing survivors.

Where are you located?

I live in Brooklyn. We don't have the money to have an office yet, so I'm mostly running my nonprofit work out of my home. One of the board members has an office in Manhattan where we host meetings and plan to host events. We hope to have an office space of our own sooner rather than later so we can more efficiently do our work.

How did you manage to go to law school without financial means?

I went to NYU for undergrad, with a scholarship from the Jerry Seinfeld Family Foundation. And the Benjamin N. Cardozo School of Law gave me a full scholarship for tuition. I had to take out loans for living expenses.

You must have been an exceptional student.

I feel like I should have done better in law school, but the school really believed in me when I applied, and they really saw the nonprofit work that I had been doing. Plus I had good grades from high school and my undergraduate studies.

I believe that giving back is a healing process.

Yes, I believe so too. First of all, I believe that with opportunity comes responsibility. When I go back to Rwanda and meet other people who survived and are my age or younger or older, I recognize the problems they have to deal with, including lack of educational opportunities or financial means to support themselves. My life in America is not perfect either, but there are many things that I don't have to deal with here. I thank God for this, and I believe I'm here for a reason.

We're given this opportunity to come here to get an education. And I feel like we should use our networks and resources to be able to help the people who did not get the opportunities we have been given. When I speak about genocide or genocide survivors, it is not just about Rwanda. When I talk about genocide, I talk about genocide as a crime. So it's about Cambodia, and it's about what is happening today in countries like Myanmar and other places around the world.

As a genocide survivor, I believe that it is my responsibility to speak for those who can no longer speak for themselves, and this is what drives me. It's one of the reasons that I feel like I survived. It is to be able to tell the story about what happened to my family and the more than a million other people who were murdered in 1994. I survived so I can share that story and hopefully inspire people to start doing more to prevent genocide. But I do agree with you that having this opportunity to talk about it and do the work that I've been doing has provided some healing for myself. But it is still difficult.

Very difficult.

Sometimes I get an invitation to go speak, and I'm like, "I don't want to talk about the horror again." I don't want to talk about the genocide because it's difficult. Sometimes when I speak a lot about it, I feel a physical and emotional exhaustion. I've learned over the years to limit how much time I'm able to do it and to obviously protect myself, but at the same time, there's a healing aspect to it.

You've been honored many times. Tell me about one that meant a lot to you.

There are a couple that I was really touched by and proud of. One of them was an award from the Anti-Defamation League, an organization whose work I admire. I admire the work they do to fight racism and anti-Semitism and the fact that they are always at the forefront of speaking out when atrocities are being committed or when discriminatory acts are happening.

The other award that I am very proud of was the one I received a couple years ago from the First Lady of Rwanda. She has a foundation called Imbuto. *Imbuto* means "seed." The organization recognizes young Rwandans all over the world who are contributing positively to Rwanda and the world. Being able to have that recognition from my native country, from the First Lady of Rwanda, was very moving for me.

But really, I do this work because I feel like I am here to do the work. Does that make sense? It's my calling. It's one of the reasons that I'm here. So even if I don't get awards, I won't sleep soundly and I won't be happy if I'm not doing this work. I do it because I really do believe that after the genocide, when you go through something like that, you get to a point where you ask yourself the question, "Why did I survive?" I was one of seven children. My youngest sibling was two or three months old, and even he did not survive. And I say, "Why me? Out of all my siblings, why me? Why not my cousins?" I don't have a complete answer to that question. I don't know if I ever will. But I really do believe that part of the reason is that I can tell the story of what happened to my family and other Tutsi families, about what happened in Rwanda in 1994. And there can be a voice for those who can no longer speak for themselves. This work for me is what I breathe and eat. I wish I could do more, but again it's always a balance because what you do also takes an emotional toll. So it's always that balance between doing as much as you can but also making sure that it's not destroying you.

I was born ten years after my siblings. That gave my mother the chance to commemorate my grandmother, who was killed in the Holocaust, by giving me her name. Sometimes I think that that is the reason I was born—so that she will never be forgotten.

Wow. It was meant to be. You're right.

Do you remember the institution that gave you your first award? It was given by part of a foundation called Pathways Women's Health, and I was the president.

Oh yes, I do remember that award. I made that connection when you asked to interview me. That award was encouraging, and it substantiated the work I was doing.

This humanitarian award was given to you and to David Gewirtzman for the work that you did together when you were in high school.

Yes. And today I continue to do that work, especially in light of the rising anti-immigrant rhetoric in this country and abroad. I teach people, particularly young people in America, that we should never have a fear of one another. It's important that innocent people are not discriminated upon on the basis of race, religion, or other things because there are good people among all groups of people. We should grant all people equal opportunities, while of course making sure that those wishing to do harm are prevented from coming into this country.

Jacqueline Murekatete (at age seventeen) with Holocaust survivor David Gewirtzman

For her work, **Jacqueline Murekatete** has received a number of prestigious awards, including the Global Peace and Tolerance Award from Friends of the United Nations; the Moral Courage Award from the American Jewish Committee; the Do Something Award from Do Something; the Kay Family Award from the Anti-Defamation League; the Imbuto Foundation's Celebrating Young Rwandan Achievers Award from the First Lady of Rwanda; and the Ellis Island Medal of Honor from the National Ethnic Coalition of Organizations, which put her name in the US Congressional Record. She has a BA in Politics from New York University and a JD from Benjamin N. Cardozo School of Law.

OLGA MURRAY

TRANSYLVANIAN-AMERICAN LAWYER, PHILANTHROPIST,
AND CHILDREN'S RIGHTS ADVOCATE

"Out of the mud grows the lotus."

AT NINETY-THREE, OLGA MURRAY IS a prime example of how much one person can accomplish in one lifetime. The third and current chapter of her life—and the one of which she's most proud—started when she turned sixty.

Olga was trekking in the mountains of Nepal where she encountered the country's poor but incredibly happy children. What started with a twelve-hundred-dollar scholarship for four boys snowballed into the Nepal Youth Foundation (NYF), a nonprofit organization she founded to build homes, schools, and hospitals for malnourished children and to provide programs in nutrition education for adults and orthopedic care for disabled kids.

Today, Olga serves as the honorary president of the NYF in Sausalito, California, and still has a fundraising role. The foundation has a sweeping mission, but Olga believes the most astonishing achievement is filling the void of education that so many Nepali children are hungry for. The organization also freed twelve thousand Tharu girls from slavery by helping abolish the Kamlari tradition of indentured servitude among farmers' daughters. Some of those children have become successful entrepreneurs.

The involvement with Nepali youth grew from the second chapter of Olga's life. One of the few women in her law school class at George Washington University, Olga was a pioneer, shattering the glass ceiling at a time when many women law graduates were able to get work only as legal secretaries. She landed a job at the California Supreme Court, where she helped draft legal opinions for landmark reforms, including civil rights and women's rights.

Olga has brief memories of a horse-drawn carriage ride to the train to begin the journey to the United States and of the last time she saw her grandmother wave goodbye to an increasingly anti-Semitic world that took the lives of some family members during World War II. Still, Olga wonders how a little girl of six, who came from Transylvania and lived in the Bronx, was recognized for her humanitarian efforts by the King of Nepal and the Dalai Lama.

But this is the story of a rare woman and a role model whose thoughts and actions stem from her heart. She builds her life on the common thread of inspiring change to fuel improvement. Her foundation's motto is "Out of the mud grows the lotus." It is a fitting description for the work that still needs to be accomplished in Nepal, in many other areas of the world, and also, perhaps, in the ensuing chapters of individuals' lives.

Olga believes that retirement should be considered a startup as the length and quality of life increases. Her secret to a happy life is the Helper's High, which is the feeling of elation you experience after giving of yourself. In other words, she said, "the memories that will fill your heart will be centered on the things you did while on the earth to improve the lives of others."

***

I understand that the most important part of your life started when you were sixty years old. When trekking in Nepal, you met the children. They were malnourished but happy, and they won your heart. How did this encounter lead to forming the Nepal Youth Foundation?

With twelve-hundred dollars, I gave four scholarships to boys from an orphanage for college. And then, I kept going back there and giving scholarships and working with kids. The foundation wasn't established until 1990, six years later.

Well, it was their resilience, their happiness in the face of the worst kind of circumstances you could imagine. And their ability to accept their hardships. And then when things went well for them, they would just become the most stable, happy little creatures you ever saw.

Even though they were so, so underprivileged, they were much happier than the average American kid, and that really touched my heart. They were grateful for everything they got, and grateful to be able to attend school. It was so different than the picture in this country. The other thing was I knew that for a small amount of money, you could change a child's life there. Save their life, do everything for them. Sometimes I say I know how it feels to be a millionaire, because although I'm not one, in Nepal, I feel that way.

In Nepal you can do almost anything with a fairly modest amount of American dollars. You need an operation? OK, here's the money. You need to go to school? OK, here's the money. You need to find an apartment? OK, here's the money. The cost at least used to be so small there that you could save a child's life for the cost of a good dinner in San Francisco. That was the truth.

Maybe unlike what's happening in the US, in Nepal there's no peer pressure, because there is no significant competition involved in children's lives.

Well, now that I've been there for more than thirty years, and now that I've worked with so many children, I think that's true in general, but I see it creeping up a little bit now. There are some wealthy families. For example, many of our kids go to one of the best and most expensive private schools in Kathmandu, and they see what others have.

When they come back from vacation and return to school, their friends have gone to Disney World or all over the world for their vacations. And I think a lot of them feel uncomfortable. It isn't that they demand that from us, but they feel uncomfortable about it. And we have started actually transferring some of our kids, at their own request, to a very good public school nearby. I think socially it will work out better for them.

There is beginning to be peer pressure in the cities. Most Nepalis live in the country; about 75 percent are farmers. In the countryside, there's no peer pressure. They're all poor. The kids in our homes at least are very grateful for what they've got; they live at a very high standard by Nepali standards.

So the kids that you support are deprived kids in the rural areas?

Well, we support kids everywhere. We've just built a children's village very close to Kathmandu, and we support lots of kids in Kathmandu. We support kids in villages and all over the place. There are needy kids all over Nepal.

Your foundation has changed the lives of tens of thousands of children, and restored sixteen thousand malnourished children to health?
Yes.

One of the most significant contributions was liberating about twelve thousand girls from slavery.
Yes.

And abolishing the Kamlari tradition. Can you tell me more about the Kamlari practice? And what does indentured slavery mean?

Indentured slavery exists where you make an agreement that you will work for somebody for X amount of money, but the money is paid to someone else. And in this case, it was the fathers who sold the girls and received money for their labor. The girls would work for about fifty dollars a year or sometimes for just a few bags of rice, whatever was given.

I can give you some of the background. This custom is not all over Nepal. It's just in five adjoining districts in southwestern Nepal, among an ethnic group called Tharu. These people were kicked off their land, probably around the 1950s. They had very fertile, large farms. No education, no schools. They lived a very communal life, and outsiders couldn't enter their area because it was infested with malaria. For some reason the Tharus are immune to malaria.

But in the 1950s, when DDT was invented, they sprayed the DDT, and they diminished the amount of malaria, practically got rid of it, and the smart people came in from the cities and all over.

Basically, they stole or bought their land, like the Indians buying Manhattan for a bunch of beads. The Tharu people ended up in shacks, living as tenant farmers.

The landlord ruled everything and did not pay them in money, but in crops. When they needed money for an operation, or a wedding, or medical care, they would borrow it from the landlord. They could never pay it back because they didn't earn money. So they were indentured for generations.

Then, in 2000, the government, to its credit, abolished this system and said, "All these laborers are free. All debts are forgiven. And for you who are still living as tenant farmers on the land you used to own, we're going to train you for jobs, and we'll give you land," and so forth. Of course, the government didn't comply with this promise, and these people had no way to eat. A lot of them were kicked off the land after they were freed. Most of them, in fact. But the problem of poverty remained.

So they started to sell their daughters. The people in the cities and big towns realized that these people needed money, and they would come and talk to the father, telling him, "If you allow your daughter to come and work for me, I'll treat her like my own daughter. I'll send her to school. She'll be so privileged." And these families literally couldn't afford to feed their children, so they let the girls go. I think it was an average like sixty or seventy dollars that the father got for the girl's labor for a year. Sometimes it was nothing. The employers just took her off the father's hands so he didn't have to feed her. They were sometimes paid by the promise not to kick the family off the land.

One year became two and three, and many of these girls spent their entire childhoods working for these people. They were not allowed to go to school. They were often beaten. They slept under the stairs. They ate leftovers. They were sexually abused, many of them. And that's how they spent their lives. So when we went in there in 2000, we estimated there were about eighteen thousand girls who had been sent away—some as young as six, seven, eight years old.

I mean, many of them were little girls. It was shocking. Many Nepalis didn't even know of this practice because it only exists in this one area, although child labor—you know, having little girls as servants—is endemic around Nepal, or it used to be. But not this bonded kind of arrangement with the father.

When we learned about it, we decided that we wanted to do something about it. The president of NYF, Som Paneru, who was then an employee, went to that area with a friend who spoke the Tharu dialect. He spoke to some of the fathers and said, "Why are you doing this to your daughter?" And they said, "We need the money, and we can't do without it." Sometimes the little girl was the only one in the family who was working.

There's a certain holiday in the middle of January called Maghe Sakranti. It's the most important festival for the Tharus. And sometimes the girls were allowed to go home for that festival. Som talked to twenty-seven fathers, saying, "Bring your daughter home for the festival. If you don't send her back, we'll make it worth your while." This was in November 1999.

Som returned to the area during the festival in January and found that almost every father he had spoken to had brought his daughter home. The fathers said, "OK then, what are you going to do for us? You said you'd make it worth our while if we allow our daughters to stay at home."

Som and I had talked about it, and we weren't sure how to reward the fathers for allowing their daughters not to return to work. We considered compensating them for the amount they had received for their daughters' labor, but we weren't sure if this was the right thing to do.

Before making a commitment, Som kind of moseyed around the villages with his Tharu-speaking friend and talked to the women. And they said, "Whatever you do, don't give our husbands money." Alcoholism was rife in the area, and they were afraid that their husbands would spend the money on liquor. Together, the mothers and Som came up with a solution: The Tharu people loved pork products, and they decided that every family that allowed their girls to stay home would be given a baby piglet. They could raise the animal, and at the end of the year, they could sell it for as much or more than they got for their labor. And in the meantime, we would put the girl in school and pay all her school expenses.

We started with twenty-seven girls that first year, and ultimately we built a movement of the Tharu girls themselves. And the government abolished the child labor practice, making it illegal in 2013.

That is such a beautiful story. That makes life worthwhile.

And if you saw these girls now—I mean, they are passionately active, they're smart, a lot of them are in college, and a lot of them have started businesses. They're quite successful.

Unbelievable! Please share a success story.

Sure, we have a lot of stories, especially from our children's home, where the kids are the poorest and the most desperate. We have loads and loads and loads of these stories. I can tell you about one.

There was a little girl, four or five years old, who was a beggar at a temple, begging alongside her father—the most adorable little girl you ever saw. Smiling all the time. So happy. Her father was deformed. His feet were turned backwards, and he was an elderly man. She was the one, of course, who generated the money, with her little smile and her cheery disposition.

When we found her there, they were living in the most horrible, horrible place. They had a room, a concrete room. It was at a temple with a lot of monkeys who ran through the room frequently. There was no furniture and just a rope across where they threw their few clothes, and a corner where they did a little cooking. It was an awful place.

We had just started our girls' home. This was 1995. We asked the father if she could come to live there, and he agreed. She came, and it was a beautiful house. We started out with ten or fifteen little girls, much like her. The father would come to visit on Saturdays. For a few Saturdays he didn't come, and the little girl got really worried. She loved her father. We sent someone to the temple to find out if he was all right, and we learned that he had committed suicide. As soon as he knew that his little girl was safe and had a future, he killed himself.

She's about twenty-six now, an absolutely beautiful young woman. College-educated, with the most warm and sparkling personality—everybody loves her. She has a really good job, and she's progressing fast in her work. I have no idea what would have happened to her if we had not intervened, but it would not have been good.

And that's a story typical to many, many children that you have helped.

Well, they're all different, but they're all in desperate circumstances. And now that I've been around there for thirty years, I see the results. I mean, I have a house there. The gate opens, and a girl comes in with her baby and her husband, and I always remember when we met her, when she was just a terribly shy, malnourished, scared little girl. That happens all the time now because I've been around for so long.

That's so wonderful that you're able to follow up on them. You can write a book yourself.

Actually, I have written a book: *Olga's Promise: One Woman's Commitment to the Children of Nepal.*

I understand that the Nepali girls have now formed an NGO to protect girls from abuse?

Yes, the freed Kamlari girls have got their own micro-lending program. They've got their own cooperatives. This includes thousands and thousands of members. This is now a powerful movement.

They protect themselves from the Kamlari practice and are very successful.

Yes. And the Kamlari practice is over now. I mean, no labor contractor would dare show his face in any of those villages today. Not only is it illegal, but these girls would run him out on a rail.

It took thirteen years to get rid of the Kamlari practice. It was a whole movement. We trained the girls to be activists and to vindicate their own rights. They learned so well. They demonstrated, they marched, they met with government officials, they appeared in the newspapers and on television, and they were the ones who, after a while, rescued the girls who were indentured. They became the most active and passionate proponents of their own cause, and we trained them to do it. They learned very well.

So that's what you meant when you said, "Out of the mud grows the lotus."

That was our original motto.

So beautiful. Can you summarize the foundation's accomplishments?

We have built schools. Mostly schools that were destroyed by the earthquake, but we also build new schools. We brought so many girls home to these village with the indentured daughters program, and some of the schools were in a state of collapse, so we had to build schools there, too, and then hire teachers. I mean, all this gets very complicated. But that's not our major mission. We built 250 schools after the earthquake, and we did build some schools in emergencies.

What is your major focus?

The focus is helping children in various ways. Education is our major focus. We educate kids from kindergarten through medical school. We educate tens of thousands of children.

What about the health issues?

We built all these little hospitals for malnourished children. We made an agreement with the government that we'd build them, hire and train the employees, and operate them ourselves for five years, and after that they would take over. Close to seventeen thousand children and their mothers have gone through that program already.

Nutrition is part of what we're about. There are seventeen of these Nutritional Rehabilitation Homes (NRH) now. We've turned over all but about five of them to the government, but we still monitor them.

We're still heavily involved in nutrition and training. We hold nutrition camps in rural areas so that families who can't get to the local nutritional home can get nutrition training, and we can see which of the kids are malnourished—sometimes hundreds of mothers come to these camps with their children. We assess who is moderately malnourished and severely malnourished, and the severely malnourished we refer to the local Nutritional Rehabilitation Homes or send them to the Kathmandu one. We give the mothers a course, like Nutrition 101—a several-hour course in nutrition, the same as we do for the mothers of all the children who come to the NRH with their children. We're also doing a lot of training. We have medical students, dieticians, nurses, and so forth who come for training in nutrition.

You decided to help a country that is totally unfamiliar to you, with a different language and different culture, and you've changed things drastically for the better. How difficult was it? How did you win the confidence of the Nepalis?

The Nepali people are very, very welcoming. They welcome foreigners, and they're very cheerful and upbeat. There isn't any prejudice against foreigners there. The second thing is, the way I succeeded is not because of me, but because I found the right people to work with there. That's the key, because Nepalis are as smart as they can be. They know what they need, and they know how to get it. We foreigners can't begin to have the kind of local knowledge that they have.

We have quite a few employees in Nepal, but we don't have a single American employee. I'm the only American there, and I don't get paid. I'm just there because I've been there from the beginning. I found the right people there, and we have a fantastically intelligent and energetic and committed staff. That's the secret, I think.

And when you are in the United States, you're still working. That's where you are funding it, right? This is where you work in order to be able to help them.

Yes. Well, this is where we raise most of the money. We have an office here in Sausalito. It's got three employees, and they take care of the database and keeping in touch with donors, things like that. We have a big staff in Nepal that carries out the program.

Do you have volunteers here?
Once in a while we have them in the office—at times when there are heavy mailings and so forth.

In many ways you are the one person who is in charge of everything in the foundation.
Well, you know, not anymore. I used to do everything here, but now we have a very good board, and we have a good staff to do these things. And in Nepal I don't really do much at all. I give advice sometimes, and I play with the kids. I give speeches at little events. It's more or less out of my hands, which is really what I wanted because that's what's necessary for continuity.

I was the president for about twenty-five years, and then Som, whom we helped with a scholarship to college, came to work for us, and now he has replaced me as president. He is responsible for its success. He is a Nepali, is totally familiar with his country and its needs, and is extremely smart. I am the founder and Honorary President. And I'm still a member of the board, so I am actively involved. But I don't run things any more now that we have grown so much.

Did it ever cross your mind that you may get exposed to some kind of viruses or bacteria from traveling?
No. I traveled a lot before I went to Nepal. That was the first time I was in Asia, and I felt comfortable there right away.

Can you explain the time you got hurt and became a patient yourself in Nepal?
I broke my leg on a trek, and that's how our whole program for disabled children started. At that time I met a young doctor who had just opened a little hospital for disabled children—the first in Nepal. He's now one of my good friends. He was the one who set my leg in a plaster cast. Later I got involved with the children at the hospital, and we began giving scholarships to children from there. I think we've educated

more disabled children than any group in Nepal.

That broken leg was a really important experience because I think I grew to love the Nepali people even more after that. That was my third time there. When I went on that trek and got injured, I was carried in a basket for seven days over the mountains by a porter.

What about life before Nepal? You went to Columbia University and proceeded to George Washington University for your law studies. At this time, it wasn't easy for women to be accepted to law school. And upon graduation it was hard to find a job. I understand that a lot of women graduates did not really practice law, but instead became secretaries.

Actually, that is right. There was just a handful of women in my law school class, and we were not nervous about our academic achievements or passing the bar, but we were very nervous about trying to find a job. Employers would inquire, "Can you type?" They even did that to Sandra Day O'Connor. She graduated second in her class from Stanford. She was the first woman US Supreme Court justice. They did it to her too.

I actually got the first job I applied for. I planned to work for one year, and I was there for thirty-seven years. So I was very lucky because I found a job I liked, and that was my only interview. I worked for the Supreme Court of California, first for the chief justice, and then for one of the justices.

I understand you had a very interesting experience with Judge Mosk?

Yes, Stanley Mosk. He was my boss for twenty-five years. He was a wonderful, wonderful judge. He used to be the attorney general. He had been the youngest trial court judge in the state when he was appointed. I think he was thirty. And then he was a very active attorney general before he was appointed to the Supreme Court. So when the chief justice I'd worked for for nine years retired, I went to work for him. And I worked for him until I retired.

Helping the kids in Nepal and the need for change is actually a continuation of caring for social justice that you experienced while working for Judge Mosk.

Well, the California Supreme Court, at least at the time I was there, was maybe the most prominent state court in the country, and it had a lot of very enterprising judges who thought of a lot of new ideas in the law. We pioneered many of the doctrines that were adopted by the rest of the country. So it was a very exciting place to work.

I helped the judge write his decisions. I think the most important case I worked on was the Bakke case, one of the first cases in the country on affirmative action, which involved the question of whether to allow race to be a factor in college admission policy. And it went to the US Supreme Court, which partly reversed us and partly affirmed our decision.

I read that you were involved in developing the constitutional doctrine of independent state grounds as well.

Well, Judge Mosk was a pioneer in developing that, at least in California. If an issue came up and it wasn't controlled by the federal Constitution, it could be decided on the basis of the state Constitution and the state laws. There were a lot of unique decisions based on that ground. He was a brilliant man, and very creative. We saw eye-to-eye politically, which is absolutely essential in that role. We had a very good relationship for twenty-five years.

You did not decide to leave the court until you went to Nepal?

Well, yes. I first went to Nepal in 1984, and I went every year after that. Judge Mosk was very supportive of my work and allowed me to leave for several months a year—unpaid leave. So I was able to really get involved in Nepal. By 1990 I said to him, "I think my heart is in Nepal, so I'll take half-retirement. For two years, I'll work six months a year and go to Nepal for the other six months. At the end of that time, I'll decide." I did that in 1990, and I finally retired in 1992.

You're helping so many children, and I'm interested to know what your childhood was like in Transylvania where you were born, and then in the US?

My father came to the US in 1927, four years before we joined him. He was a craftsman and made beautiful furniture. He established himself in business not long after he arrived in America with thirty-eight dollars in his pocket. Later he became a citizen and then sent for me, my mother, and my three other siblings. We arrived in 1931 to New York, and that's where I grew up, in the Bronx. I lived there pretty much until

I was seventeen, when I left home. It was during the war. I graduated from high school when I was sixteen, in January of 1942, just a month after Pearl Harbor.

I've always dreamed about traveling, but there were no commercial airlines then, though I think Pan Am flew overseas. And it was during the war, so I traveled all over the country until I was twenty-one years old. I'd land in a city, and I'd get a job, and when I got bored there, I'd go to the next city and the next job. Then, at twenty-one, I started college. I graduated when I was twenty-four. And then, for two years, I went to work for Drew Pearson, who was a very important, muckraking columnist in Washington at the time.

I loved the job of answering his fan mail, which was quite fantastic. But after two years, I thought, *This is not a career*, so I decided to go to law school. I went to George Washington University. When I told Mr. Pearson that I was going to leave, he said, "Don't leave. You can come to work any time you are free and answer the mail. You can come at midnight." So I worked independently for another three years for him. I graduated in 1954, came out to California, and took the bar.

And then you got married?

I got married a year after I passed the bar exam. That was in July of 1955. My husband had two sons; they were twelve and ten at the time. We divorced in 1961, but I remained close to him and his sons. I've failed in two things in my life. One is retirement. The other is divorce because we stayed very close.

He died very young, in 1976. One of his sons has two boys, and I'm now a great-grandmother. I have three great-grandchildren.

Do you have any memories from Transylvania?

Very few. I remember our house a little bit. A little cottage. I think I remember my grandmother, just a few things. I remember the horse and carriage we took to go to the train that would take us to France, where we would board a ship to the United States. I remember our dog chasing the carriage, and my grandmother crying.

It was very smart of your father to move to the United States. What prompted him to do that?

He just felt that there were no opportunities for his children where we were living. It was pretty anti-Semitic, and he'd been through the First World War. Many of the people in Europe thought that America was the golden land.

My father was wonderful. He was a great character and very inventive. And the way he got here, it's too long to tell you, but it's sort of typical of how he operated, you know? He was very gentle, but he knew how to get what he wanted.

In 1927, he found out the name of the American consul in Bucharest who was in charge of issuing visas. My father had a shop where he made beautiful furniture. He made a leather couch and two leather armchairs and put it on the train addressed to this guy without any return address. And then, a couple of weeks later, he said to my mother, "OK, I'm going to Bucharest to get my visa."

He arrived at this big mansion and knocked on the door. The butler saw this little workman and said, "I'm sorry, the consul is not home." But my father looked beyond him into the salon and saw his furniture in a place of honor in the room. And then he said, "Well, I'm the person who sent that furniture, and I just wanted to be sure that it arrived in good shape." The consul was actually there, and he heard the conversation and said, "Oh, come in. Come in. Nobody in your country has ever done something so wonderful for us. The furniture is so beautiful. I am so appreciative."

My father went inside and looked over the couch and chairs, pretending to be looking for nicks and scratches. And then, when he finished, the consul said, "I'm so grateful to you. Is there anything I can do for you?" And my father said, "As a matter of fact, there is. I'd like to have a visa to go to America." And that was a time when people from southern Europe were considered to be undesirable immigrants, so they had a very strict quota.

The consul said, "I can't do that. The quota is spoken for for years to come. There are no vacancies." My father, I guess, looked disappointed. The consul said, "Well, come back next week." So my father stayed in Bucharest. He went back the next week and the next and the next, and the butler opened the door. Nothing, nothing, nothing.

Around a week before Christmas, the consul was at home and when my father arrived, he invited him in and said, "I'm going to give you something, but you have to swear that you'll never say how you got this or who you got it from." It was a visa. It must have been somebody who died or something like that; that's why it was available. My father had to rush back to our town and get ready. He collected thirty-eight dollars, and with his violin, he left for France. He was never separated from his violin. He played the violin and the cello all his life.

This is such an incredible story, and you almost didn't tell me that story.
 Well you know, it's just too long, so it's not in my book. Within four years of the time he arrived in New York, he was all set up in business. He had some of the wealthiest clients because he did such beautiful work. He was an established man. He had a bank account and a business, and excellent recommendations from influential people, and he sent for the family.

He's the kind of European guy that I met in Israel. That gentleness that you're describing, a person who plays the violin and doesn't separate themselves from it. It's so touching. And he goes to America with it.
 He told us later that he played music in the steerage at the bottom of the ship where all the really poor people were. He played the violin for them.

You must have missed him when he was away for the few years.
 I hadn't seen him since I was two, and I didn't know who he was. And he had never seen my little sister. My mother was nine months pregnant when he left for America, and my sister was born four days later. He had to be across the border by December 31 under the terms of the visa.

Well you know what? It must have been really a bad situation there for him to leave your mom nine months pregnant.
 It was. And my mother, she was so brave to agree to it. So he had never seen my little sister. She was four when we came, and I was six. He had this beautiful apartment furnished for us. And when we got to the apartment and my mother went to bed with this strange man, we were furious and howled outside their bedroom door for a long time. In

Europe, we slept with my mother, and we couldn't understand why all this was changing.

This is an immigrant story, and I'm writing about an immigrant's experience. Do you remember any difficulties of adjustment as a child in America?

Not really. My parents were very smart. Of course, my mother didn't speak any English, and we didn't know a word of English when we arrived. My parents just said, "Out, out on the street. Play with the other kids," to the four of us. We arrived June 6th, 1931, and in September we started school. I never remember learning a word of English. We spoke perfect English by September, just from playing with the kids on the street.

So basically your father has had the immigrant experience, and when you came he was all set. For four years he was building a nest for you, and when he was established, that's when he brought you over. And at that time, you were able to get visas because he was American already.

Yes.

You've got so many honors. Your work is so well known. When I keep telling people, excitedly, that I'm going to interview you, they say, "Oh, of course; we've heard about Olga." And I've heard about you from Isabel Allende (see page 19).

Yes, she's a good friend. Actually, I think she has talked about me a number of times. I gave a TED talk, and that was also a result of her exposure.

So, tell me about your encounter with the King of Nepal.

It was an incredible experience to attend the ceremony where I received a medal from the King of Nepal. I wasn't the only one. There were a hundred people getting medals at the same time, but it was really quite an experience. You go onto the palace grounds, and there are men on horseback with red uniforms and black plumed hats and black boots, and they parade around in front of the honorees. And then at the ceremony, the king puts the medal around the neck of men, but he gives it by hand to the women. That's the kind of society it used to be.

And then we were invited to a party later that afternoon. It was amazing. We were out in the garden, and there were these beautiful tables with beautiful food, and cigarettes on the tables. And then these high silver gates flung open, and down the marble steps with the statues of lions and tigers carved out of marble on each step and a red carpet down the middle came the king and the princess. And I just thought, *Oh my God. What's a girl from the Bronx doing here?*

So that was nice. And then I went back to the house and put the medal on each child, and took pictures with them. He was an unpopular king, and the kids kept saying, "Well, he's not my king. He's not my king."

What about your encounter with the Dalai Lama?

He used to give out an award called the Unsung Hero of Compassion. This was the first year that he gave it. Again, I was not the only one. There were fifty people. It was like a teaching session. They gave you the award, and a silk scarf, and a beautiful book, and they talked about you, and they printed this very nice book about the backgrounds of the honorees. And then after lunch, he gave a talk which just confirmed to me what a wonderful person he was.

He was quite a cheerful person and had a great sense of humor. They asked for questions from the guests, and one woman asked his advice about some trouble she was having with her teenaged son. There was a silence for a moment, and then he said, "How should I know? I'm a monk."

What was the most important honor that you received?

I think the one I liked the best was from the Dalai Lama. I thought it was the most meaningful because there were forty-nine other people there who had done wonderful things, and it was moving.

I'd like to know what you mean when you say "Helper's High."

Well, if more people knew about it, I think more people would spend more time helping others. It's a feeling you get when you're doing something good for people. I mean, it's better than drugs, or alcohol, or anything else. It makes you feel good. It's just a feeling that you're doing something for somebody else outside of yourself.

It gives you hope for humanity, when you do it and you see improvements, and you think things aren't so bad. Things can change. Things can get better. I've seen that so, so, so often. I'm not as cynical about human nature as maybe most people become at my age.

It's hard not to be cynical given what's going on in our country today.
Well, I'm not cynical. I'm just so aggravated and angry a lot of the time. I'm sort of like the uber anti-Trump person. I'm very interested in politics. I think about it a lot. I read about it a lot. In Nepal, I read three newspapers every day. Bad things are happening here.

Why do you think we got into this kind of situation, where the most unlikely person became president?
Well, I think it was a combination of not taking into consideration the anger of a certain segment of the population. I was an enthusiastic supporter of Hillary Clinton, and I still am. But Hillary Clinton wasn't appealing to a lot of people.

I think those two things, and the fact that I think most people didn't think it could happen. I think America is losing some of its stature in the world.

It was a tremendous pleasure to talk to you. The last thing I'm going to ask you is, do you have a message for people who are retiring today?
Well, it's that life doesn't end at retirement. The secret, I think, to a happy retirement is involvement. And the best kind of involvement, from my viewpoint, is helping other people. It makes you feel valued, like a valuable person in society. It's a thrill when you see what effect your actions have had. When you retire, it's not the end. It can be the beginning of something good or better than your working years.

Retirement can be a startup.

Olga Murray's passport photo

Olga Murray is a recipient of the 2001 Unsung Heroes of Compassion Award by the Dalai Lama, and a medal of honor in 2002 from the King of Nepal. In 2005, she was honored as a finalist by the World of Children Award. In 2005, the Nepal Youth Foundation received the California Association of Nonprofits' Award of Excellence for the Indentured Daughters Program. In 2006, Olga Murray won the award for the Mannington Stand on a Better World.

ARGINE SAFARI

ARMENIAN-AMERICAN TEACHER OF THE YEAR WINNER

"It is great to perform, but when you make someone's life more meaningful and better, it is a completely different feeling."

TO BECOME A TEACHER OF THE YEAR in New Jersey, an instructor must meet several requirements, including the following:

Be an expert in your field who inspires students of all backgrounds with the ability to learn.

Create a strong culture of respect and success.

Demonstrate leadership, innovation, and educational activity locally and nationally.

Have the respect and admiration of students, parents, and colleagues.

Demonstrate poise, eloquence, and the ability to maintain a demanding schedule.

One music teacher earned this distinction for far more reasons than described in the guidelines above. Of the 220,000 educators who work in the state's K–12 charter or public school districts, more than 2,500 were nominated by administrators, teachers, staff, parents, and students as Teachers of the Year in their district. Four were ultimately chosen as finalists for the state honor.

Argine Safari rose to the top, culminating with a trip to the White House in April 2017 with the forty-nine other state winners. "Through music, I teach my students to pursue their dreams, recognize beauty, have more love, compassion, respect, integrity and understanding," Argine says. "Through music, I teach my students how to be truly human."

She started playing the piano at the age of seven. As a freshman in high school in Armenia, her music theory teacher, Rita Israelovna Petrosian, discovered her unique ear, talent, and strength of character, and she was instrumental in inspiring Argine to apply to the prestigious Moscow P. I. Tchaikovsky Conservatory. There, another teacher, Valentina Nikolayevna Kholopova, drove her hard, underscoring the principles of discipline, dedication, and perseverance Argine's family had long preached and which she has incorporated into her lifelong philosophy: "When you love what you do, you don't realize how hard you work."

A Grammy-nominated educator and the 2010 Princeton University Distinguished Scholar, Argine has learned to blend the structured

Russian disciplinary method with a warmer, caring, and freer American style of education, combining perseverance with joy and dedication with the love of music. In 2013, she co-founded and developed a nonprofit youth theater, Stage Scene and Song Performing Arts. Argine and her partners have been running this award-winning program where young participants receive intense training in all aspects of musical theater, culminating in performances of fully staged musicals, often to an audience of amazed parents seeing a child's artistic side for the first time.

Argine and I sat down for a casual conversation in New York City, where her journey to America began.

I would like to congratulate you on your wonderful award of the Teacher of the Year of the state of New Jersey for 2016–17. This is such a great honor. Tell me about your story as a musician and how you wound up in the United States.

I was born in Armenia, Yerevan, to a very musical family, and grew up with my twin sister, Gisane, with whom I shared my musical endeavors. Our house was always open to everyone to come and to enjoy music, and I remember my dad, who is very musical, playing the piano and singing. Ricky, our Doberman Pinscher, was so musical that he would sit near the fireplace to enjoy the fire and the music. These are some of my most favorite childhood memories.

My sister studied violin, and I studied the piano. I remember adoring my father and wishing I could play like him. He played by ear but could also read music. Friends and relatives used to come over and ask him to play this, play that, sing this, sing that. It was just fun, a wonderful time. But my sister and I studied music professionally. For seven years we attended a music school, and then after that, I continued my studies at a specialized music high school. My sister went to a different school, and at that point we split professionally, but we always stayed in contact with each other, no matter what.

At the high school, one of my biggest influences was my theory and Solfeggio teacher who taught me the most important life lessons. Soft-spoken and kind, Ms. Petrosian was a brilliant musician, a hardworking single mother, and most importantly, a remarkable teacher. She encouraged curiosity in her students. She taught us how to connect the most complicated music theory concepts to the real life. She pushed us to be the best we could possibly be and made each and every one of us believe in ourselves. But the most important lesson I learned from her is that with passion, drive, and hard work, anything is possible.

One of my first projects was about a musical form. As I started digging deep into the topic of my choice, the prelude form, I got excited to learn about the evolution of this form, and before I knew it, my project turned into a research paper. Flipping through sixty pages of my handwritten work, Ms. Petrosian gradually raised her eyebrows in amusement, gasped, slowly looked at me, and said: "My dear child, there is nothing you cannot accomplish if you work hard." I stood there in wonder. *What does she mean? Why is she saying this?*

Day after day, Ms. Petrosian made me work harder than I could have ever imagined. She gave me the toughest assignments and expected more from me than from any other student in that class. She knew right away I was hungry for challenges, so she accepted her own challenge of supporting me in my passionate journey of discovering music and what it meant to me. She encouraged and helped me in my struggles, making sure I never lost faith in myself. Three years later, I became a student in the dream school for anyone pursuing a music career, Moscow Conservatory. Ms. Petrosian changed my life in the most profound and insightful way.

Do you think that the changes in music genre are influenced by the historical situation and economy in the world?

I think there are many reasons for music evolution. The influence comes from many countries and cultures. For example, Chopin's preludes bring influence from Poland, and his difficult preludes are a wonderful way to express musicianship. In the same breath, Liszt, Brahms, and Rachmaninoff wrote preludes reflecting their respective cultures and countries of Hungary, Germany, and Russia, and they are also extremely difficult to play. These approaches are very different from the original Bach preludes which were preludes and fugues.

Preludes started originally as an introduction, like the prelude and fugue by Bach. Then later, the prelude became an independent form, a very involved form. A romantic prelude is very different than a

Baroque prelude. For example, Rachmaninoff's preludes are large piano compositions with their own structure—no longer introductions to something else but their own independent compositions. They are some of my favorite music.

I was just fascinated to know that a genre of music can actually develop over time and how the historical influences are so important in its development. One type of music could start a certain way and develop into something else.

It would be fascinating to listen to music together with you and for you to explain how the piano piece evolved. Do you still play piano?

Yes. Piano is my favorite musical instrument.

Was your music school training very intensive?

Yes. When I graduated music school, there were juries and exams at the end of the year, so we were supposed to perform by memory. It was very challenging. It's nerve-racking to know that you have to memorize everything. What if your memory skips a bit and you play something wrong? And I've had situations like that. You just have to find yourself, wiggle your way out, and somehow move on. The idea of my teacher was "Never stop. Keep going, keep performing," even though we knew that there would be people in the audience that would realize the mistakes right away.

When you play, you immerse yourself in the music and forget everything around you, and you don't even realize that time passes, just like other art forms. The accomplishment gives you such self-confidence and happiness.

Oh, yes, absolutely.

When you were in school, did you work long hours? Describe a day in your high school in Armenia.

I started playing piano at the age of seven, and I went to a specialized music school at the age of fourteen. It was like a regular high school in the morning where you studied academics, which ended early in the afternoon, and after that there was music training the rest of the day. Rehearsals and performances were a major part of my education, and many times they went into the night. My professors were very famous. They were big names in their respective fields. Some of them were still performing on music stages, and others were accomplished music researchers.

If you want to be a musician, you need to know that at an early age; in order to be accepted to my specialized music school, I had to know that I wanted to pursue music professionally.

Therefore, this decision had to be made with a lot of caution and soul searching while seeking advice from parents and teachers. This school was akin to getting free private music lessons for many years from the best teachers my country had to offer. All you had to do was to be dedicated, driven, and ready to sacrifice your daily routines. Having a little bit of talent did not hurt either!

The teacher that I mentioned to you was my inspiration. I guess she was able to realize that I had that gift in music—a good ear. She created a very specific curriculum for me, and she pushed me and guided me in a different direction because she saw something in me that I didn't know myself. I loved the challenge, and I loved being singled out and guided by her.

Whatever work she gave me, I just did it, and I did it with joy because it was challenging and enjoyable at the same time. But I loved working, and when you love what you do, you don't realize how hard you work.

What role did your parents have in your life as a musician?

Both my parents are physicists. Though being a scientist, my dad was a tremendous musical inspiration for me. My mom was the one who was a strict parent, a Tiger Mom. I wouldn't say that I was afraid of her; she never once raised her voice. My sister and I just had a tremendous respect for her and also admired her. It was enough for her to look at me in a certain way and I got the message. If she did, I would feel that I did not meet her expectation. We both felt that, my twin sister and I.

We had a very specific tradition in our house. We had to clean the house and help with all the house chores. Over the summer, we always did some extra schoolwork, studying math and languages. My mom was very strict and stern. You just couldn't get by. You knew that whatever you did wrong, she would pick up on it. She kept us so organized and disciplined, and I think in a sense what I learned from her are her superb hardworking skills. She's an unbelievably thorough person and a perfectionist.

Because they were both scientists at the time in Armenia, they were not getting paid much. The economic situation was very harsh and unpredictable. My dad was supplementing his income by helping doctorate students write their dissertations. My mom would design and make clothes for others. She had a knitting machine, and she would stay up all night working until she finished her orders. I remember clearly that if something didn't work well, she would just start all over and say, "No, it's not perfect. It's not going to fit her well." She actually knit my wedding dress!

Your mom was a really incredible role model. You grew up in the capital of Armenia. What was it like?

Yerevan is the largest city, with just over one million residents, but it always felt like a small town where people knew each other. You would always see a friendly face on the streets, at venues, in people's homes.

When the time came to decide my next steps, I applied to study at Moscow Conservatory. Moscow is very different from Yerevan. Moscow is one of the largest cities in the world, a huge urban city where everything moves at the speed of light, it seems.

Was the church an intimate part of one's life?

That is a very good question. Armenia was a part of the Soviet Union at the time, and religious affiliations and practices were not allowed. When I was growing up in the '70s, no one could claim that they were practicing Christians, Jews, or Muslims. However, my grandma was very religious because her father was a priest. You know that, in Armenia, priests are allowed to marry. Her husband, my grandpa, was very active in the society and had a very good position in the government. As such, he and his family could not have been associated with any semblance of religion. Therefore, my grandma kept it all a secret. But despite persecutions and fear of jail time, she still attended church every Sunday. I remember how even when she passed away, people from the church came to our house and sang religious songs and hymns to honor her days as a church choir singer. That was a very moving experience, because even though we knew she was religious, we never realized that she literally had a second family outside of our home. She told us stories from the Bible, and she was very scholarly. She wrote books with her reflections on the Bible, the way she saw it. Stories from the Bible were coming alive in her notebooks, and she would make connections with these stories and our lives.

That is how I was brought up, not worshipping "Jesus is good," but it was more like what I can learn from the Bible story or Old Testament or New Testament, and how it reflects on today's life. What kind of reflection does it have on me? My grandma was a Protestant and attended a Gregorian church—a special religious branch of Christianity only found in Armenia since Armenia was the first country in the world to accept Christianity as a state religion back in AD 301.

Yes, the Donation of Constantine. At the time of the Soviet Union, you were not allowed to practice religion. The famous Marx statement that religion is the opiate of the masses was carried on so that religion was forbidden.

In the '70s, it was Brezhnev and his Politburo cronies that instilled the anti-religious sentiment to more than 200 million people. Everything changed when the Perestroika happened. My parents were always politically aware and were never fooled by the Communist propaganda. But until Perestroika, nobody really believed that the Soviet Union would fall apart because the principles of Socialism had been so deeply embedded in our culture for the past seventy years. So, when the Soviet Union collapsed like a deck of cards in the '80s, it was akin to a Great Flood—all that was hated was washed away and the rebuilding process had to start from scratch. I was in my late teens.

How did you feel about that at the time?

Well, honestly, we all knew there was something big happening. We didn't realize how big it was. Gorbachev, at the time, was new and was seen as a very controversial figure by many in the establishment and some people in the Soviet Union. Others, like me, were hoping that he could turn things around.

I also want to mention another catastrophic event that happened during my first year of studying at the Moscow Conservatory in December 1988. The famous Armenian earthquake centered in the small town of Spitak and devastated many surrounding towns and villages. It took thousands upon thousands of lives. It was huge. I was tempted to go to Armenia to help with the cleanup process, like a lot of my classmates did, but instead I decided to volunteer at the local hospital in Moscow where some of the victims with the most severe injuries were flown in—from Armenia and Spitak, in particular. I witnessed some really, really heartbreaking cases. I will never forget this child who lost his arms and legs and his entire family. It was terrible to watch, but what was amazing was his incredibly positive spirit. He had strong dreams of becoming a doctor.

People from Spitak have a very strong spirit, are very positive, and possess a great sense of humor. I don't really know what happened to this child because he was transferred to a different hospital, but I doubt that he survived. He was only eleven years old. When things like this happen in front of your eyes, it's almost as if you are being transported to a different place. You realize that all these little, inconsequential things that are happening in your life are just that—very little and meaningless. One learns from others how to survive in difficult situations and how their strong spirits help them survive.

Just like the Jews during World War II, Armenian people suffered from the 1915 genocide. We know how it feels to lose and to be lost. But we also know how to move on and to survive by holding on to each other. I personally lost people in my family because of the genocide. My father, aunt, and her sister, and the survivors were able to tell the story. They walked through the deserts in order to survive and passed the stories from one generation to the other. They emphasized how strong the spirit was that held them together. We grew up learning about this. It was part of our history. You can never erase it from your life.

There was hatred toward the Ottoman Empire, not toward the Turks. Unfortunately, the Turks have erased the genocide from their history books. In Turkey, they burned all the evidence of the 1915 genocide, as if it never happened. We, the Armenians, pay great respect to the German people, who kept educating their children about the atrocities of the Holocaust by studying it in schools and building museums as a testimony. Unfortunately, this is not the Armenian story. Turkey has never acknowledged the 1915 genocide. Millions of people were killed, mutilated, tortured, disrespected, and misplaced. This was especially devastating since the Armenians were always a very small nation. Out of two million Armenians who lived in the Ottoman Empire, about 1.5 million Armenians were murdered. As a result of a huge displacement during the 1915 genocide, the Armenians are now scattered around the world, but our history keeps us together.

When I became the New Jersey State Teacher of the Year, many people in Armenia expressed their pride to me. It was a big deal for them. They made me feel like a representative of my nation. I lifted their spirits. I feel very honored to be Armenian because I strongly believe that it is a very talented nation in many ways. We are great inventors and great writers, artists, scientists, and musicians. I'm proud of our history.

Immigrants are always proud of their nationality. Although America gives immigrants the opportunity to excel, it is the spirit and the strength that an immigrant brings to America. Tell me about your Russian experience. It appears that during the Perestroika, it would have been the best time for you to be in Russia and study music in such a highly respected school. And at that time, the Soviet Union failed. Why did you leave when things looked up?

Well, when the Soviet Union fell, the situation became extremely unstable. Not only economically, which always was the case, but also politically. You know, you cannot erase seventy years of the Soviet regime. It takes years and years to change this mentality. Especially in Russia, where chauvinism and Russophobia always went hand in hand. It was in Moscow where I met my husband, whose father was Armenian and mother was Jewish. My future husband and his family always felt a particular discomfort from the authorities due to their ethnic and religious backgrounds.

In Russia, when you apply to universities, you have to state both your parents' nationalities and religious affiliations, just as in the case of the Jews. Russia is very peculiar when it comes to allowing other nationalities to take advantage of what they have to offer. For my husband, it was difficult to even get accepted into the university. Though he lived in the Soviet Union all of his life, his mixed nationality and religious background weren't welcomed on many levels.

So the thing that stood in the way of your husband's progress was that he was Jewish?

That's part of it. He is half-Jewish and half-Armenian, with a darker skin and hair than most Russians—not Russian-looking at all. Though he had many Russian friends, was fascinated with Russian history, and perfected his Russian to a point where he spoke better than most Russians, he still did not belong. He and I felt very comfortable among our friends, colleagues, and like-minded people, but once we would have to leave this comfort zone, things would change in an instant. On the streets of Moscow, my husband and I had to fend off Russian nationalists—and many times the authorities—from verbal and potential physical altercations.

It was a very big accomplishment for me to be accepted to the Conservatory because it was a very select group of non-Russian people that they were willing to accept. There were people applying from the entire world, and their unwritten rule is to accept your own first. I guess it is a good thing that I wasn't really aware of it, otherwise I probably would have been discouraged to apply. So, great recommendations from my teachers from the Yerevan school and the high marks in the placement exams couldn't sway the authorities to make a wrong decision in my case. I got in!

The school's academic policies were so strict that they did not accept any excuses. I made sure I went above and beyond my studies, including having my child listen to my final recital one day before she was born! After I gave birth, a few days later, my teacher, Valentina Nikolayevna Kholopova, called and said, "Congratulations on your baby. I will see you tomorrow, with twenty more pages of your final dissertation." I didn't see it any other way. I didn't think any other way. I was like, well, I've got to do it while I'm breastfeeding, while I wasn't sleeping. I accepted this as if it was my obligation. No objections.

I think that that taught me toughness. It taught me discipline. It taught me perseverance. It taught me not to take any excuse and not to give any excuses. It taught me that no matter what, I'm going to just do my work, and I'm going to work my hardest, and I'm going to try to do my best no matter what I do and no matter where I go. And those are the values I try to pass on to my students.

Are you still in touch with that teacher?

Yes! She is a world-renowned scholar. She invited me to do a presentation at the International Music Conference in Moscow Conservatory in February 2016. Currently, she is advocating to have my article published in the Conservatory's Music Education journal. She is still very, very active. After I gave my presentation at the Conservatory two years ago, she came up to me, took my hands, and humbly said: "How I wish I was a student in your class!" Can you believe that? She is an iconic figure in the world of musicology and does groundbreaking research in the field of music theory and music analysis, and yet she has a humility that is absolutely admirable.

That is wonderful. Well, we understand this Russian mentality in teaching. I had an experience with my own daughter, Jordana. She was learning ballet with a Russian teacher who was a known prima ballerina from the Kirov Ballet who planned a rehearsal on Mother's Day. As you know, it is not accepted in America to have rehearsal on Mother's Days. It so happened that my daughter was invited the afternoon of the rehearsal to a birthday party. When the rehearsal was still going on at three o'clock, my daughter asked permission to leave, and the teacher disallowed it. So Jordana stepped forward and said, "Excuse me, but I have to leave because I have a birthday to go to, and therefore you're going to have to get yourself another ballerina. I'm leaving." She was only seven years old. Imagine if that would have happened in Russia.

Good for her.

You know, Kalleria was a wonderful teacher and she loved my daughters, Jordana and Ariel, but she was very strict. We used to invite her for Passover celebrations, and one day she came with a book called West of the Sun and East of the Moon. *It contained stories full of illustration. She said, "This is for you. Every story illustration could be inspiring a ballet dance," and she left. I didn't know that it was a goodbye present. Shortly after, she passed away. She was a great teacher, but very strict for the American mentality.*

I survived it. At the time, I didn't realize that the Russian style is not always right. I took it as the fact, but I think that that experience taught me to combine what I learned there and to adopt what is expected here in America. Here, a teacher gives some freedom to students and the ability to make their own decisions. Sometimes it is too free because occasionally it's done to please the parents, which is another extreme that I don't agree with.

When I was growing up, there was a structured repertoire. It was a very strong system designed to reveal and foster talent. We were judged by a jury. We were required to adhere to a repertoire which included a Baroque piece, a classical piece, a romantic piece, and a contemporary piece. Those were requirements for every repertoire.

I think that what I learned there, I have to fit into what's going on here. The combination of both makes sense to me. A kind of unique representation of a teacher who has high expectations and demands for her students and herself, but in the meantime, I know what it is when a student is discouraged, when a student is forced to learn a musical piece that he doesn't enjoy. I don't want them to quit. I want to encourage them. A teacher has to inspire joy and love for music.

I had to adjust to different cultures. Kids are coming from different places, and need to have their voices heard. They like to be a part of the decision making. They are the leaders. They have freedom here. I didn't have that when I was growing up. And kudos to this country for providing that to the young people and giving them opportunities that we never had. I want to cherish that, and I want to bring that into my vision, and my teaching, and my way of approaching things.

So how did you end your journey in Russia? You sought asylum in America?

We took our thirteen-month-old daughter and ventured into the United States after waiting for more than five years to be vetted and approved by the United States government. It was dangerous and unsafe for us to live in a new Russia. Even several years after we moved to the United States, my husband's cousin fell victim of a hate crime back in Moscow, which devastated our family. Neither Armenians nor Jews felt safe.

The Russians let the Jews leave Russia at that point, right?

A lot of Jews immigrated to the United States and to Israel. However, it took years before the migration was approved. During the darkest years of the Soviet Union, people were changing names to sound more Russian so they would be left alone and given opportunities. When the migration started during Perestroika years, the reverse happened—many Russian people would change their names to sound more Jewish so they could move to Israel.

Did your husband practice Judaism?

No, he did not because they were afraid. His mom would occasionally go to synagogue in Moscow since she was proud of being Jewish. She did not have to disguise her religion, though, since no one suspected she was Jewish as she was fair skinned with blonde hair. She looked Russian to the authorities.

Still, I remember how hard and unpredictable it was. At one time, my future husband and I took a bus and were confronted by a group of older, drunk adults making aggressive comments toward our appearance and assumed nationality. Unfortunately, this was a regular occurrence. The streets were not safe; the authorities were not protecting us, if not abetting the criminals. We had to leave and seek asylum. We arrived in the United States on a refugee visa.

Can you tell me about your new life as a refugee in the United States?

It was in 1994 when I first moved to Brooklyn. I was a newly minted immigrant. I knew that I needed to improve my language skill, so I went to college, for which I got a scholarship. I graduated with a bachelor's degree in business from Brooklyn College and started working in the business field, but I gradually took some music gigs such as musical directing and conducting. First, I worked as an accompanist and quickly found a part-time regular job, then I was asked to lead the youngest group of students. Eventually, I did conducting and arrangement for them. Today, they are a sought-after Grammy award-winning chorus.

At the same time, I did all kinds of performances. But what's interesting is that I met a young woman from Moscow, very talented. Her name was Oksana. She was working in a church and was looking for someone to cover for her. I had never played a church service before, but I said I would try. That is how I started taking lessons in organ playing and singing, and I started to lead the services in various churches, singing in different languages. To this day, I'm a church musician as well—I am an organist and a choir director in Woodcliff Lake, New Jersey. But I really am a piano player. Unfortunately, I don't practice as much because I'm so busy teaching. For example, I was just invited to play Gershwin with an orchestra, but I had to think for a while before accepting it because I would have to dedicate a lot of time to practice and to prepare for performances. Once you don't practice as much as you used to, your skills are not the same.

Does your daughter play?

Yes, Beata is a very good pianist. She graduated from Manhattan Precollege in voice and piano, and she loves it. She's extremely bright in many ways. She decided to practice law and recently graduated from law school, passed her bar exam, and was already sworn in to become an attorney in the state of New York. And she is only twenty-five!

I also have a son, Areg, who was born here and plays the trombone. He's now in high school, and I am his choral teacher. He actually started to play the piano, but he hated it because he had a Russian teacher who was very strict. At nine years old, boys need excitement, entertainment, and joy to continue pursuing music. He was not going to obey just because his parents said so.

It is nice that your kids are continuing in your footsteps.

Oh, yes. They're both very musical.

Do you ever get to see your mother and father?

They actually moved to the United States. They did it because my dad was granted a very special scientist visa as an outstanding scientist. That's how they moved here. But I still have my twin sister in Moscow.

Does she like it there?

She loves her job. She's a violinist. She works in a top-notch orchestra, and she travels the world.

Does she come here to perform?

Yes. She can't move here, though. It's very difficult to join a major orchestra here. It's very competitive. Her kids are also very bright musicians. But to come here would cost them a lot of money to attend a good school. There, they are accepted to private academies and tuition is free. Very affordable. Maybe they'll come here for college.

After you went to business school, how did you proceed?

I worked in business—even on Wall Street for a short period of time. At the same time, I was doing those musical gigs working as a church musician and in off-Broadway shows. I needed music in my life. I took my daughter with me everywhere. She was a part of the musical gigs I put together. She grew up learning all this and understanding it. It was an important part for her and me, and it brought us closer.

But then 9/11 happened. I had a private student in Brooklyn who was a brilliant eighth grader at the time and wanted to apply to LaGuardia High School of Performing Arts, which is a tuition-free school, but highly competitive. Unfortunately, her father was killed in 9/11. Her mother was working full time and was left with four children. Clearly, she couldn't afford private lessons anymore. I made it a goal for myself to help my student succeed and continued teaching her, preparing her to get into the school of her dreams. When she was accepted, it was the thrill of my life. I realized that I had the strength and the power to change somebody's life. It was an incredible feeling. I love performing, but it is a different feeling when you help someone else, when you make someone else's life so much more meaningful and better. She gave me back more than I gave her—a realization that I had the power to succeed as a teacher. I had no doubts at that point that I had to become a teacher full time.

We moved to New Jersey in 2000, and I decided to teach in a public school. I said, "I'm going to apply for the license. I'm going to get the certification. And then we'll see what happens." I took classes on child psychology and pedagogy, and I passed the necessary exams to become certified. I had to learn band, orchestra, and choir K–12 repertoire because the music teacher certification requires you to be prepared to teach any instrument and any kind of music, at any grade level. That is very different in Armenia and in Russia where music teachers are more specialized.

While still working on my certification, I started applying for several teaching jobs, and one of the schools that I applied to is the one where I'm still teaching presently. When they offered me the job, I suddenly realized how challenging it would be for me to teach in an American high school, with such a different culture than the one I grew up in. Also, I knew that teaching in a public school would be much different than in a private academy, which is what I was used to. In Brooklyn, the kids came for audition and the expectations were high—from performances with local orchestras to gigs with the New York Philharmonic. We had Michael Jackson, Elton John gigs. In fact, the day before 9/11, we had a performance with Michael Jackson in Madison Square Garden.

I didn't know whether I was making the right choice by accepting a job in a public school. I was wondering what the kids would think of me. Such a big culture change I had to make. But I decided to take the job, and today, thirteen years later, I am teaching still at the same school. I never looked back, and this was one of the best decisions I have ever made in my life.

At Pascack Valley High School, I had an opportunity to build the program from scratch. I had a vision of developing a high-quality music program that would be open to everyone, and I had a dream that I could reach every child in my school. That every child would have the opportunity to take my classes. Of course, it is still a big work in progress. Students need to fit music into their very busy schedules. I want them to take an elective in chorus or band or whatever they wish to, but their schedules are limited. Studying music is always a challenge for these students, and I cherish every moment I get to spend with these amazingly talented youngsters.

One thing I try to teach my students is an ability to focus on one field and become better at it, as opposed to spreading themselves thin. I also teach that perseverance and passion are very important to become successful. It has been proven by a lot of research that people who persevere and are committed to one field or area of study have a higher chance of success.

So, you're Grammy nominated.

I was Grammy nominated as an educator, but I was also teaching at Brooklyn Youth Chorus when they won the Grammy Award for their performance of John Adams' music dedicated to the victims of 9/11. I was very proud of the students I taught at that time and of the fact that they won the Grammy! I felt an incredible sense of pride and accomplishment, but I also could not believe it was actually happening!

I didn't mention that I have a nonprofit youth theater, Stage Scene and Song Performing Arts, that I started with two of my colleagues. This company is not associated with my school; it is an after-school and summer program that offers high-quality acting, singing, dancing, directing, and musical-directing training, culminating in a full production of a musical. We believe that the performing arts transform, enlighten, and empower its participants and audiences. The arts cultivate problem solving, collaboration, communication, imagination, and creativity. We engage and embrace students who are culturally, educationally, and linguistically diverse, and we provide a perfect playground to inspire individuality and self-worth while still fostering a mutual respect for peers, a tremendous sense of community and camaraderie, and an appreciation for contribution. It gives me pure joy when, after working with our participants for four weeks, they are able to produce full productions and their parents walk out after the performances and say, "I didn't recognize my own kid!"

Tell me about your visit to the White House with the other state Teachers of the Year.

I was honored to be a part of the elite group of outstanding teachers from every state, gathered in the Oval Office in April 2017. As we all surrounded the seated president at his desk, standing in a circle next to the First Lady Melania Trump, Vice President Pence, Second Lady Karen Pence, and Education Secretary Betsy DeVos, I thought of the unprecedented honor that was bestowed upon me. Here I was, a refugee who came to this country with nothing, representing the incredible educators of the state of New Jersey in the official office of the President of the United States. This was nothing I could have ever possibly dreamed of. At that moment, I thought of my favorite quote from Nelson Mandela: "It always seems impossible until it's done."

Millions of thoughts were going through my mind. I was thinking of the heavy responsibility that we embrace every day: changing children's lives, one child at a time, to make their future brighter. It is our purpose, our mission. I was thinking of the field of education as one with tremendous sources of frustration, especially in today's world when our nation is more divided than ever. But for every frustration there is a student whose life so easily trumps these challenges. So I thought of my students who are the singular reason why I was standing in the Oval Office, full of pride and tears at the same time. They are the reason why teaching is the best profession that can be. I thought of those who have shared their own struggles and triumphs with me.

I thought of Valery, who overcame her depression and eating disorder and who founded her nonprofit organization. Val believes that every teen's life is worth fighting for.

I thought of Ben, who unexpectedly lost his father back in September. Ben was able to overcome many obstacles and will be attending Montclair University as a music theater major in the fall.

I thought of Aaron, my gay African-American/Puerto Rican student who struggled with his image but learned to become confident and strong when he discovered that he had a gift. Aaron is an incredible performer who is able to move his audiences to tears and make them laugh at the same time.

I thought of Chandni, who was bullied her entire life because of her heritage but had the courage to proudly accept my invitation to perform an Indian dance during one of my concerts. This performing experience gave Chandni confidence to organize a walk to raise awareness of Indian farmer suicides.

I thought of Nick, who suffered from a learning disability and dreamed of making friends throughout his school year. Nick's performance at the graduation recital was so powerful that the entire football team gave him a standing ovation.

I thought of Dan, who was born deaf but dreamed of becoming a musician. Today, Dan is a proud public school music teacher who inspires his middle school students to pursue their dreams no matter what.

Each of these brave young men and women have made an impact on my life, and I carry their stories with me wherever I go. I am forever grateful for the lessons of courage that I learn from them. They challenge and inspire me, they make me laugh and make me cry, and they impact me more than they know. My students give me great hope that the future is bright. They are forever a part of my life, and I am forever a part of theirs.

I am a proud American public school teacher. I long to inspire my students to pursue their dreams, the way Ms. Petrosian inspired me. I cannot imagine doing anything else than teaching because I truly believe that we have an incredible power to influence our students and their future. As a music teacher, I also have a unique platform because the power of music is penetrating and everlasting. Music is the force that keeps me going, and this force motivates me to inspire my students to stay strong and never give up. Music's transformative power is evident in the way my students grow and mature, and it gives me pure joy to watch them blossom. Through music, I teach my students to pursue their dreams, recognize beauty, and have more love, compassion, respect, integrity, and understanding. Through music, I teach my students how to be truly human.

Argine Safari in her classroom

In addition to being named the 2017 New Jersey Teacher of the Year, **Argine Safari** received a Fulbright Distinguished Teaching Award in 2019, and as a result, conducted music education research in Finland and was hosted by the Sibelius Academy of Music, University of the Arts, Helsinki. In addition to visiting more than thirty K–12 schools and conservatories, she presented programs on education issues, conducted masterclasses, clinics, and seminars, and facilitated round-table discussions in Finland, Russia, France, and Germany. She also received an NEA Foundation California Casualty Award for Teaching Excellence in 2018, a Lowell Milken Center for Unsung Heroes Fellowship in 2018, the New Jersey Education Association Arts Educator of the Year in 2018, the Evangelina Menendez Trailblazer Award in 2017, the Distinguished Scholar Award from Princeton University in 2010, and many other academic, musical, and community honors. She has been a keynote speaker addressing some of the most challenging issues in education today and is currently pursuing her PhD in learning, instruction, and innovation from Walden University.

DORIS SCHECHTER

AUSTRIAN-AMERICAN ENTREPRENEUR, RESTAURATEUR, AND PHILANTHROPIST

"We have the third generations of families coming to my store. For me there is such a beauty about that. I've done this and I have achieved this . . . to be a people person, to be proud of who I am and what I stand for."

SOON AFTER KRISTALLNACHT IN VIENNA, in November 1938, Doris Schechter and her parents went into hiding for four years in Guardiagrele, in the Abruzzo region of Italy. The town was a capital of copper and wrought-iron crafts and was named after Nicola da Guardiagrele, a medieval goldsmith and artist.

It was here that Doris' life became a puzzle that she continuously tries to solve. She has a few mementos and memories, and the rest she has learned from stories she's been told about her early caregivers and the people who helped her family escape the Nazis.

Now a mother of five and grandmother of sixteen, Doris has lived in the United States for seventy-six years. She has created a successful "generational" restaurant where the public—and specifically the Jewish community—enjoy baked goods and cooked delicacies. Sometimes, her meals are the first food a Jewish person will enjoy upon deplaning in New York. (An Israeli customer once told her, "If you come to Jerusalem, you will meet many people who would reciprocate a Sabbath dinner for you!")

We sit down to talk in Doris' apartment, across from the Museum of Modern Art. I don't think the location is a coincidence. Here she can be close to other creative minds, muses for her productive life as a businesswoman, author, playwright, and filmmaker. Blonde curls still ring the face of the woman who, as a little girl, posed with a hotdog when she landed in New York along with other European immigrants fleeing the Holocaust.

But today, even among the bright intelligence and quest for life that shines from her face, there is a sadness in Doris. She continues to connect the past with the present, remembering the time she lost her beloved father, struggled to assimilate in American schools, and, at the urging of her mother, devoted the only self she knew to her growing family. She's still learning about herself, thanks to recently finding her birth certificate in Austria and seeing photographs and family mementos in Italy that crystallized stories she heard but could never truly make her own.

She's looking for answers for herself and countless others, and she is on a quest to thank the people who helped her survive as she tells stories that should never be forgotten.

You were six years old when you came to America with your parents and your younger sister.

I came along with 980 survivors, and the following poem written by one of the passengers describes the overwhelming emotions transpired by catching sight of the Statue of Liberty.

"Into the Light, Safe Haven," 1944

Thank God for you, Henry Gibbins, ship of dreams filled with
my bedraggled brethren dark and fair, tall and short—
all frail-boned and gaunt—
each of us a survivor reborn in the wake
of conscience, reborn on this buoyant sea revered for strong
currents and changing tides, fresh air filling the sunken chests
and ashen lungs of those who'd escaped the fires of Auschwitz-
Birkenau, Bergen-Belsen, Buchenwald, Dachau, Treblinka…
Yes, thank God for you, Henry Gibbins—
your sky-crowned decks surrounded by sea-speckled rail—
a far cry from barbed wire!
And during hours of German bombardment, the shelter of
stalwart bulk, mahogany halls,
tier upon tier of canvas hammocks—
warm blankets and soft pillows helping to smother my
nightmares, set in motion sweet dreams;
dining hall, with cornucopias
of vegetables and meats, kaleidoscope
of treats swelling shrunken bellies, smoothing withered souls;
and treasured beyond belief—glistening white toilets!
You are America to me!
The America of my dreams!
Home of the free and brave!

I was born in April 1938. I was six months old when Kristallnacht happened. That event changed the trajectory of my whole life. That's when my father knew that Vienna was no longer a place for the Jews.

Jews were being picked off left and right. So my father persevered to find a safe country for us.

What was your family life like in Vienna?

My father worked as a textile engineer. My mother worked for a very famous retail house. She loved her job. We were a middle-class Jewish family that lived in the second district. My mother used to say it was referred to as the Matzah Island because all the Jews lived there. My mother came from a business background, and my father came from an intellectual family. They loved their life in Vienna. My father was loved and respected by all who knew him. He died when I was six years old.

Tell me about your journey leaving Vienna.

My father intended for us to end up in France because he heard that it was safer for Jews. But as the story goes, I got sick in Italy on the way to France, and my father didn't want to take a risk. So we wound up staying in Italy, which is amazing because everyone that went on that boat to go to France was picked up and sent to Auschwitz.

My mother and I were sent to a small town in the center of Italy called Guardiagrele, along with other refugees. My father, who was sent to a concentration camp in Italy, asked permission to join us and was permitted to do so, which was the miracle of all miracles.

According to my father and my mother, we lived in an apartment that belonged to a nice lady who later in my life I reunited with. Her name was Rosalia. My father thought that this is where we would be for the duration of the war, but things changed when the Nazis walked into town in November 1943. And my father wound up hiding in the forest.

What did you live on?

The local government took care of the refugees' needs and gave us a certain amount of money to live on. In this town, there were fifty Jewish refugees who were being taken care of by this organization. My father accounted for us by reporting to the mayor of the town every single day.

We spent about five-and-a-half years in Italy. I remember a young woman named Rosalia who was a very important person in my life. She was probably seventeen, and I used to call her Nana. She would always look after me. Imagine that a refugee was not allowed to go to school, but she didn't care about that. She went to the local Catholic school and said, "I want her to go to school like all the other children." You have to remember that my father was an Orthodox Jew and he never compromised his dietary laws. He ate vegetables or pasta, nothing else. He never gave up his identity or who he was. People remembered that about him. Many years later when I met this woman, she said, "I think your father was a rabbi." I said, "My father wasn't a rabbi." He must have conducted a service for whoever wanted to pray for Sabbath. I know that Rosalia had very strong and warm feelings about my father. She loved me very much and sent me to the Catholic school.

I remembered having to cross myself. I knew that it was alien to me. I remember a very vivid memory as a child, getting so nervous about it that I peed my pants.

Another memory that was substantiated later when I visited this town ten years ago is when my childhood friend took me to the school and showed me the gated room where a naughty child was put.

Another childhood memory is getting sick; my father got permission to take me to Rome to have my adenoids removed. That happened without anesthesia, and I remember a chair with a white basin and the blood pouring out. I guess I must have been a lovable little child because the nurses bought me a doll. This picture of me with the doll was found by Rosalia in the ruin of the building that we lived in, which was bombed by the Nazis after we left, and she handed it to me when I reunited with her.

I remember that in the hospital was the first time that I ever had contact with a telephone. I found it so fascinating. They explained to me that we are here, and you can talk to someone all the way at the end of the street or the other side of the street. I've loved the phone ever since.

At one point, when the Nazis took over the town, we had to cross the border for safety to join the Allies along with some Italians. I remember that the area was very mountainous. It had a very circular feeling. I remembered telling my parents, "Run, run, the Nazis are coming." I knew that they were a tremendous danger.

At the checkpoint, the Nazis asked for our papers, and my father didn't own work papers. A very nice Italian man gave him his own work papers because they didn't have his photograph. He said, "Let me give you this and you can make them believe that you're me." That worked. I still have that.

I remember the cave we stayed in—I don't know for how many days. It was dark and scary. In his memoir, my father wrote that the Italians realized how needy we were and shared some of their food with us. Eventually we came back to Guardiagrele. My mother had just given birth to my baby sister, which made it even more difficult.

We ended up eventually in Bari in a displaced persons camp. My father ended up working for the Office of War Information for the United States Army, where he would translate Goering speeches.

I think at that point he must have heard about President Roosevelt inviting us to come to the United States as invited guests for the duration of the war. Then my parents had to sign a paper saying that once the war ended, we had to go back to where we came from. That's when Ruth Gruber, a young Jewish journalist, together with Eleanor Roosevelt, lobbied to allow the refugees to stay in the United States of America. I will tell you later how important Ruth Gruber became in my life.

We were among 982 refugees who were brought to Naples to embark on the boat *Henry Gibbins* to go to the United States.

Later when I met Ruth Gruber in the United States, she told me that the man who had to interview the thousands of people in order to decide who could get on the boat had a nervous breakdown. He said, "I can't be playing God any longer; I can't do this."

This reminds me of the story of the creation of the orchestra in Israel.
Yes, yes! His name was Mr. Uberman.

Mr. Uberman, who was building the first Israeli orchestra, went back to Vienna to choose members to join his orchestra. The story is that while he was auditioning, he did not look at the candidates' eyes while listening to their music because he knew that the ones that he would reject would end up in a concentration camp. Getting back to the boat, do you have any recollections?
Yes, I was always seasick. I always had my head in my mother's lap. My mother tells me that I must have had this tremendous affinity for my father because I would go to the soldiers and say, "Do you have a shirt for my father?"

We landed on the American shore on August 3, 1944. When the photographers saw me, they took a picture of me eating my first hotdog, which was later published in twenty-six newspapers in the US. Amazingly, through this publicity, my extended family already living in the US discovered our existence.

We were sent to Oswego, in upstate New York, where we wound up in a gated area.

Later on, I found a letter my father wrote that I was scared to show Ruth Gruber. In this letter my father said, "I would never have left Italy had I known I would wind up in a camp again, because freedom to me is everything. I gave up my freedom to come to the United States, but if I had known that this would happen, I would never have left."

I think that my father said this when he was dying of spinal meningitis in a hospital in Syracuse when he felt that he would have had a better chance of being alive had we stayed in Italy. For me, his death was the biggest trauma. I think I was always a very good child, and very obedient. Even to the point that when we were crossing the front and I lost my shoe in the mud, he said: "This little five-year-old never grumbled; she just went with the flow and never complained."

All of this was probably on the promise that when we came to the United States, we would have a whole new life. Well, that didn't really work out because he died, so that promise was gone.

We stayed in Oswego for eighteen months. We were not allowed to leave. But my father, who found a hole in the fence, sneaked out of Oswego to be reunited with his cousins in New York and fell in love with the city. I think that's where I got my love for New York. Thank God that he did that, because he died shortly thereafter.

After Eleanor Roosevelt lobbied for us, we were dispersed throughout the United States. We were allowed to come to New York City. My aunt and my uncle lived there, and my father's family lived in Washington Heights.

I was then six years old. I found myself without a father, and with a mother who had lost her husband, her country, her language, and was alone with a six-year-old and a baby.

At the time of the war, my European family was dispersed throughout the world. Some went to Israel, some to France, some to

South America. My grandmother joined us from Belgium, and we all lived in Rego Park, Queens. Then my aunt and uncle decided that we should all live together, and we moved to Queens, on 167th Street.

I entered fourth grade when I went to P.S. 131. All of my friends lived in Jamaica Estates.

We were in Jamaica, which was very middle class, very nice. Certainly very lovely, but I was different than everyone. I was "the other." Different culture, different sensibility, different points of view within the family. And I didn't speak the language. I went to summer camp when I was six or maybe going on seven. It was a terrible experience for me because I didn't know whether my mother was really going to pick me up after camp ended. I had a lot of trauma and fears. Everyone made fun of me because I had an accent. That's when my priority was to get rid of the accent.

I didn't speak the language well, and I was different. Also I didn't have a father, and that was very painful. I think that it really encumbered me in so many ways. You know, when a father dies suddenly, somehow or other you feel responsible for his death.

It's so amazing from the psychological point of view. There were so many things to overcome, and then on top of it you have a tremendous feeling of shame and guilt in not really knowing who you are. I think that my mother, as a survivor, had her own emotions to deal with. Coming from a certain type of family and background, she was under the impression that because I was young and had my whole life ahead of me, I didn't suffer emotionally like she did.

I was different from my friends, having been raised with lots of restrictions and envying the freedom that I was denied.

All my friends were going to college, and I remembered thinking while I was still in grade school that it would be so wonderful if I could become a doctor. That was one of my earliest thoughts and dreams. Then I dashed on—how could I be that presumptuous to think that?

I had low self-esteem. First of all, I don't remember saying to myself that I'm smart enough to do this. My mother thought that my sister was the brilliant one. I think that I really did well in grade school, but then I had so much baggage in high school. I thought so little of myself.

According to what I extrapolated from my mother, the only way to get out of my situation was to get married. That was maybe the way to the American dream, I thought. When I was eighteen I went to FIT (Fashion Institute of Technology), and I fell madly in love with this man. I said he's gonna be my husband, and three months later he was. I thought he was my knight in shining armor.

Yes. That's the fantasy of a young person. Then you find out that he's human. We had five children. I was thirty when the last one was born. We managed to have a comfortable life.

I had a Chevy convertible, a dog, five children, a house in Kings Point. Then all of a sudden, I got into such a depression after Dana was born. I remembered looking in the mirror and seeing that my eyes were black. I got so scared that I couldn't even see my soul. That's when I went into therapy with a Viennese-American analyst. She really helped me out.

Her name was Hanna Kapit. She was Austrian and understood my background. She was unbelievable; she helped me find my direction and gave me the strength to do something for myself.

So what did you do for yourself?

I turned an avocation into a vocation. I always loved to bake. When I moved into Kings Point and achieved the American dream, I realized there was something missing from it. People were getting divorced left and right. If that happened to me, what would I ever do? I couldn't afford to provide for my family myself.

With the five children, it was really scary. My uncle came from France, and he was educationally a high achiever and was the authority on medieval Jewish history. He came to visit me and was aghast that I didn't finish my education. Then I really had to find the road to become an independent woman.

How did you do that?

With the help of my analyst, I was encouraged to join my friend Marsha to start a baking business with carrot cakes. We were baking at home. I was very good at getting customers. Marsha would make the phone calls to find out who was interested in buying. I would be devastated if they said nothing.

So you were the ambassador of making friends? She was the marketer?
Right. Our housekeeper baked the cakes and put them together.

You were on the delegating side? You got the other people to do the hard work?
We became big and we opened a store in Kings Point, Long Island.

That's where I met you, when I used to come with my little girl to get cookies?
Right. My store was next to my home, and it was very convenient. I always dreamed of becoming famous, and we moved our store, My Most Favorite Dessert Company, to Madison Avenue, New York City. And I immediately got great reviews.

That went very well. I remember the delicious cakes.
I had to pay my rent, so I extended it into a full-fledged restaurant, and my dilemma was whether I should serve meat, because a lot of my customers were religious Jews with specific dietary restrictions. Being a Jewish woman, what was important to me was being able to serve everyone, including the Jewish community. That was very important for us.

Rabbi Luchstein said, "Everybody knows who you are and what you stand for, but we need you to be under supervision." For a while, I stayed open on Sabbath, but having served the Jewish community, I felt shame and felt like an imposter. That's when I followed the rules of the Jewish religious tradition, and I changed the whole opinion of what kosher means. Nobody really thought that if you're kosher, your baked goods are delicious. So I changed the level of people's opinion about that.

One day, a converted woman to Judaism walked in my store and said, "I love your restaurant; I love your cakes. Would you like to write a cookbook? Because kosher food has a different meaning in your restaurant." That's how my first cookbook, called *My Most Favorite Dessert Company Cookbook*, came to fruition.

Because I was paying such high rent, we moved to the theater district. That's when it really became a full-fledged restaurant. The journey was tedious and was very trying.

A large percentage of the clients were Jews?

Jews, religious Jews—actually on Madison Avenue I had everyone. People loved my place. They loved the food, and they did love it on Forty-Fifth Street also. We had to expand the menu, and we had some interesting chefs. In the process, I was able to get back to my roots, meeting people from all over the world.

I remember being in Italy with my oldest daughter, Laura, when she engaged in a conversation with a religious man who felt lost. He mentioned that he was on the way to New York, and she invited him to visit the restaurant. He said, "I know that place. I love it."

Then we moved. I opened up on West Seventy-Second Street between Broadway and West End. One day a woman from South America came into the store with her two gorgeous daughters and said, "I will never forget the engagement party that my friend from London threw for me in your restaurant. And here I am, with my daughter who is getting married herself."

Having these very deep roots with people was so important, to be part of their lives. To be part of their lives here in New York City, having food that they could have and enjoy.

We now even have the third generations of families coming to my restaurant. For me there is such a beauty about that. I've done this and I have achieved this. Family and friendship are so very dear to me and so important. To be a people person, to be proud of who I am and what I stand for. I always say the reason that I am who I am is because of my formative years in Italy. My restaurant unknowingly became a mission. It became a place to come back to, a "generational" restaurant with legacy.

I saw your documentary film Ahead of Time: The Extraordinary Journey of Ruth Gruber. *Tell me about it.*

I was the executive producer with Patti Kenner and my friend Denise [Benmosche]. Actually, for many years I would meet different documentarians that wanted to work with and do Ruth's story. But nothing happened.

How did you meet Ruth?

I was at a Hanukkah party at my friends Allyne and Fred

Schwartz's. Fred said to me, "Doris, I met a woman that you should meet. She actually was the journalist assigned by President FDR to accompany the 980 survivors to New York, including you. Why don't you call her?"

Fred knew that I was on the *Henry Gibbins*. He knew that I was an Oswego refugee. He met Ruth at the opening of the Safe Haven Museum in Albany, where she must've told the story. He recognized the story because of me, since we were good friends.

My daughter Laura was there. She said, "Are you going to call her?" I was too timid to call, so she called her.

She said, "Oh my God, it was so easy to get her. I found her number and called her. She said, 'Hi, I'm Dr. Ruth Gruber.' I said, 'I'm Laura. You brought my mother to the United States with her family and I would love to meet you.'" Ruth said she would be delighted.

We met her at my restaurant, and we had a wonderful time together. She told me that when she was working for the *Herald Tribune*, FDR told her, "I have a special mission that I want you to be part of. It would be a good idea for the State Department to do something for the Holocaust in Europe."

There was a commission to allow one thousand refugees to come to the United States. Once that was all put together, he said, "We're going to send you." She had gotten her doctorate in Cologne. She spoke German; she spoke Yiddish. She was the perfect person.

That's how she got to go on this boat. When we met in my restaurant, we bonded immediately. Then she took me to her house to look at photographs. I sat in there crying my eyes out, and she never questioned or intruded on my privacy or emotional status. She was so understanding.

She said, "You lost your language, you lost your country, you lost your father. It's a lot to cry about."

Nobody knew me better and understood me more than Ruth. She was in my life, and I in hers.

Also, several years before I met her, I read this extraordinary book, *Raquela, A Woman of Israel*, and it turns out that Ruth Gruber wrote that book. Raquela become a role model for me. Raquela had a beautiful summer home in a beachy area in Israel, which my husband and I explored in a visit.

Ruth and I became such close friends that I considered her my adoptive mother. My daughter Laura said her dream in her life would be to go to Israel with Ruth.

One day, Ruth called and said to tell Laura that her dream could come true. "You and Laura should come to Israel with me." We did. It was so extraordinary to see Israel through Ruth's eyes. She was very knowledgeable. She was the only American journalist that covered the exodus. Later we traveled with her to Poland and other places.

Fascinating. So you did a documentary about her life?

We did a documentary about her life. Patti said, "You know what? I'm tired of everyone wanting to do something. Ruth is now ninety-six years old, and I'm going to do this documentary."

We had to go through emotional debris, so to speak, to get to where we wanted to be. But we persevered and we got through it. We had a dream team, and the movie was done.

It was a beautiful movie.

It got seven awards. First of all, it premiered at the Toronto Film Festival, which is very prestigious. Then it was shown in Berlin. I opened it up in Rome, and I showed it in Pescara, Italy. That was a good feeling for me—that was really full circle. We showed it in Alaska. It's been all over, and it's still going.

I understand that in the quest to recapture the time you were in Italy, you go to Guardiagrele every year to visit. Tell me about the first time you went back.

I go back because I always think about my childhood and about the angel in my life, who saved me in the little town of Guardiagrele. One of the first times I went back, I was accompanied by my family, including my mother. That's when, to my surprise, the postman pointed to the house that Rosalia lived in. Rosalia was the woman who gave my family love and friendship in Guardiagrele. About ten years ago, I decided to contact the mayor of Guardiagrele. Shortly after, he came to the US and I told him my story. When he returned to Italy, he was interviewed about his story by TV announcers and journalists.

Not long after that, a woman called him and said, "This story that you're telling about meeting Doris—she's the little girl about whom my mother, Lucia, talked about all my life."

Remember when I told you about the time that we lived in an apartment that belonged to an Italian family, and we had to cross the border for a while to escape the Nazis who came to Guardiagrele? I was then five years old and that woman, Lucia, was twenty-two. She was a friend of Rosalia's. Lucia offered to take care of me while my family went into hiding. The story was that my mother was doing her job, washing clothes outdoors in the piazza, and she was crying. Lucia asked her, "Why are you crying?" And my mother said, "I'm ready to give birth at any moment and the man that promised to take care of my child changed his mind. He said it's too dangerous. It will draw attention to his presence as a Jew in this town." Lucia looked at my mother and said, "Don't you worry. I have a son who is blond and has blue eyes, and so is your daughter. I will take care of your child. She will be safe with me. You go on with your newborn and when you come back, you'll reunite with your daughter."

My mother was so grateful. But after she gave birth, she came back to Lucia and said she decided to take her chances. "I can't leave my child with you. But here is a picture of little Doris, to keep you company." She gave her a picture of me, and I guess Lucia told this story to her daughter frequently.

Later on, throughout my life, when I used to annoy my mother, she would say, "I should've left you with Lucia."

Lucia put my picture in a locket and she wore it her entire life. That story prompted me to go back to Guardiagrele and reunite with her. I took a picture of her wearing my face on her heart. She was ninety-six years old. I forgot to tell you that Rosalia's son also said the same thing, about how his mother frequently talked about me.

It is amazing the effect you had on people when you were five years old. How did the mayor hear about you to begin with?

I was in Italy, in Tuscany, when I decided to write a vegetarian cookbook. I came up with the idea to dedicate the book to the citizens of Guardiagrele in gratitude for saving my life.

So I called Elizabeth Poetsecana, who was a journalist and a translator in Italy, and asked her to write a letter for me to the Town Hall of Guardiagrele. That's what she did. We first emailed it, and then I sent a hard copy. I sent it out on a Monday. On a Thursday I got a phone call. "This is the Town Hall of Guardiagrele, and I would like to speak to Doris Schechter."

We got connected, and the mayor invited me to come over. He said, "Why don't you come here? I know all about your father and your family." So Laura and I went. I cannot describe the surprise when I saw a large picture of my mother along with other refugees on the mayor's office wall. I looked at him and said, "This is my mother. How is her picture hanging here?" He said: "I am a historian, and I researched the events of the time of the war and the behaviors of the citizens of Guardiagrele. I researched the time of the war and the people who found refuge in Guardiagrele. I found some of them to enlarge in order to commemorate their existence. What a pleasure it is to meet a daughter of one of the survivors."

What are your aspirations now?

I'm involved in doing a film about three extraordinary people in France. The movie is about a priest, a hat designer, and a Jewish-Polish engineer.

It is such an extraordinary story because it really shows what people did without compensation, only out of the generosity of heart, only out of respect and love for their human brothers and sisters. To me this was a very important project. Right now we're thinking of rewriting the script. It doesn't happen overnight; it has to evolve.

There are some very important Holocaust films like *Schindler's List* and *Sophie's Choice*. To me those were the most extraordinary Holocaust stories ever. It was very intimate.

Your new project involves Verdi's Requiem. *Tell me about it.*

I realized many years ago that Verdi's *Requiem* was my most favorite piece of music. For me, everything is on an emotional level. I felt so connected with this music that I even told my kids when they were little that in case I died young, they had to have Verdi's *Requiem* played.

Incidentally, thirteen years ago I met a maestro called Murry Sidlin who founded the Defiant Requiem Foundation. The foundation was prompted by a story that fascinated Murry. The story is about a chorus that played Verdi's *Requiem* sixteen times, in Terezin, a concentration camp in Hungary. The orchestra, which was made up of a piano and a chorus, was led by a musician by the name of Rafael Schechter. Unfortunately, they all perished. Murry then produced a documentary which, while playing the *Requiem*, narrated the story of that orchestra. It was shown in Avery Fisher Hall in the Met, as well as in Vienna. The foundation's mission is to commemorate the orchestra and to help Holocaust survivors in the US.

I went to see it twice in Avery Fisher Hall. It was extraordinary. Then I found out that it was going to be performed in Vienna. While I was in Vienna, I met a human rights attorney who I asked to help me find my birth certificate. And she did. That was a very emotional moment for me.

Being personally and emotionally connected to the *Requiem*, you can imagine how the story of the Terezin orchestra has touched me, and I made a vow to make it my life project to have the documentary-concert performed at the Vatican.

I went to see Verdi's *Requiem* the other evening at the Metropolitan Opera House with James Levine conducting. I was reading a translation of the libretto, and I realized even though I never really knew the translation, the emotions I felt just coincided. I was sitting there crying.

What was the sentence that affected you?
"Dear God have mercy on me, deliver me from this hell." I realized then why this music meant so much to me.

In anticipation of an upcoming big birthday, I see tears in your eyes.
There was a lot of struggle.

Yes, but there's more. You had a mission to give back to the kind citizens of Guardiagrele who saved your life. But I don't think you ever considered the impact that you made on their lives. You gave them the gift of saving the life of a little girl and her family. Don't you see? This is the reason why Lucia still carries your picture in a locket near her heart.

Doris Schechter created an innovative kosher restaurant and bakery, My Most Favorite Food, which she continues to manage along with her family. She is the author of two books, *My Most Favorite Dessert Company Cookbook: Delicious Pareve Baking Recipes* (HarperCollins, 2001) and *At Oma's Table: More than 100 Recipes and Remembrances from a Jewish Family's Kitchen* (Penguin, 2007). Her third book, about vegetarian cooking, will explore her journey of arriving in the United States. Doris is also the executive producer of the documentary *Ahead of Time: The Extraordinary Journey of Ruth Gruber* (2009). She is working on a movie based on the book *Incredible Mission,*

Doris, as a child refugee in Italy

about three protagonists in 1940s France and their love and respect for their fellow man. In October 2019, Doris helped arrange for fifteen hundred New York City students to attend a performance of *The Children of Willesden Lane.* The play is based on a memoir written by Mona Golabek about her mother's escape from Nazi-controlled Austria to England on the Kindertransport and the love of music that helped her survive.

AROON SHIVDASANI

INDIAN/PAKISTANI-AMERICAN ARTS PHILANTHROPIST

"You don't have a soul unless you are involved in the arts, because through the arts, you learn history. You learn emotion. You learn tolerance. You understand other people."

Photo Credit: Kimberly M. Wang

AS I WALK INTO THE NEW YORK apartment of Aroon Shivdasani, I am flooded by the spiritual aura that fills the space. The living room continues with a Zen-like garden. I notice on the left a welcoming Indian statue of a human-sized servant. He's dressed in a perfectly ironed uniform. "He never works," says Aroon, "but his presence satisfies the Indian friends who visit and are used to an abundance of human help.

"And so, once I introduce him to them, there are no more questions asked," she says, giggling. "Life is different here in the USA. Much simpler. Much freer. We are happy here."

On the right side of the room, a sculpture of a woman with a shaved head rests peacefully in a designated alcove. Aroon explains that this represents a woman who does not hide under glamorous hairstyles. She'd rather expose her external beauty without décor. The sculpture's disjointed body presents the pelvis and legs through a space, its lower extremities draped with a sari transformed to pants worn by Indian fisher-women, to facilitate working. Around her neck are images of Indian male gods. Her head is held high, wearing these male gods as trophies.

Aroon, who lets her white hair decorate her young, intelligent face, is all about inner strength and spirituality. She shares those values with American society through the Indo-American Arts Council (IAAC), a nonprofit arts foundation she created. Twenty years ago, there was little representation of Indians in the arts in America. But today, due to Aroon's hard work and persistence, the image of the Indian in the arts is evolving. Under the IAAC, Aroon established an Indian film festival, a dance festival, a literary festival, a traveling art exhibition, numerous music concerts, and theatrical presentations.

As we talk about her childhood fleeing what is now Pakistan, her mother's influence on her love of art and music, and her goals to instill multicultural acceptance in her own children, I try to extract from Aroon stories of struggle as an immigrant to the US to no avail. She credits her success to a simple concept: good attitude. "If you have the right attitude, you gain respect," she says.

Settling in the United States in her early twenties, she instantly felt at home. She befriended her American neighbors, enrolled her kids in the American school system, continued her own education, and taught drama and creative writing.

At the same time, the IAAC allows her to share with American society a broad awareness of Indian visual performance and literary art. She aims to blur the ancient vision of the Indian arriving on the white elephant, taking us instead on a different journey into the world of mixed myth and reality of Indian culture, to a world that is elsewhere and here in the same time. I get the impression that no matter where Aroon is planted, she is a hero.

You were named one of the top influential global Indians by the Economic Times *in 2015 and are a recipient of many other important awards. It seems like the foundation for what makes you who you are today was laid in your childhood. Who were you as a child, and how did India shape your adulthood?*

My family fled from what is now Pakistan in the Partition of India in 1947. My father was a *zamindar*, a feudal lord, and he owned forty thousand acres of land. As a zamindar's wife, my mother didn't work. She was simply his wife. My mother's family was always extremely involved in the arts. Mummy sang, acted, danced, wrote poetry. She was madly interested in literature, which translated into her major at university being literature and drama.

When my parents fled to what remained as India, they had to start from scratch. We were just babies then. We're Sindhis, from the state of Sindh, which was originally part of India. But now, with the partition of the country, Sindh became part of Pakistan, and we, as Hindus, were forced to flee to India.

We were placed in a boarding school in the foothills of the Himalayas called The Lawrence School, Sanawar. My mother started teaching there to be close to us. It was a fabulous school. We were four siblings and we all attended that school. My mother's upbringing, combined with what we learned in Sanawar, formed us as individuals. There were children from almost every state of the country. It was a bit of an elite school, but the point is that everyone else was leveled. It wasn't that you are Punjabi, a Sindhi, or a Gujarati. It didn't matter. You were either my friend or you weren't. You liked the person or you didn't. We were all human beings.

The studying part of school was important, but so were sports and the extracurricular activities. We studied from the crack of dawn until lunchtime. After lunch, we had to have hobbies, a musical instrument and one other hobby. It could be art, a musical instrument, dance, or theater. Between the extracurricular activities and prep (homework), we had time for sports.

When I was at university, I was on several sports teams, part of the theater group, and a member of the College Union Council, all as a result of my early education.

We learned to do everything. Of course, we were encouraged to excel, but one had to be at least a jack-of-all-trades. Through team sports, through the arts, you understand the other human beings. You learn tolerance. You see the genius in people, and you also learn to be kind to those less fortunate. It's an all-encompassing feeling.

My father was a kind, gentle human being, but he was very firm. When we were sitting at the table, if we didn't have table manners, he would send us to the pantry. My mother was the nurturing one. I think I have her DNA. She insisted that even during the holidays we learned music and dance. She used to take us to museums, art galleries, theater, and concerts. She always said: "You have to be a complete human being. You cannot understand the world purely in school."

When I left Sanawar, I went to a high school in Bombay (The Cathedral & John Connon School), where I made lasting friendships. Later, at the University of Bombay, I met my husband. He was at the Indian Institute of Technology (an engineering college) while I was at St. Xavier's College (majoring in English Literature). We met at the age of fifteen, and the rest is history!

At the time we were growing up, the world wasn't the way it is today. In India now, we have communal riots and Hindu-Muslim tensions. I grew up in a serendipitous world. I think we were very protected in some way, because it just didn't occur to us that there were differences between Hindus, Muslims, Jews, Buddhists, Christians. It really didn't matter.

I am now seventy-one years old, and it's a slightly different world. When we went to parties in our youth, our parents needed to know where we were going, to whose house we were going. They needed to know their parents, and they needed to know that the boys were going to pick us up at a certain hour and drop us back home by our curfew time. We were three sisters and we all went out together. Our parents mandated that either all three of us went or no one went.

It never occurred to us that this was something to rebel about because we were always so happy! We always had such a loving home, such wonderful friends. I do believe we led a very serendipitous life. We were exposed to everything. Our minds were stimulated by lectures, the theater, movies, world affairs, etc.

The environment has really been very influential in the way you have conducted your life and your affinity to art.

Yes, it was both my parents as well as all the academic institutions I attended. At university, I was on the College Union Council, in the drama society, I played sports, and I involved myself in every aspect of college life. They encouraged you to participate in everything. You didn't just attend classes and go home. All the extracurricular activities were extremely important.

I'm not going to tell you much about my father's influence because Daddy was at a nuclear atomic power plant, the Tarapur Atomic Power Plant. He used to be there during the week and came home on weekends. He was an amazing, wonderful, loving father, but he actually left a lot of responsibility of bringing us up to my mother. He adored my mother. A few years ago, he died of esophageal cancer, and even when he couldn't speak, his eyes would follow my mother around.

Did they have an arranged marriage?

Yes and no. Certain classes of people just meet. My parents and their families knew each other, and so they were, I guess, introduced. I think it was love at first sight—more for my father than my mother. They adored each other, but my father couldn't see beyond my mother. Their relationship was just beautiful.

My mother died at the age of ninety-four, but she was always "present." She was my best friend. She was so knowledgeable. We would talk about everything. When she died, I was shocked. I put her on a flight to Canada on a Friday. On Sunday, she was absolutely fine, talking about a movie she was watching on television. On Monday morning, my sister called me and told me to come up to Toronto immediately. Mummy had fallen.

Were you there when she died?

Yes. She was in the hospital when I got there. Her eyes were closed, and she was lying back. The doctor said, "She can hear you. She can speak to you." One side had gone completely paralytic. I held her hand and said, "Ma, it's Anu." (My family calls me Anu.) She squeezed my hand. She knew I was there. My biggest regret is that I was always busy. Mom would say to me, "Darling." I'd say, "Ma, not now. I'm busy." Now I think, "Why didn't I sit and spend more time with her?"

Did your parents immigrate with you to the US?

No. We left India in 1968. My husband and I were going steady for four years through university and got married immediately after. My parents left India when they realized all their children were overseas. They left India because they wanted to be close to us. We are a very close family.

We went to England where Indur, my husband, did a post-graduate traineeship with Westinghouse and then received his master's degree at Imperial College, London University. I worked at the *Observer* newspaper doing media research. I don't know whether this is a thing in the rest of the world, but in India, there's the "only-son" syndrome. Indur's parents pressured him to return to India. So we decided to go back home. It was 1970.

At that time, a lot of our friends passed through London en route to the US for further studies. They'd say to us, "Why are you going back now? Come on, see the world!" We were still in our early twenties. Our things were all packed, our trunks were with the shippers, addressed to India. Listening to our friends, we applied to both Canada and the US to immigrate. Canada came through first, so we called the shippers and had the address changed to Toronto. This was just adventure, nothing else.

We got jobs and worked there for a couple of years. We traveled a lot. But the calls from home never stopped: "What are you doing now? Come back and get a real job." Once more, we packed. Before leaving, we visited friends studying in Cambridge (at MIT and Harvard). One of them wanted their car driven to Los Angeles. We volunteered to drive it there for him and traveled the US in that van, sleeping in the back and camping. After delivering the car in LA, we made our way back to New York and bought a ticket to India. This time, we traveled through Europe. By the time we reached Rome, we said, "This is it. We don't have any more money to go any farther." We flew to Bombay.

We lived in Bombay for three years. My husband joined an elite corps called Tata Administrative Services. He was everyone's blue-eyed boy. We were also very idealistic. Indur did not want me to get a regular nine-to-five job. He wanted me to "give back" to the country. I worked as a volunteer with an organization called FREA India (Front for Rapid Economic Advancement of India), with the Spastics Society, and several similar organizations.

However, our wanderlust hadn't been quenched. Our friends were visiting us from the States. They stoked this fire and, being young and foolish, we gave up our comfortable lives and set off on another journey West.

My husband sent me first because my parents were now in Canada. My brother and both sisters were overseas too. My younger sister was studying for a doctorate in fine arts at the Accademia di Belle Arti in Italy. My older sister lived with her husband in England, and my brother was in Seattle. We are a close family, and now I was the only one in India.

So you went back to Canada?

Yes. We first stayed with my parents, got jobs, and then moved into our own apartment. I started doing my master's at the University of Toronto. Simultaneously I worked with the Bear Theater Company. We loved our lives in Canada. My husband was with IBM in Toronto, but then he was offered a job in McLean, Virginia, with a management consulting company, so we moved to the US. We were very adventurous.

Yes, and young.

Yes, and by now, we wanted children. But I couldn't have a child now. My older child, Sacha, is Canadian. She was only five months old when we adopted this beautiful, beautiful baby. I remember when we went to pick her up. We drove up, walked into this place, and I could hear her screaming and crying. The social worker, Betty, walked in with a baby. The baby's nose was dripping, and tears were running down her cheeks. She had a high fever. I held out my arms. She snuggled up, quiet in one second, completely quiet. I knew this was my baby.

Later that year, my husband went to India to see his father who was very ill. He left in October and returned after his father's funeral in early January. I got pregnant with my younger daughter, Misha. We couldn't believe it. Now I had two miracle babies.

In the United States, we lived in Virginia for three years. It was again a beautiful three years. My children were babies. While they were in school (until noon), I worked as a docent at the Corcoran Gallery of Art.

I joined another group of young mothers. I wrote for a neighborhood newsletter, joined a mothers' co-op, and generally had a wonderful life enjoying my toddlers. If Indur and I wanted to go out, we'd leave Sacha and Misha with one of the mothers in the co-op. My children played, had dinner, and went to bed with their kids, and we'd pick them up and bring them home at night, and vice versa with any of the mothers in the co-op. It was wonderful because they made such good friends. They're still friends with those little ones, and I am still friends with those mothers. In 1983, we left Virginia for Westchester, New York.

In New York, how was the process of assimilation? A lot of literature and movies describe the struggle of Indian immigrants, like Chitra Divakaruni's Mistress of Spices *(see page 69), and other movies and books have been written about the struggle of Indian immigrants. I was wondering if you ever felt like "the other" in the United States.*

I think we were lucky. There's luck, and there's also attitude. You don't look for trouble. Some people presume that there are problems; they presume there will be discrimination. I just presumed that I was accepted, and so did my husband. I think that presumption and that attitude flows through to the children. As far as they were concerned, they were American, and they had no problems. Westchester, where they grew up, was a Judeo-Christian society. I was very insistent that my children did not discriminate against any one religion. They should always know what's happening in each different religion and way of life, whether it's a mosque, a synagogue, a church, or a temple. I actively invited friends from every faith to our home and made friends with the mothers. It got to the stage where every weekend, my kids at a certain age were going either to a bat or a bar mitzvah, or to a confirmation in church.

Once, I remember, we were in a grocery store, and the rabbi from the synagogue said to my daughter, "Misha, I haven't seen you in our temple." I asked Misha what that was all about. She explained, "I go with my friends to the synagogue, and the rabbi thought I was Jewish."

Are you a practicing Hindu?
We're not actively practicing Hindus. However, we were born Hindu. My children were born Hindus. We perform all the rituals, and we celebrate Diwali and all the holidays. By the way, both my children have married Jewish boys. At both weddings, we had both ceremonies, the rabbi and the Brahman. We live in a society where one assimilates to one's environment.

Attitude is very important. When we were in England, there was discrimination. I remember going to rent a place. The lady said, "Oh, you could pass for Welsh." I said, "I don't want to pass for Welsh!!" She said, "Do you cook curry? If you don't cook curry, I have the place for you." We just ignored these ignorant people.

Do you think that besides a positive attitude, it is about the fact that you mingled with people who, like you, were in a good socio-economic state and were educated? Did you also cling exclusively to other Indian nationals?
That could be too. That could be because I know that we never lived in a purely Indian neighborhood.

How did you come to form the Indo-American Arts Council?
When we came to New York in 1983, my children were little, and I was consumed with exposing them to the world. I took them to different countries every year. We did everything characteristic of that country: the politics, the art, the dance, the music, the food. We ate only the local food, and when we returned, I'd have them make a scrapbook of what they saw and did. We started traveling with them when they were four years old.

The arts have always been very important to me. I noticed that in New York there were no Indian art galleries, no Indian art. On television, you never saw an Indian. In theater, there were no Indian playwrights, and you never saw an Indian on stage. In film, nothing. It was shocking that one of the oldest civilizations of the world was invisible in New York! The hospitals were full of Indian doctors, the universities had myriad Indian professors, but there was no art.

Thus was born the Indo-American Arts Council—to build an awareness of hitherto invisible Indian arts in the performing, visual, and literary arts.

Now we've got an amazing reputation. In May [2018], we completed twenty years. I started the first Indian theater festival with the Lark Theater. We invited the maestros of Indian music to perform here. We presented Indian fashion shows. We did it all. Now the country is full of film, dance, and music festivals from India. We were the pioneers. Look at the amount of Indians on television, in movies, all this . . . but there was not one when I started.

Now there is the Chicago Film Festival, the Indianapolis Film Festival, the Dallas Film Festival, and the Washington Film Festival, all inspired by the IAAC in New York. The people who started them all recognize us in New York as pioneers.

After 9/11, Mayor Rudy Giuliani asked people in the arts to revive New York.
After 9/11, we responded to Mayor Giuliani's call to help revive a shocked city. We are New Yorkers. We're Americans. We wanted to do something to bring people together. One screening wouldn't do that, so we produced a festival. We opened with Ismail Merchant and James Ivory. Ismail Merchant is an Indian-American. James Ivory is a Brit-American. We opened with them, and we closed with Mira Nair's *Monsoon Wedding*. In between, we had other films. This was our tribute to New York.

That's beautiful. How did you market it? How did you attract people?
It wasn't easy, but I was very lucky that I have friends in the arts, like Salman Rushdie, Mira Nair, and Madhur Jaffrey. They helped attract people. You always need somebody to bring people in. People recognize Salman and Mira, and Ismail Merchant is big in the Indian community. People know him. Madhur Jaffrey is a cookbook writer, a director, and an actor. People knew her. The way I got people to attend these festivals was by getting well-known Indian personalities to attract the audience. People bring people, and then you build up your mailing list.

You are a natural in marketing. You're friendly, and you have such a bright and warm, open personality. It's like sunshine.

I have a very passionate mission—to ensure that one day Indian performing visual and literary arts are as familiar to mainstream America as Pavarotti or Isadora Duncan. When I started the IAAC, the arts aficionados knew only two Indian artists: Ravi Shankar in music and Satyajit Ray in film. They knew no one else! Now, I think, people are becoming aware of our artists.

I believe that you actually don't have a soul unless you are involved in the arts, because through the arts you learn history, you learn emotion, you learn tolerance, you understand other people.

Now Americans see the Indian person as a culturally creative person, different from the common perception of a taxi driver or businessman. You introduced us to the Indian culture. In some way it's also self-serving because it exposes future Indian-American generations to their heritage. The next generation will feel differently about their heritage than you do. I believe that the culture is also changing in India.

It's developing. Not only do we have a history, a humongous history, but it's been changing over the years, and it's been developing. India has had so many different people conquering the country that we've got their histories, too, that have become part and parcel of our culture.

Like Nepal and Bhutan, Sri Lanka, Bangladesh, all these places, they have their own traditions.

They do, but they also have a basis. . . . The basis is India and Hinduism. In the festival, they all participate. We started with saying just India, but then we expanded it because we realized that the whole subcontinent basically consists of the same people, whether they're Hindu, Muslim, Buddhist, Jewish, or Christian. If you look at them, until they tell you something, you can't tell the difference.

Totally. That is the same for many countries.

Yes. Every country has that. Even in a small country, there's a difference between North and South. In general, you're an Indian. We include everyone from the subcontinent in our festivals: India, Pakistan,

Sri Lanka, Bangladesh, Nepal, Bhutan, and Afghanistan, the whole subcontinent. India is like Europe under one head. The cultures in each state are different. The way of wearing a sari in each state is different, as are the clothes and the food.

You encourage actors from all the subcontinent to perform.

We put out Calls for Submission for each of the festivals—the books or the videos of the movies or the dances or whatever comes to us. We have curators for each festival. It's very important to have the artists come and represent their work after the performance. We have post-screening or post-performance discussions. We have workshops. We have panels so that people can ask questions. The director or the actor or the performer can talk to the audience, tell them the history behind what they're doing, why they're doing it, how they're doing it, how long it took to put this together, what the cultural background of it is. All that is very important.

You have very intimate relationships with the actors and the writers.

Everything has a Q&A. Recently, the Cohen Media Group asked me to have a screening of *Shakespeare Wallah*. It's Merchant and Ivory. I said, "I will only do the screening if I can interview the director and actor after it; otherwise it's pointless. They can go to the theater and watch it." The audience wants to ask them questions. First I have a discussion with the person, and then I open it up for questions from the audience.

Do you feel American?

That's a strange question. Yes and no. Yes, I feel American. I think this is an amazing country, and it is my home. However, my heritage is Indian. It's given me a lot. I should explain this, when I say it's given me freedom. It's not that I didn't have freedom in India. In India, we belonged to a certain class, a certain community. Everyone knew what you were doing or saying or whatever. It impacted your family.

You feel freer here, and it touches your everyday life.

I don't know. It's strange. I feel I can do whatever I want. I don't have anyone putting any constraints on me in any way. It's not like people purposely constrained me. However, in India, it's pretty much like living in Grand Central Station. There's always somebody sweeping or somebody cleaning or somebody in the kitchen asking you what to make for dinner. There's never enough privacy.

Are you still involved with what happens in India?

Absolutely. We left India initially in 1968. I've spent more of my life outside India than in India, although my roots are there, and I'm still very concerned with what is happening in India. I often go to visit.

You're also very involved in charity. You care about orphans and women and abuse?

I do. I have been on several of those boards. When anything happens in India, we jump forward. When there was an earthquake in Gujarat, I raised money for it by doing a live art auction and inviting Bill Clinton. I went personally to Gujarat to see the earthquake area; I met the people on the ground, asked them what they needed, and earmarked that money to go to building houses, building wells, and helping the weavers—because we always have to give to the arts also. The weavers in Gujarat lost all their looms because of the earthquake.

When there was an earthquake in Latur, Maharashtra, I personally went there, saw what happened, and accompanied AmeriCares to distribute relief supplies. We had nowhere to sleep, nowhere to do anything. We were just there with the rest of them. This is what I mean when I say that I'm American. We raised money by presenting a play and sent the money we raised to build a whole village for the victims of the earthquake.

When there was a tsunami, I produced an event at Christie's—an art auction, a fashion show—and I invited Hillary Clinton to help raise money for the victims of the tsunami. Everything is through the arts.

In response to communal violence between Hindus and Muslims in India, I organized theatre director Michael Johnson-Chase to convert author Shashi Tharoor's book *Riot* into a play to present all the various extreme factions as well as the voice of reason. It was an effort to start a dialogue to make sense of this violence. We presented this reading at The New School to an amazing crowd. Unfortunately, we also had New York City police as well as campus police on guard to quell protests by both factions outside the theater. Basically we're the same people. Look at our skin. You can't tell whether I'm a Hindu or a Muslim or a Jew. Who knows? I can tell you what I am, but you don't know that until I tell you. We need people to understand that.

The new generation doesn't make distinctions. Our children don't make distinctions.
No, they don't. I think because we have made sure they won't.

We laid the groundwork, but our parents were a little bit more of the mind that a Hindu should marry a Hindu, a Jewish person should marry a Jewish person. But it is changing for the better. There is still a kinship when you meet an Indian girl, isn't there?
Yes. There are things you don't have to explain. You don't have to explain things where they are immediately understood.

I experience it when I meet another female doctor. We know what we went through, and we know who we are and what we do. When I meet an Israeli girl, I have a warm feeling before I get to know her. When I get to know her...
You decide whether you like her or not.

It's not the same when you meet somebody not of your own tradition.
Absolutely.

You're maybe more guarded at first.
Yes, I guess.

How do Indians in India feel about Americans? During the Second World War, America supported Pakistan. India did not help the US against the Russians.
India has been very upset with the US for a long time because that whole region was India. Saudi Arabia and Pakistan have the most terrorists in the world. Yet America supports Pakistan, sends arms to them—supposedly to fight the Taliban, but they use them to fight India. They're all on the Indian border, all American-made arms to fight India. India was very resentful of that. Although things are changing.

India is very strong now.
　Yes, it is.

Indians have been able to thrive to become one of the strongest countries, economically, militarily. But you've elevated the esteem and respect of Americans toward the Indian community by exposing the talent and colorful Indian culture. I believe that our relationship with India is improving.
　You are right. Both Clinton and Obama are very popular in India.

Indians as well are benefiting from America's advances. Is there an American culture in India?
　Yes, of course they know American movies, food, clothing. However, Indians are very comfortable in their own skin. I love this country. I don't think I could live in India anymore. You go there and slip right back into the life you left behind. You get looked after. You don't have to do anything. You slip right back into meeting all your old friends like you never left. However, after three weeks, I get antsy, and I have to leave. I want to come back home to New York.

Aroon Shivdasani is the retired executive and artistic director and founder of the Indo-American Arts Council, an organization dedicated to showcase, promote, give visibility to, and build an awareness of Indian and sub-continental performing, visual, literary, and folk arts and artists in North America; while simultaneously working to support important social and humanitarian causes in India and the US. She believes fervently in Indian artists' contributions to the amazing

Aroon Shivdasani, center, with filmmaker Mira Nair and novelist Salman Rushdi

cultural diversity of New York's artistic landscape. Among her myriad awards, in January 2015 she was named one of the top 20 Global Indian Women by the *Economic Times*, India. In March 2018 she was honored by the Society of Foreign Consuls, New York, for her "outstanding achievements and contributions to Community Empowerment," and in July 2018, she received recognition awards honoring her for being "a pioneer of Indian Arts and Aesthetics in North America" by the Consul General of India, New York, and the new chairman of the IAAC. In May 2019, Aroon received the India Pride Award Honour from the India Heritage Society.

ASHLEY TABADDOR

IRANIAN-AMERICAN LAWYER, PROFESSOR, AND FEDERAL IMMIGRATION JUDGE

"How can I possibly fight for a better community, a better country, if at the first chance that I'm being challenged, I would fold because it was convenient to close my eyes?"

AFSANEH ASHLEY TABADDOR WAS BORN in the capital city of Iran in 1971, amid the stirrings of civil unrest and the country's revolution. She grew up in a Westernized household where her parents emphasized education and personal and financial independence. Dinner-table conversations were always politically charged, and Ashley grew mindful of the world around her. Conscious of its social and political complexities, she wanted to be part of the discourse that made the world a better place.

In 1979, the Islamic Revolution replaced almost twenty-five hundred years of Persian rule with a religious establishment under the Grand Ayatollah Ruhollah Khomeini. Ashley's innocent activities, such as playing in a co-ed school environment, wearing jeans, and failing to wear a head-scarf, became criminal. She was confronted by the military police as a ten-year-old for her resistance to the newly established rules.

Initially, her family had been supportive of the revolution. But as the suppression grew under the Ayatollah's rule and the government turned its attention to her grandfather's connections with the previous regime, Ashley's parents decided that it was time to leave. They were smuggled into Pakistan and then abandoned as refugees. After several troubling months, they arrived in the United States on Christmas Eve 1982, hoping for a miracle. Ashley had just turned eleven.

Ashley and her family settled in the San Fernando Valley. As a child of immigrants, she knew she was different and was expected to be the best in her class. She was a passionate and hardworking child, and with the gender restrictions placed on her in Iran now lifted, Ashley began working toward her dream of making a difference in the world. She was drawn to the brilliance of the American political system of checks and balances, protecting against abuse of power in support of a more just society. She graduated as valedictorian of her high school and went on to earn her BA cum laude from the University of California, Los Angeles, and a JD from the University of California, Hastings College of the Law, where she began her speedy ascent into the world of law.

Immigration became her specialty by chance, but after seeing how it transformed people's lives and resonated with her own experiences, she found her calling. She now serves as an immigration judge in the courtrooms of Los Angeles and hears politically and socially complex cases, some of which involve deporting hundreds of families and children to their home countries.

In 2014, Ashley successfully sued the Department of Justice for discriminating against her on the basis of her heritage. The case highlighted the importance of ensuring a diverse bench and protecting the independence of judges from discriminatorily motivated attacks.

And now, as the newly elected President of the National Association of Immigration Judges, she has been involved in protecting the purity and integrity of law by fighting for the independence of the immigration court.

Away from the bench, she allows herself to have fun and laughingly refers to herself as a "Valley girl." This friendliness and approachability and her glamorous appearance disguise the humility and the weight she carries when she makes critical decisions regarding the lives of other immigrants.

In an invigorating conversation in her home court of Los Angeles, Ashley engages me in her immigrant past, working for human rights and women's rights, being mindful of the current administration, and working relentlessly to make sure that the scales suspended from the hands of Lady Justice remain steady and balanced.

Your Honor, I believe that hard work and perseverance are the secrets to success, and the environment that one grows up in plays a big role in that journey. Would you share with me your childhood memories of growing up in Iran?

We left Iran when I was ten, around 1982. We came after the revolution, which happened in February of 1979. I have a lot of memories from my childhood in Iran. We lived in Tehran, which is the capital of Iran. My parents had moved to a newer neighborhood as I got a bit older, because my father, who is an orthopedic surgeon, was able to establish his own clinic. They were able to finally purchase land and slowly build a home in a new part of town known as *shahrakeh gharb* which translates to "the Western town" and has now been renamed after an Arabic mosque.

We grew up in a Western family. Both my parents had been educated in either Europe or the United States. While growing up, there was a lot of emphasis on education. Basically, the only thing that was ever expected of me was that I would go to school and be dedicated to my education. There was also a lot of emphasis for me to become independent. I was lucky that my grandmother and my mother, and a lot of the women in my family, really valued an independent woman. So from a young age, I was always being told how important it is to gain both financial and individual independence so that you never feel like you have to make compromises with your life based on others, particularly with the relationships that may impede you from reaching your potential.

I went to a French private school for kindergarten, first, and second grade. And then the revolution hit. I remember distinctly that the schools were shut down, and we had to go to a segregated school, girls separated from boys. We were going to school at different times of the day.

When the revolution hit, we were actually quite happy. My family was in favor of the revolution because the Shah was considered a dictator, and he had a horrible reputation for suppressing dissidents. So he was not well-liked. I remember as a child watching the demonstrations on TV and feeling the air of enthusiasm in the people around us. But shortly after the revolution, I could tell that things had changed for the worse, that what was expected to happen didn't happen. Even though I was young, I could tell that things were not working out the way people wanted. Within a couple of years my parents decided that we had to leave. The situation had gotten pretty severe, and it was becoming particularly difficult for girls.

My parents were having some issues with the government as well, but they never really shared the details with me. My dad left, but my mother was in Iran with my brother and me. And we no longer had permission to leave the country. So they had to make arrangements with a smuggler to have us cross the border into Pakistan. In Pakistan, we were actually abandoned by the smugglers because there was obviously no accountability. They just tossed us across the border and abandoned us. My mom had to work with my dad from overseas to get us out of Pakistan to Spain. At the time, Spain was the only country in Europe that was allowing Iranian nationals to enter without a visa. They changed that practice shortly after we arrived. We stayed in Madrid for a few months until my dad was able to secure visas for us to come to the United States as visitors.

And that's how I remember arriving in the US, at JFK, on Christmas Eve, December 24, 1982.

How long were you, your mother, and your brothers away from your father before arriving in the US?

My dad left Iran about a year and a half before we joined him. He left because my grandfather needed open-heart surgery. My uncle was a neurosurgeon at Johns Hopkins and had made arrangements for my grandfather to be operated upon. And so my father was able to get a visa to join my grandfather, who needed someone to accompany him.

Plus he was a man, so it was easier to leave Iran.

That's right, he did not need extra permission from a spouse, and leaving his family behind was a guarantee that he wasn't leaving the country permanently. He really sincerely was going there to help his father with every intention of returning, but while he was in the US, things just became progressively worse. Like I said, I don't know the details—they've never shared them with us—but I know that at some point after he came to the US, my mother called him and said, "Look, I don't think we can stay here anymore. See if there's some way we can come there, move there, and I'll make the arrangements."

After the revolution, you suddenly had to wear this hijab, which symbolizes the biggest visible change evolving in Iran.

Yes. It happened initially step by step. Once it got to the point that the new leaders felt they were pretty rooted and had some control, it became clear that women had to wear hijabs, cover their hair, and be modestly dressed. Girls who wore pants, particularly jeans, which was considered Western-style clothing, were frowned upon. I had a couple of experiences with the military police who confronted me because I was wearing jeans and running around without a head scarf playing in the streets.

You were not allowed to talk to the boys.

We were obviously segregated at school, so there was no longer the co-ed interaction. But it hadn't gotten to the point yet where we were not allowed to be with anybody from the opposite sex. We were kids. I was nine or ten when I was playing with friends and had to deal with the military police roaming the streets looking for what they thought was inappropriate behavior and inappropriately dressed girls.

I understand that in school the police questioned the kids regarding their parents' behavior at home to see if they were breaking the newly set rules.

That is interesting. We definitely knew that there were many families who had run into problems with the police because the children had inadvertently spoken of activities at home in front of teachers who then turned them in to the police. That was something that the kids did without realizing it. Kids were being kids at school sharing stories of what they did over the weekend or what was said or what was thought. The parents would then be confronted with those unintended consequences. At some point, we were very much aware that you need to be mindful of what you say, to whom you say it, and where it is said.

That's a lot of pressure on a child.

Yes. You had to have that sensitivity and become more mindful of your public versus your private life.

Did you speak English when you arrived in the US?

No. I had gone to a French school from when I was two or three until I was about seven or eight when they closed the school. I grew up with French as a second language. By the time we came to the United States, I had forgotten that as well. And the only word I knew in English was "no." So it was a challenge to try to learn the language.

How did it feel being in a new country and in a new school without speaking the same language as the other children? Do you remember being isolated or did you make friends right away?

I was lucky in certain ways. When we came, it was halfway through the school year. Even though I had completed fifth grade, by the time we made it here, the school officials decided that it was probably best for me to start fifth grade again, mostly because the American school system graduates you into the junior high model after the sixth grade, where things get much more complicated. And in hindsight I think they were right because those extra months really helped me focus on learning the language.

When they put me in the fifth-grade class, there were two other students who were Iranian-born. One of them is my best friend now. The other one became a best friend for a long time, but we have since grown apart. Every day they would take me out of class for about an hour and bring one of the Iranian girls to help me with English. So there was a lot of emphasis on motivating me to learn the language as soon as possible. I've always been a very extroverted, very verbal, very interactive person. So I do remember feeling exceptionally frustrated that first year because I couldn't communicate the way I wanted to communicate.

And you sometimes had the answers and couldn't really express them.

Yes, and that was frustrating. Without being able to put a sentence together, I couldn't adequately express myself. There were times I got picked on because I didn't speak the language or some sort of interpersonal scuffle occurred, and I couldn't defend myself. But all in all, I'm grateful. In large part I was pretty well received, welcomed.

The Iranian hostage situation had ended in 1981, a couple of years before I started school in the States. So the same animosity didn't exist against Iranians that my cousins had experienced during the hostage situation. By the time I was twelve, I moved to junior high school.

I remember the hostages were kept 444 days. At the time I was doing my fellowship in New York Hospital, and I did diagnostic studies on the Shah of Iran. There was no animosity toward the Shah. Maybe because the new government of the Ayatollah was so oppressive, and also because he was very sick. When you arrived in the US, where did you live?

We lived in Northridge in San Fernando Valley. So I'm a "Valley girl."

You're not blonde.

Nope. But I can definitely relate to the old '80s movies, the outfits, and hairstyles of all the Valley girls and the accents.

It makes you fun. When you grew up, did your parents keep mingling with other Iranian nationals?

My parents have always been very social, and they've always had a very large set of friends. We grew up with extended family and extended friends of the family who in large part were Iranian. In school I was interacting with everybody from different backgrounds and had friends from different backgrounds, but most of the adults around me were Iranian.

We tend to attract and be attracted to the people who have the same traditions. As an immigrant, you compare yourself with your American neighbors, and you realize they're different.

One of the things I remember about those first few years is definitely a major urge to assimilate. There was a lot of emphasis to learn the language. Because we had a very Western upbringing in Iran, there was a lot of comfort in accepting the modern Western values. We are Iranian by nationality and heritage and culture, but because of the background of my parents, a lot of what we did was similar to what an average American would do. There was a lot of home gatherings and food and social events and maybe sports or things like that. But perhaps the difference was that we never really watched football on TV.

I also remember watching American comedies and not quite understanding the humor.

Yes, and it took some time to understand those changes. But there was absolutely a lot of push to learn the language, to make sure you take advantage of all the opportunities. And in large part my parents really didn't try to stop me from exploring and learning.

I believe that immigrants take advantage of opportunities that American citizens take for granted. I remember when I was a child, I had role models among my peers, and I was proud when they chose me to be their friend. Did you feel this way when an American girl befriended you? Sort of like the feeling that I want to be her friend so I can be more like her, and I might feel less different? The urge to assimilate?

That's a good question. I was somewhat clueless to those things. I knew that I wanted to learn the language, I knew that I wanted to be able to excel in school, and I also knew that I was different. But it didn't bother me. It was not something that I felt was an impediment or in any way felt that I needed to apologize for.

It was a natural thing for you to be who you are?
    Yes. So in that way I was comfortable in my own skin.

Because as a grown-up now, getting into the brain of the child is very difficult. But I remember as a child in Israel, I always was very proud when the best student in the classroom became my friend, or the best athletes would choose me to be their buddy. It made me feel good about myself. I felt stronger. Now for you, as an immigrant coming here as a child, there were different parameters. Wouldn't you want an American friend to invite you for Thanksgiving? Was there a social hierarchy in Iran? And how did it translate to being in America?
    I was, in hindsight, completely clueless about it. I remember when I was in the fifth and the sixth grade, I didn't even understand the concept of the cool kids versus the not-cool kids. When I had a birthday party, I invited everybody. It didn't even cross my mind why some of those invited did not come.

Maybe you were more comfortable all around because you were comfortable in your socioeconomic environment.
    Yes, my parents were definitely in the upper middle class. They were not financially in the same category as many of the affluent Iranian immigrants that preceded them. They had to sell their home and, coupled with a small savings, make a fresh start here. It wasn't a situation that we were living off of any sort of inheritance or anything, so I never grew up in the lap of luxury. We valued education so much that the feeling was that if you were well accomplished, and if you were highly educated, it was going to be OK. I never really thought of it in the context of "I need to get the coolest friends" or "I need to be associated with the most popular group."

It is well known that children of immigrants have the impetus to be successful. Sometimes challenge can be a driving force. Education, especially for immigrants coming from certain countries, is a value they hold forever. It is one thing that cannot be taken from them. It's true for Jewish families, it's true for Asians—because they know this is what's going to get them ahead. Were your parents a big part in your drive to succeed?

For sure, yes. I've always been focused on education. My mother was a perfectionist. If I came home with an A-minus, the reaction was "Well, what went wrong? What did you not get right?" I had to get an A or an A-plus. There was a huge push to make sure I excelled at my education. My mother would say, "You have no other responsibility in life other than this, which is something we've done so that you could focus on your education. And that's all we expect of you." I've had an internal drive for it too. I've always wanted to be the best that I can be. In many ways it worked that it was consistent with my own values. You can argue whether it was so internalized that I could no longer differentiate theirs from mine.

Well, obviously your parents were highly educated, and unlike other immigrants, they managed well here. As you know, some immigrants are very famous and successful in their own country, and when they come here, they are suddenly nobody. Often for immigrants, the tragedy is that they have to start from scratch. That obviously wasn't the case with your parents.

That really helped us. Because my dad is a doctor and a surgeon, and he had done his residency in the United States, he was able to come here and essentially pick up where he left off. He passed the boards and renewed his license. He was lucky to have a transferrable profession that was and is respected. So that made a big difference.

Do you think that if you stayed in Iran, being a daughter of a famous successful surgeon, you would've been able to achieve what you achieved here? Obviously your internal drive would've been the same, but maybe the opportunity would have not been there for you.

I feel really, really fortunate to be here. I'm sad that the revolution happened. I'm sad to see what happened to Iran. It breaks my heart to see the people who are struggling in that environment. But I feel so fortunate that I was able to leave and come here, of all places on the planet. Honestly, every day in many ways, regardless of whatever's happening in this country, I'm mindful of that; I'm still grateful.

The question of what would have happened if I stayed behind is hard to answer. We were raised in a very politically and socially conscious environment. The dinner-table conversations always focused on what was happening in the community, what was happening here, being mindful of where you are and trying to make the world a better place. And I read a lot about women who are excelling in Iran, even during this regime. And seeing the statistics of those who have gone through master's programs and PhD programs and particularly in math and sciences, I realized that they have been able to achieve so much. But at the same time, when you look at the social constraints and the professional constraints that are placed on them, it's heartbreaking.

They are able now to go to the universities, but they cannot really get a job. There are few Iranian women who you can name that are a part of the administration.

The economy is so unstable that it cannot absorb the number of people coming out of the universities. And unfortunately, at this point in Iran, while it's amazing to see the high level of literacy and to see the number of people graduating, unlike here where education is definitely one key to success, there it doesn't necessarily mean that you're going to be able to find a job or be able to support yourself. So you will hit walls left and right that will prevent you from really being able to reach your full potential or actualize your dreams or really make a difference. So yes, I definitely think that I would not have been able to reach the goals that I wanted to.

It seems like you've never had a chip on your shoulder as an immigrant; you never felt insecure as a result of the fact that you were different, "the other," in the United States. But it appears to me that most immigrant women feel somewhat insecure on uncharted ground, and that insecurity drives them to work harder and to succeed.

I've always known I was different. But I didn't necessarily feel insecure about it. I remember in high school I got involved in student government. I ran for senior class president, and I won. I think I was just so blind to all these forces, so I just went for it. Sometimes it worked, and sometimes it didn't, but I didn't pause to think that any failure was because I was different.

So, on the other hand, sometimes being different has been an enrichment and a source of strength.
I can see that, yes.

To take it further, maybe in your case you felt superior in a certain sense to your American friends, a feeling that stemmed from your self-confidence.
I feel that I've always been lucky to have that self-confidence, and I think it comes from honestly having been loved and respected growing up. I never had a situation where my parents would tell me, "You can't do this because we say you can't do this," or "You can't do this because you're a girl." I was always treated as an equal to them in many ways. If there was a rule to follow, they would explain the rule, and they would want my input. Sometimes they rejected it; sometimes they accepted it. But I always felt that I was being respected and that I was being supported. I certainly felt loved. Being loved and trusted contributed to me feeling secure regarding my capabilities to achieve my dream.

It sounds like a part of your success was your desire for your parents to be proud of you.
Yes, absolutely, 100 percent. I think I needed the validation, and the fastest way of being validated was to be the best at everything. And what is better than to be validated by people who supported me and helped me become who I am today?

You've been an immigration judge in Los Angeles since 2005. Prior to that, you were an assistant US Attorney for the Central District of California and a trial attorney with the Office of Immigration Litigation, Civil Division, in the Department of Justice. Quite an achievement for anyone, especially a woman, especially for a first-generation immigrant to America. This is very unique.
Surprisingly, at least with Los Angeles, we're lucky to have a good number of women judges, women immigration judges. And I'm proud to say that our supervising judge is actually an Iranian-American woman

herself. She's younger than I am. And it's nice to see the way that she's succeeded. She has a very interesting story. She grew up, I think, in South Africa. Her parents were a part of the United States Agency for International Development. So in that way, I'm lucky that in this one small community, we do have a good number of women judges, particularly women immigrant judges.

But as a general statement, I think you're right. When you look at courts across the country, the number of women on the bench or immigrant women from the Middle East or maybe from a non-major religious background is very minute.

Why did you become a lawyer?

I always remember my time in my eleventh- and twelfth-grade civics classes and AP history classes. It just resonated with me. Coming from Iran, having gone through the revolution, having seen the impact of a corrupt and inept government, either before or after, I was so drawn to the American political system. I cannot underscore how much I found the entire system to be an ingenious way to try to balance the forces, the human nature forces, in an attempt to come up with a fairer or more just system.

And then we learned a lot about the civil rights movement. As I said, I grew up in a politically and socially conscious household. My grandmother was always talking about the importance of being mindful of underserved communities, and she instilled that mindfulness in me. Studying the civil rights movement, studying the political and social dynamics of the American political system, and just given my general personality, I knew I wanted to go to law school. We did a couple of mock trials. I was lead counsel; I was doing opening and closing statements. And one of the teachers came to me and said, "Have you thought of becoming a lawyer?" "Yes, I've thought of becoming a lawyer." So I was lucky that I've always had a sense of self; I've always had a sense of purpose; I've always had a sense of where I want to go. And so very early on, I knew I wanted to go to law school. I knew I wanted to work for the federal government. I knew I wanted to deal with issues that impact the larger community. I just knew all of that. I can't explain it other than that.

And you worked very hard. Because you had a goal, you had passion and perseverance.

I don't think I ever thought of it as a choice. I just felt like it was so clear.

You have grit, which translates to courage, resolve, and strength of character. Having a talent is getting one above grit, but both are needed for success. If one wants to be an extremely good painter, one has to have a talent, of course, but that's not enough. A combination of clarity of goals, self-critique, passion, and perseverance are the keys to success.

I do think it's a combination of the factors you mentioned as well as your natural makeup. I took for granted how much clarity came to me so easily. As I've crossed paths with many others, I've seen that not everyone has that clarity. I have always taken it for granted that you should always be looking inside, you should always be examining yourself, you should always be looking to see where you've been. You should always be looking to see how you can make the world a better place.

Did you have any role models?

I've always been interested in reading memoirs of people who've succeeded and have in some way done something different. Every kind of book I can read of people coming from different backgrounds and going through challenges, overcoming challenges, just personal stories really inspire me. But having said that, I can certainly talk about [Supreme Court Justices Ruth Bader] Ginsburg, or [Sonia] Sotamayor, or my grandmother and mother. I've been constantly looking for role models everywhere. I've been trying to look at people's stories, look at people's lives as sources of inspiration and lessons. I've always attributed that, to be honest with you, to my lack of creativity. I'm an exceptionally linear, very structured, very-two-dimensional-in-many-ways kind of person. I've never had the level of creativity that I see in other people. I've been drawn to other people's stories as ways to try to learn from and define myself.

I think it's so similar to the way I have been through my life. I've also been very linear. I had my goal, I worked very hard, and I got to use the left side of my brain. I tried to see what my right cerebral brain had to offer, so I tried to paint. I tried to write. And it enriches my life. We all do the best with the tools that we have, but I like to explore.

You're involved in many charities and associations. You've dedicated your life to public service. You have been involved in many speaking engagements to students. You have been a leader and a role model to your Iranian community. You belong to many women's organizations, legal associations. You obviously care about women's rights.

Yes, absolutely.

It's very difficult for you to see what's going on in Iran, where a woman is worth just half that of a man, where a woman cannot go out visiting another country without the permission of men, or if they get divorced, they can't take their child unless the father approves. Do you have plans to do anything about it? What can you do?

I'm very sensitive to women's rights issues or human rights issues, not just in Iran, but across the globe. I feel very powerless regarding what's happening in Iran as a country. But I feel very powerless about so many other countries and so many of the issues that we're facing. And that's why I do so much and try to impact what I can impact. If I can mentor students, if I can do speaking engagements, if I can be part of an organization that helps, if I can in any way directly do something, I will do it. But other than that, I just keep abreast of what's happening. And that's it. You sort of have to know where your field of influence is.

Well, the truth is that you have the nature of an activist, as you've proved from the way you've handled a very difficult situation that you had to confront. You fought, and you didn't let it go.

You can say I'm a fighter.

Unfortunately, they don't have you in Iran, because you would have done a lot of good.

Or I would have been in a jail waiting for my execution.

Why did you become an immigrant lawyer?

For me, the image of a lawyer was someone who was in a courtroom. I grew up thinking that if you're going to make a difference, it's through the legal system. I said I really liked working for the federal government because early on I was exposed to it as an agent of change for the betterment of the community.

The reason I went into immigration law and immigration court was frankly a little bit of a happenstance that turned out to be a very fortunate opportunity. I had an upper-level law student who had finished a summer internship program with the Department of Justice, and he came to me and he said, "You have to apply. It's a great opportunity to work for the federal government, and it's a very simple application." I thought it's very unusual for the federal government to have that kind of opportunity in LA, outside of D.C., and they had a higher number of openings than other agencies, so I applied for it. And I was fortunate to get it.

I came in and I absolutely loved it. It was everything I was looking for. It's one of the most complicated areas of the law, so I felt like I was constantly being challenged. And then it resonated with me because I see what an important role that immigration court played in people's lives. And I was mindful of the fact that for a number of years before we gained our green cards and then citizenship, we were here without status. And even though I was younger, I remember how much it impacted my parents, how nervous they were, how anxiety-driven they were. And so I think either consciously or subconsciously, it really resonated with me, and I came back. I applied for the law clerk position, came back as a law clerk, and really enjoyed it. I was lucky enough to excel. The chief judge then accepted my application to come to D.C. and be his attorney advisor. And the rest is history. But that's really sort of how I fell into the world of immigration law, and it just works. It resonated.

I want to get to the subject of the ban on immigration. But I believe that you don't handle people who want to come to this country. Rather, your cases are regarding deportation of people who are in the United States.

Yes. Currently, I'm very, very committed to maintaining the independence of our immigration judges. So that's the way that I try to keep the system honest. You asked me before what I can do regarding human rights for women in Iran. I recognize that my influence is only so far. I can do what I can do within my sphere of influence. So my sphere of influence is in the immigration court as an immigration judge, to make sure that my decisions are made in an independent fashion and that the other judges in the courtroom are also given that protection.

When it comes to immigration, people who are in the United States are afforded different rights and responsibilities than people who are outside the United States. And the sphere of influence, the jurisdiction, for example, that the immigration court has, has to do with people who are physically in the United States. So in situations where the government picks up somebody or in some ways identifies them as someone they want to deport, for example, or remove from the United States, they have the option of bringing them to the immigration court. When they bring them to the immigration court, the laws are different than, let's say, the "Muslim ban" that you were referring to. Those types of executive proclamations address people who are seeking to come to the United States from outside the United States. So there's a clear division.

In immigration law, generally speaking, the border is a huge divide. If you're outside the border in many different ways, especially if you don't have many ties in the United States, you're considered in a completely different category.

So the immigration proclamations or executive proclamations or anything in that regard dealing with people outside the United States is out of my jurisdiction. And when you ask, "Well, what do you do in situations whether you agree or disagree?" I focus on what I can do with what I can do.

I'm the president of our National Association of Immigration Judges, which is dedicated to fighting for the independence of the court, recognizing that there are a lot of forces that are trying to put their finger on the scale. And it's our job to fight against those forces so we can make sure that the people who come before us get their day in court. So that's what I'm fighting. That's where I believe I can make a difference. That's where I believe I can keep the system strong. I can make the system honest and help make the world a better place. What I think about the immigration ban is really outside of my sphere of influence.

Are your hands tied in this administration?
Well, right now, one of the challenges that the immigration court

has is that we are placed in the Department of Justice. The court is in that unusual situation of being technically in the Executive Branch under an enforcement arm. So the Attorney General is ultimately and technically our boss, and the Attorney General is wearing a law enforcement hat in many ways. And there is an inconsistency there when the courts are being used as a pawn in the political debate that's happening in the community. That's where our issues come up. That's why I'm such a strong believer in our organization in trying to keep that bubble of protection around the immigration court and trying to make sure that we're not used as pawns.

I can give you an example. In the previous administration, as part of their executive policy-driven decision, they decided that they were going to place the cases of all the kids, all the recent arrivals of the kids and the adults and children, in front of the line. This wreaked havoc in our system—with a court that has about three hundred judges and six hundred thousand cases, to all of a sudden try to rearrange dockets, try to bring in all of these people who are just arriving and put them in front of the line of people who have been waiting in line for years. It really, really challenged the system. And it called into question the integrity of the system because they were using the system as a political pawn.

Similarly now, we're seeing it with this administration. And I'm talking now again as a representative of our organization. The challenges we're seeing is that they're detailing judges to these courts because they want to make a statement about the high number of arrests and the high number of detentions. And so they're trying to use us again in that political way.

Thousands of cases have to be rescheduled so that we could send a third of our judges to these other courts. They've publicly stated that now they want to implement quotas on judges.

Can you imagine trying to have a deadline and a quota of how many cases you're supposed to finish in how much time? These are the kinds of challenges to the independence and integrity of the system that I'm dealing with.

That sounds like a lot of pressure.

The integrity of the system is constantly challenged. These are the things that I'm most passionate about because it's where I can at least have a direct impact, where I think I can do my part in the big picture to try to protect the integrity of the system.

It's interesting that you have two parts as a person, as a whole. I see the little girl who came here with her family and grew up here and has this tradition, and the history of a tradition of a thousand years ago, coming to this country that is really new. And then there's the other part where you're so entwined in the judicial system of this country, which makes you so American in many ways, because of who you are and what you do. I think that the past enriches you, and the present makes you strong.

This is my country. I feel very strongly about it. I'm invested in this country. The part where I get mad is when I feel there are people who in some way are trying to define "American" in an exclusionary way. And I won't allow that. This is my country. And I want to make it a better place, I want to make it an inclusive place. I want to make it one that everyone can be proud of.

You felt betrayed by the government that you trusted. Can you explain what happened?

This is something that happened in the last administration. It came up after I was invited to a White House event for Iranian-American community leaders. I was given all the clearances from work and everything else, but afterward I was told, "Well, you should consider recusing yourself from all cases of Iranian nationals." I tried to confront them about it; I asked, "How is this any different than an African-American judge hearing civil rights cases, a Jewish-American judge hearing a Jewish or Palestinian case, or a woman judge hearing women's cases?" The examples are many. And that was when it was elevated into an order, and they forced me to move cases of Iranian nationals off my docket.

That's when I knew I had to fight this racially discriminatory action. I filed suit, and after several years of litigation, they ultimately capitulated and reversed the order, acknowledging that I hadn't done anything wrong. They also paid the attorney's fees and damages. But they never really explained why they fought the case for so long when it was so obviously wrong. Throughout the process, every time I would push them, they kept saying, "Oh, it's just to avoid an appearance of impropriety."

But what appearance of impropriety? What is inappropriate about an Iranian-American leader being at a White House event? I believe it has to do with the word *Iran*.

It was an unprecedented decision. It was an indefinite order. Even though in practice it had a negligible effect in terms of the number of cases—I had a handful of pending cases, and we don't get too many Iranian national cases anyway across the country—it was just a matter of principle.

And only 1 percent of your cases were Iranian nationals?

I don't even think it was that many.

Wouldn't it have been easier to just recuse yourself? After all, they didn't take away your privileges of being a judge. You could have continued to see immigrants from the entire world. You were fighting for three years for justice. Wouldn't it have been easier to just say, "I won't see those Iranians." Why did you insist on fighting for so long?

To me it was a no-brainer. There wasn't even a moment of pause. The very integrity of my job as a judge was attacked. You can't possibly say something like that and then at the same time claim that you're treating me the same or that somehow I'm equal to the other judges. You have now created a second-class judge. It doesn't matter that it was six cases or eight cases or one case. It has nothing to do with the actual number of cases. It has to do with the principle.

I believe also that you have done a favor so that other judges will not be subjected to similar accusations. You didn't want the government to have a precedent, and you continued fighting.

I was very mindful of that. I really did not want that to be a precedent because initially they claimed that there were other precedents, and when we pushed them and they had to divulge the actual cases, those were not precedents. They were in no way similar to my situation. So again, I really felt very strongly that this was something that had to be corrected.

You showed tremendous integrity by doing it.

I hope so. But I really believe it is of paramount importance to have an independent judiciary, an independent judge. You can't have somebody who's not part of the system, who's not a party before the court, who's not in any way in that chain of command, come and tell you that you have to recuse yourself from these cases. You just can't.

How can I possibly be part of that system? How can I possibly fight for a better community, a better country, if at the first chance that I'm being challenged, I would fold because it was convenient to close my eyes? Yes, nobody would have known actually, because nobody could. It was such a minimal amount of cases. If I had just been quiet, nobody would have known. Except some people would know in the administration, and I would know. So if they did that to the next person, the next group of unfavored minorities, they would come back and say, "Well, we did this before and nothing happened." I could not possibly let that happen.

You've summoned the courage of Shirin Ebadi.

Oh no, she's in a completely different class of people, head and shoulders above me. She stayed behind. She fought.

She was a Nobel Prize winner, the first Iranian woman judge, and after the revolution she was demoted to be a clerk. She then retired. She objected and said, "That's not who I am." She wrote a few books and many articles where she preached her opinion regarding human rights.

And then she fought and got back her license as a lawyer and opened a private practice, fighting the government again. Standing up for the rights of people in Iran. There were murder cases, women who had been stoned. And she was behind these people stating that the Koran stands for justice.

What was ingenious about her approach is that she ended up using the system against itself. She knew more about the Koran and the religious influence of the Koran in the legal system than many of the judges and lawyers. If you read some of her books where she talks about what she did, she would cite the Koran to the judges, cite the Koran to the government prosecutors and say, "These edicts that you are issuing have no basis in these religious books that you are citing as your authority." This is what obviously caused a lot of problems for her because they didn't want to be challenged; they didn't want to be called out. And she really suffered for it.

By the end, she was in house arrest?

She ultimately had to leave the country. The government sabotaged her marriage. And she and her husband ultimately divorced or separated. And she had to leave. I believe she lives in London.

She fought also because she has two daughters. And she just wanted them to have a better world, a better life. But how many of us are confronting power and are not scared of being jailed or killed, especially under that kind of regime?

That's why I think she's in a completely different class. I'm privileged to be here. I'm privileged to have a system that in large part respects you for fighting through the proper channels. Are there personal prices that I've paid for it in certain issues and certain intangibles? Yes. But I knew that; I knew that was going to be part of it. It is what it is.

Afsaneh Ashley Tabaddor is an immigration judge, president of the National Association of Immigration Judges (NAIJ), and an adjunct lecturer in law at UCLA School of Law. Judge Tabaddor has testified before Congress and appeared on national news outlets, including CNN, ABC, and C-Span.

Ashley Tabaddor at the National Press Club, 2018; photo by Noel St. John Photography

She is the recipient of judicial excellence awards by the Mexican-American Bar Association (2018), the Armenian-American Bar Association (2014), the Arab American Lawyers' Association of Southern California (2014), and the Iranian American Bar Association (2013). She is an active member of the National Association of Women Judges and the Pacific Council on Immigration Policy. The views expressed by Judge Tabaddor do not necessarily represent the official position of the United States Department of Justice, the Attorney General, or the Executive Office for Immigration Review. The views represent Judge Tabadoor's personal opinions, as well as opinions that were formed after extensive consultation with the membership of NAIJ.

GORDANA VUNJAK-NOVAKOVIC

SERBIAN-AMERICAN BIOMEDICAL ENGINEER
AND MEDICAL RESEARCHER

"Professional accomplishment and the love for my family work together for me. What I learned is that my work is never done; the door is never closed. Being in academia becomes a lifestyle rather than a job, and I'm immersed in it."

WHILE WAITING PATIENTLY FOR MY meeting with Professor Gordana Vunjak-Novakovic in her lab at Columbia University, my mind reflected back to 1996 with the birth of Dolly the sheep. Dolly was cloned in Scotland via somatic cell nuclear transfer, a process that involved injecting a cell nucleus from the mammary gland into an unfertilized egg whose DNA had been removed. The egg provided the nutrients to this multi-potent stem cell to replicate and multiply with the DNA provided and form a clone. The ability to transform a somatic cell (any cell other than a reproductive cell) to a multi-potent stem cell solved the ethical problem that the use of embryonic stem cells once posed to stem-cell science and regenerative medicine. I quickly realized that Dolly the sheep paved the road to an entirely new kind of research that is now being pursued by Gordana and many others toward advancing patient care.

Gordana, a pioneer in the field of tissue engineering, and her team have made strides to successfully regenerate human tissues to replace parts of damaged organs using somatic multi-potent cells, an area known as regenerative medicine. A second arm of this research is to transform biological research to health care, through studies of human diseases and testing of new therapeutic modalities. The new technology is named Organ-On-a-Chip (OOC), which uses miniature tissue and organs grown in the laboratory to emulate human pathophysiology and develop new drugs to cure disease. Such an approach falls into the realm of precision medicine, as the patients are treated as individuals, not as a collective group, and are considered for their genetic diversity, ethnicity, sex, and age, and state of health or disease to develop drug regimens that are optimized for a specific person's biology.

Gordana was born in the Serbian capital of Belgrade. Growing up with her engineer father and her lawyer mother, she was encouraged to pursue and develop her sense of creativity and innovation. After completing her PhD in chemical engineering at the University of Belgrade, with long stays in Germany where she completed many of her experiments, she switched her interest to biomedical engineering and followed her childhood passion for medicine. With a Fulbright Fellowship, she joined MIT's Department of Chemical Engineering and moved to the United States with her husband and young son. At MIT she had the privilege of working with renowned biomedical engineer Professor Robert S. Langer, a life-changing experience that led her to join and become a professor in the Biomedical Engineering and Medical Sciences Department at Columbia University in New York. She was recently appointed University Professor, the highest academic rank at Columbia University reserved for only a few active professors out of four thousand; she is the first engineer in the history of Columbia to receive this highest distinction.

As our interview continued and Gordana spoke about her students, it was clear that she is equally passionate about teaching and mentoring as she is about science. Her unique method is to provide freedom of thought, leading to innovation by the fresh, unbiased approach of her young students. Nothing is more important in a world of fast-changing science, technology, and medicine than the ability to think creatively and without fear of failure. Her lab is a nursery of some of the greatest talent in engineering for human health. That's where stem cells are guided to form healthy organs for people to have a longer, better quality of life, while providing a context for training the next generation of leaders in the field.

You immigrated to the United States in 1986 as a Fulbright Fellow after earning a PhD in chemical engineering from the University of Belgrade in Serbia. What prompted you to move to the United States? Was it a result of political unrest in Serbia?

I didn't really immigrate in '86–'87. A year before I received my PhD in Belgrade, I had a baby, and I was offered a job to stay as faculty member at my home department. But I got into a professional crisis when I realized that I didn't want to pursue "classical" chemical engineering for the rest of my life. Although I had always liked medicine and biology, I did not study medicine because I thought I didn't have the stomach for it. But the love for medicine always remained in my life. I was fortunate to get the Fulbright Fellowship, which allowed me to pursue bioengineering at MIT. So I moved with my entire family to Boston. There I found my profession-al vocation in pursuing tissue engineering, a field that had just taken off.

My mentor was Robert Langer, with whom I wound up working together. I was going back and forth to Belgrade several times a year and in 1993 I took a year's sabbatical, thinking that I would eventually go back to Belgrade for good. As I started to make progress, I also realized that the University of Belgrade could not support the work that my field required in order to progress. In addition, very shortly after I arrived in Boston, the political situation in Belgrade got worse.

After seven years of going back and forth, we settled for good in Boston. A few years later, I was offered this position in Columbia, which I accepted because of the very special work being done there, a once-in-a-lifetime opportunity to build a new program in stem cells and tissue engineering. So today I have two homes: Serbia and the US. I still go very often to Belgrade. Serbia is my home country. But since 1993, we've been here continuously.

Did you leave your parents behind?

Yes, my parents stayed back and many of my family members moved to other countries around the world.

So you were in the United States, getting news about what was happening in your country and being aware and concerned about the civil war of former Yugoslavia.

Yes, but I was still traveling back to see our parents to make sure that they were OK, in spite of the difficulties.

You must feel fortunate knowing that today, under the present government, the situation has changed with regard to specific immigrants that are forbidden to have their relatives come over or to go visit them.

Yes. I was grateful that I was able to travel and be of help to our parents. We've been helping them through the years. I think it's a very fortunate situation.

In your academic life, was there gender discrimination?

People very often ask me this question. But I never felt a disadvantage being a woman in Belgrade, or in the US. It's completely neutral. But I know that a lot needs to be done in general. I am very invested in promoting women in academia. As women advance professionally into independent and leadership positions, the pipeline becomes more leaky.

I'm actively working on plugging this leaky pipeline. I am aware of the fact that as one moves from undergrad to graduate school to higher levels of training and finally leadership positions, in any segment of life you have less and less women involved. This is a huge problem. I personally at times felt a bit strange, as I'm sure you did being the only woman in the room.

One cannot consider this a normal situation. This is less obvious in academia than in some other fields. In my own lab we're fifty-fifty. But in the faculty, it's not really fifty-fifty. It so happens that in my department there are a significant number of women. In fact, my dean of the School of Engineering is a woman, and she is the one that is actively promoting diversity of our faculty. There are about ten or twelve women deans at Columbia. But I'm not unaware of the issue of inequality.

My discussions with other MIT graduates revealed that there was a real drive to change the situation for women in academia, and women organizations have been formed for financial and academic equality, which had a domino effect for many other universities in the US.

I was at MIT at the time when Professor Nancy Hopkins, a neuroscientist, set a benchmark for fair treatment for all women professors in science so they can take the same share of laboratory space and financial support as their male colleagues. The president of MIT at the time, Charles M. Vest, strongly supported the movement.

On a personal level, I was very fairly treated. I was invited to Columbia to build the program, and I was promoted. I was given an endowed chair very quickly, and last year I was elevated to a University Professor. I cannot complain. On the contrary, people are really, really nice to me. I'm paying back by mentoring my junior colleagues. I'm very serious about helping people from my lab and all around me to advance in their careers, and I'm encouraging them to live a life besides their professional one.

So being a mother and pursuing one's career while enjoying both.
Women are often worried about taking positions with high responsibility if they're planning a family, assuming they will need to take a lion's share of responsibility for their children. It is an inequality

of a different kind, which is now changing with the millennials. I never heard a man wonder if he can have both an academic career and a family. Until women feel that they can dedicate their life to pursue their dreams without feeling inhibited by motherhood, or vice versa, the problem will persist. However, we have made tremendous strides in recent years.

Yet I cannot complain. It would be very untruthful or hypocritical if I say that I am disadvantaged because I'm really not. Nobody told me what to do, and I controlled my own life.

You pursued your passion and improved the quality of life of others. How did you manage to balance the roles of scientist and mother?

I often give talks about the work-life balance. Over the years, I have learned that family is most important and one's work is most important. They are at the same level. I really strongly believe that I am a better mother and wife because I am accomplished professionally. And I am a better professional because I have a full life. I feel better about myself and the work I do if there is the fulfillment of having a family. Professional accomplishment and the love for my family work together for me. What I've learned is that in academia my work is never done; the door is never closed. It becomes a lifestyle rather than a job, and I'm immersed in it.

The other thing I've learned is the realization that there is never a good time for anything—to write a book, to give that big talk overseas, to have a child, to move, anything. Because I am so busy, there is a never a good time to do things. And so I've learned how to keep my goals while changing my strategies, and to optimize daily in order to accommodate.

Women are able to multitask, and we are flexible.

Another skill I learned as I grew older is to say no nicely. When I was young, I was always accommodating and would attend everything I was invited to, do every review, and write every invited paper. Now I've learned how to say no to 95 percent of the invitations I get. I also have learned how to get all the help I can and to delegate as much as I can. I've learned to run a lab in a way that I get the absolutely best people I can, the greatest talent, and give them freedom to pursue their dreams. Because they're smart, they should not be micromanaged. It's some kind of art and science balancing this life.

It's very true that delegating, giving freedom, and at the same time being on top of what's going on, directing, and showing the way to success is a talent. Basically, it is the art of being a good teacher.

It's very important for the trainees—graduate students, postdocs, clinical fellows. We have quite a few fellows who are spending their research portion of the training here. I think that if I didn't say, "Go find the question that you really want to study and make a difference in some area of science and life," then I would not get the results I'm seeking. They usually go into a couple of months of thinking, defining questions, trying to find out what they want to do for their PhD or postdoc. Once this process is over, they have a sense of ownership. This is their project. This is their idea. They are being prepared for real life.

Nobody should be subordinated, and everybody should be allowed to think and act freely. The very interesting thing about training that I'm finding, especially in this area of medicine and engineering, is that the field is developing quickly. These young people who are in their early twenties will be at the peak of their careers in medicine or science twenty years from now.

Because the advances in science and technology are so fast and unpredictable, we do not know how the world will look then. We are training them to resolve undefined, unknown situations.

Especially in the field of bioengineering, which is exploding and with its ability to cure disease and to prolong our life span, it will dovetail with unforeseen economic problems. You haven't told me yet, why did you study engineering in the first place?

My father was an engineer, and he was very creative. He was a person developing new technologies, building factories. He was creating products that you can see and feel. He collaborated with many people around the world, and he was my role model, and so I followed his path. My mother was completely the other part of the scale. She was a lawyer and liked humanities. Many of my family members are in the medical field, including my son. But we did have in the mix some engineers and people in the humanities. The point is that education was a very important issue in my family.

The path to success is education.

It really starts at home. In my laboratory, we have high school kids that come from underprivileged communities. They're all smart kids. They don't have enough support, for reasons that are not their fault. I believe this can be compensated through opportunities and training and mentoring. It was nice to follow some of these kids all the way to medical school, for example. I believe that we should provide opportunities for talented kids to develop their aptitude.

Columbia is very big in accepting underprivileged kids who show perseverance and talent.

Columbia University is huge in that.

What's great about New York is that you can find opportunities for socially responsible research right here around you. It is an enormous advantage being here. It is a small world on its own. It is important in the world of science for people to interact and to exchange ideas. New York offers that.

You must have had some kind of difficulties adjusting to this world, coming from Serbia.

Yes, the style of work here is very different. I found that I had to be very resourceful, and hands-on, and find my way to solve practical problems. Coming from Serbia, I had the training to ask why something happens, and then develop the ability to answer it. So it was difficult, but I was able to handle it. For example, I never took multi-choice exams when I was in Serbia. There is a written exam for every class here; it is a standard. We took oral exams. This is another adjustment I had to make.

Oral exams—I remember them. You sit in front of the professor and answer questions on materials you had dedicated a year studying in a foreign language while hundreds of students are listening to your answers.

Yes. That was adjustment. But I also brought knowledge that some other people didn't have. I felt that I had something to offer that was lacking here.

Absolutely. In 1993, regenerative medicine took off. The concept of tissue regenerating or engineering was introduced. You're a pioneer in this field. Since then, bioengineers have made significant strides in the medical field. Can you explain the goal of tissue engineering and how it improves the quality and the length of life?

Yes, everything you said is exactly right. It is serendipity to be in the right place at the right time with the right person to meet. For me, that was the father of the field, Professor Langer. I was standing on the shoulders of a giant because he gave me this opportunity to enter the field, which I didn't even know about. When he asked me to join in the research of tissue engineering, I asked him, "What is it?" I ended up bringing in a new dimension to the field, the use of in vitro environments we call bioreactors to culture cells and form tissues in laboratory.

The initial concept was to place cells into scaffolding materials, implant them into animals, and see what happens. But I took the path of engineering tissue from a cell. It involved taking living cells, combining them with biomaterials, and providing conditions similar to those present in our body to construct a tissue that can replace the defective or missing organ in our body. For example, we can now replace a missing bone that was damaged as a result of trauma, or surgery, and heal the defect that was formed. So the idea is to address this problem of dysfunctional or missing tissues by providing biological substitutes to make the tissues themselves and sort of fix the defect. This has been pursued for twenty-five or more years now.

You're making it sound easy. A lot goes into providing that optimum environment to a cell that you scientists obtain from a functional tissue in a patient's body to transfer it to an embryonic cell, meaning to strip it from its function and make it susceptible to become and differentiate to any tissue that is needed. From what I understand, there are strict criteria, which, as you said, took twenty-five years to provide the environment—or what you called a "scaffold"—to create a tissue to repair the heart, liver, bone, etc.

Yes, there are specific criteria that need to be met to provide a scaffold that will allow the cells to form the tissue type in question. The resulting tissue construct is implanted, for example, to repair bone. It has to be biocompatible not to illicit an inflammatory immune response, strong enough to match the properties of the original tissue, to be produced in the precise anatomical shape, and to be biologically functional.

So you learned how to nourish an undifferentiated cell to use bioengineering to cure disease.

There is now another arm of tissue engineering that started to develop some six or seven years ago. We make micro-sized pieces of functional human tissues and connect them with vascular flow in a physiological meaningful way to study disease or to do drug testing in human models. These platforms are called "organs on a chip" or "tissues on a chip." This is a completely new development in the field that is enabling the modeling of disease and the developmental testing of drugs.

How do you do that?

We start from small samples of blood that we use to isolate adult stem cells. Then we induce these stem cells to make heart cells, liver cells, skin cells, bone cells, and so forth and so on. Then we can make a patient-specific combination of tissues—for example, bone, lung, and liver tissue. We can combine these tissues with a bioengineered tumor to test the intended effects of anticancer drugs on tumors, as well as unintended effects on other tissues and vasculature. This way we can improve treatment regimens and optimize the dosage of the drug for treating a specific patient.

In August 2006, Time *magazine wrote an article about using stem cells for regenerating tissue. At the time, President George W. Bush allowed federal money to continue embryonic stem cell research to already developed lines but excluded supporting new ones. I also remember the political and religious argument regarding usage of embryonic stem cells. The debate was around the moral issue regarding the destruction of life versus prolonging life. In 2012, the problem was solved by Nobel Prize winner Shinya Yamanaka.*

Absolutely. The debate about embryonic cells for regenerating tissue is gone because Dr. Yamanaka discovered that any cell can be brought back to an embryonic-like stage and then be used for tissue engineering.

But there is also something that one has to give up. There were advantages for using embryonic cells versus non-embryonic cells.

This is true. Going back to the so-called Bush lines, there were two problems with human embryonic cells. One problem was that it was unclear for many of these lines how exactly they were obtained and whether those cells were biologically altered, and whether their phenotype was normal. There were ethical problems and technical problems. At the end of the day, there were only two lines of embryonic cells that were actively used. Nevertheless, the field learned a lot from working with embryonic cells. But since Yamanaka's discovery, we are finding that pluripotent stem cells are very similar to embryonic. Some scientists still believe that it is easier to demonstrate certain scientific findings in embryonic cells. We don't use them anymore. I used them at MIT because that is what was available at the time. We were getting them from this federal repository in Wisconsin, and the cost in those early years was very high. Today we have a very different situation.

Yamanaka actually established this process of generating stem-like cells starting from somatic cells. Cells from skin, blood, or any part of the body can now be turned back into embryonic-like state. This discovery changed everything, in two ways. First, there are no more controversies. Second, you can do patient-specific studies that could not be done using embryonic cells. Today we can make patient-specific bone, patient-specific skin. Yamanaka really opened the door to something important. It was a paradigm shift; everything changed in 2011–2012.

And today, what is powerful about adult stem cell-based tissue engineering is that it is patient-specific because it's customized to the patient's genetics, state of health or disease, gender, race, and age. And we can now study the changes that cause the disease and experiment with the effects of drugs to cure the problem, all in human tissue models studied in vitro. Basically, you can run a clinical trial on a chip for a specific patient population.

Is there a danger for a tissue that was engineered and transplanted to develop into a tumor, cancer?

This is a frequent question. This is actually part of the safety studies, baseline studies that need to be completed under the supervision of the Food and Drug Administration. We look into these aspects very carefully. But then, there may always be some longer-term effects that you just miss because you don't look long enough. The honest answer is we don't know for sure. But we are seeing in experimental studies that the cells respond to their environment. So you expect that if you put the bioengineered tissue construct into the bone, it will not become something else. It will become bone.

Do you study the genetic mutation in the diseased tissue?
Yes. For example, we study genetic mutations in the diseased heart. And we have a heart tissue from the cells of the same patient where we removed the mutation that we study, too, as a healthy control.

Being a pioneer in your field and receiving honors such as being the first woman engineer to receive the Director's Lecture at the National Institutes of Health (NIH), do you feel gratitude toward the United States? It has provided you with the possibility to achieve something that you could not in your country.
Sure, absolutely. I was very grateful and very humbled about being elected to the National Academy of Engineering, the National Academy of Medicine, the National Academy of Inventors. This is certainly a personal recognition, and I feel good about it. But it's also a recognition of the profession, and of my team. Any recognition one of us gets in our lab is also a recognition of our team effort.

What do you think about the unfavorable sentiments toward immigrants today?
I never personally felt disadvantaged, and I was brought up to be blind to race, ethnic background, and gender. I was brought up to completely accept people for who they are and not where they come from.

You grew up in a homogenized society?
Absolutely, and a very tightly knit society. I have a lot of understanding for people who come to this country and then experience difficulties. My lab is like a mini United Nations. The students come from all around the world, solely based on their academic merit and passion for science. It is the norm for us. Nobody feels like a foreigner because most of us are foreigners.

Do you feel any changes in the financial resources from the present government for research and development?

We get our funding mostly from NIH. Until a few weeks ago, NIH had no budget. Functioning through more than half of the fiscal year without a budget makes you very conservative about giving away funding. As a result, the pay lines are very low. The grants that we would normally have funded were not funded, because they were very careful. Now it turns out that the budget went up. There is a lot of uncertainty in this situation. We don't really know what the next year will bring. For science and its translation to clinical applications, continuity is extremely important. The stressful situations and uncertainties about funding support are not helping anyone because you cannot function normally if you don't know what will happen in one month, three months, or six months.

Your work certainly will improve the well-being of humans without discrimination of gender or race.

Gordana Vunjak-Novakovic, PhD, is University Professor, the highest academic rank at Columbia University reserved for only a few active faculty out of four thousand, and she is the first engineer in the history of Columbia to receive this highest distinction. She is also the Mikati Foundation Professor of Biomedical Engineering and Medical Sciences, and on faculty in the Irving Comprehensive Cancer Center, College of Dental Medicine, Center for Human Development, and Mortimer B. Zuckerman Mind Brain Behavior Institute. She directs the Laboratory for Stem Cells and Tissue Engineering, serves on the Columbia University President's Task Force for Precision Medicine, and the Executive Leadership of the

Gordana Vunjak-Novakovic as mace bearer in 2017, after her appointment to University Professor, the first engineer in the history of Columbia University to earn this distinction

Columbia University Medical Center. In October 2019, she was among the class inducted to the American Academy of Arts and Sciences. The focus of her research is on engineering human tissues, including heart, lung, bone, muscle, tumors, and vasculature for regenerative medicine and studies of development and disease. She has trained more than 150 graduate students and postdocs. With her students, she founded four biotech companies that are based in New York City: epiBone (epibone.com), Tara Biosystems (tarabiosystems.com), Xylyx Biosolutions (xylyxbio.com), and Immplacate (immplacatehealth.com).

FABIOLA WILSON

HAITIAN-AMERICAN US ARMY MAJOR (RETIRED)

"For those who think that women are mentally incapable of enduring the devastation of combat, I would say that women have been dealing with so much between discrimination and the servitude-type life, and we've had to fight for our rights. History has proven that we're mentally tough enough to endure life's challenges, whether it be combat or not."

FABIOLA WILSON WOULD GROW UP without her mother until she was almost six years old. She lived with her godmother in Haiti, a tiny nation on the island of Española that has seen enslavement, genocide, revolts, US occupation, dictators, and political deceit. Earthquakes and epidemics, including AIDS, further impoverished Haiti and spawned massive immigration.

Fabiola's mother, Iramise Blaise, was among these immigrants in the late '70s and early '80s. She landed in New York and took a job as a nanny for an American family with two girls. When Fabiola joined her, they moved to Brooklyn. Iramise continued to work hard and support her daughter, and Fabiola strove to integrate with the community and learn English.

Fabiola became an officer in the US Army. She has been deployed to conflicts, including Bosnia and Iraq, and as a medic she has seen firsthand the ravages of battle, helping injured soldiers and civilians.

Fabiola is a fighter in the ongoing War on Terror and an administrator who seeks to streamline medical operations. As a woman in the Army, she sometimes deals with men who would prefer that women stayed home, or at least not hold leadership positions over them.

When we sat down to talk, I learned that Fabiola joined the Army because she wanted to travel and take advantage of new opportunities, just like her mother did when she left Haiti for New York. She promised her mother that she would continue her education and focus on the medical field. Now, however, Fabiola tells me she might retire a year early. President Trump's disparaging remarks about Haiti have left a bad taste in her mouth, and she's no longer sure she can work for someone like him or for an organization that blatantly disregards and mismanages minority soldiers.

———

Do you have any recollections of the years when you were separated from your mother and lived in Haiti, from the time you were born to the age of six?

Well, the fortunate thing about the separation is that I don't recall it clearly, I was so young. But by virtue of the information my mom and my other family members have given me, and the pictures I have seen, my early years, raised by my godmother, were happy ones. My godmother filled the void with love and affection.

I remember that when my mom came to retrieve me, it was a happy moment. When I arrived in the United States, I was wearing a beige dress with floral prints with lace trimmings, and my hair was made up in two braids.

My dad passed away when I was around six. He, too, moved to the US while I was a child, so I hardly knew him. The few memories I have of him were warm and joyful. I have a picture hanging in our family room of him sitting with my mom. Even though I was very attached to my godmother, the transition to my mom was effortless as I recall.

While residing in Haiti with my godmother, my mother went to Israel and learned to become a chef. Then she ended up in the United States. Years later, working as a nanny to an American family, she had me join her, and I went to stay with her in that home. But before that, we landed in Brooklyn and were received there for a short time by my family, my older sister and brother from my mother's previous marriage. Thereafter, I remember taking the Long Island Rail Road to join my mother at her place of work in Locust Valley, in New York.

My mother was married when she was seventeen, and her husband was accidentally shot by the Haitian police. I was told they were pursuing someone else; it was a matter of being at the wrong place at the wrong time. This is how I have a half-brother and sister, who are eighteen and twenty years older than me, residing in Brooklyn and Florida.

Do you remember the first few years in the United States?

I remember the two little girls my mother took care of. I remember a glimpse of the school that I attended with them. I remember having fun. But I had difficulties with the language, and I remember that it was very frustrating. I wanted to communicate with the other children and have fun and really immerse myself in everything, but not knowing the language was a barrier. We stayed with this kind family for a year, and then my mother decided that we should move to Brooklyn where the environment of a public school would provide an opportunity for new immigrants to learn the language.

Were you discriminated or bullied as a result of being "the other?"

I know the language barrier was the issue. For me, any circle has always been fine, but I think it was more the language barrier. In Brooklyn I had the assistance of translation and the teachings of English and Creole. My mother was frustrated because her English was not up to par to assist me with my difficulties. So that was the determining factor for us to move to Brooklyn. It was a difficult decision for her, she told me later, to leave the family and the two little girls she was attached to. But she felt that the situation was setting me back more than it was helping me. Moving to Brooklyn was also a difficult decision because the teaching was not as phenomenal as it was in Locust Valley's private school. My mom said that she wished we could've stayed, because she really loved and missed the girls. She's always made that very clear and carried the pictures of the girls with her.

Tell me about your life as an adolescent.

I went to Lafayette High School. It was an engineering and nursing school. My mother wanted me to take the medical route, so I enrolled in the nursing program. Part of the program was volunteering in a nursing home, and the other part was working in Coney Island Hospital. I really enjoyed my high school. I received a scholarship for Hunter College for nursing, but I did not pursue it because I decided to join the Army, to my mom's disappointment.

What made you join the Army?

The initial thought, I honestly couldn't tell you where it came from, but I was intrigued with the idea of traveling. Like my mother, I was hoping to experience different things that life had to offer. I inherited the travel bug from her. The Army recruiter came to my high school. Friends of mine who were seniors the year prior had joined the Army and the Navy. Out of nowhere I decided that I was going to join the Army and travel. No one else in my family ever had done anything like this. I promised my mother that I would fulfill her main concern, that after joining the Army I would continue my education. I promised her I would go to school, and I would work hard at it on the weekends, lunchtime, or nighttime, and whatever it took. That's what I did.

So how was the experience when you joined the Army?

I did the initial paperwork on August 31, 1995. I graduated from high school and attended basic training on July 2, 1996, followed by the Army's initial training to be a medical specialist, a combat medic. I was able to fulfill my mom's dream for me to stay in the medical field. That was the equivalent of a civilian emergency medical technician. I enjoyed that tremendously. While I was a medic, my first duty station was Baumholder, Germany, from December of '96 to '98. After Germany, I went to Fort Hood, Texas, which is in the Killeen area. Three years later, I re-enlisted to become an orthopedic specialist. The Army provided us with all of our training, which occurred in Fort Sam Houston, Texas. The training had two parts: phase one was in San Antonio, and phase two was working in one of the hospitals and on-the-job training in Fort Bliss, Texas, in El Paso, close to the Mexican border.

Was there a time when you felt that your life was threatened?

While I was assigned as a medic in Germany, I deployed to Bosnia from 1997 until 1998. I was there for four months. It was a NATO mission. There were lots of land mines and bombings that had occurred prior to our arrival. One of the Army's missions was to help rebuild, evacuate, and provide resources to the Bosnians. It was a combination of a dangerous combat zone and a humanitarian mission.

I was scared because it was my first non-US territory combat zone experience, and we had to have our weapons with us. Before we left the post, we had to put our ammunition into our weapon and be prepared for any attack because not everyone wanted us there. We were outside of our secured locations and very vulnerable once outside the gates. That was scary.

We were pleased that we returned home with the amount of soldiers we left with, with no life-threatening disfigurements or attacks against us. So for me, I can say I was blessed in that aspect.

When you returned from Bosnia, did you apply to orthopedic school?

Yes, three years after I left Germany. I completed phase one and two of orthopedic school, and I went to work at Reynolds Hospital in Fort Sill, Oklahoma. I was in Oklahoma from 2000 until 2002, taking care of broken bones, missing limbs, and various orthopedic matters.

From 2004 to 2006, I was a full-time student and was enrolled in the Simultaneous Membership Program, which was the reserve portion of my transition from an enlisted soldier to an officer. It consisted of training one weekend a month and two weeks per year. That way, they paid for all of my college tuition. I earned my bachelor's in interdisciplinary studies and military science and was commissioned as a second lieutenant on May 5, 2006.

In exchange for the education, what was your commitment to the Army?

I was committed for four years for every two years of schooling. My first duty station was in South Korea, at Camp Red Cloud, then Camp Stanley. I stayed there for two years. These two locations were among the most northern military posts in South Korea, also known as Area One by the military. It was approximately an hour-and-a-half drive from what was called Camp Casey, near the border of North Korea. I worked for the 2nd Infantry Division Surgeon, with duties consisting of strategic planning, future and current operations, medical licensure accountability, and maintenance.

We also tracked the medical training of the doctors, nurses, and noncredentialed soldiers. We participated in field trainings that were conducive to preparation for attacks from North Korea: how to evacuate the family members who were there with the soldiers if North Korea were to plan to attack us, or prepare for any natural catastrophes or manmade disasters. So there was a lot of planning, especially for the division, on contingency plans pertaining to North Korea being involved.

What was your rank there?

I was second lieutenant. It was my first duty station as a commissioned officer.

What are your memories of that time?

I learned a lot. There were times I felt overwhelmed because it was meant for a more senior-level officer.

As my time in Korea was close to an end, Smiley Wilson III, now my husband, whom I met in Baumholder, Germany, in February of 1997, found my email address in a group message that was sent by a mutual friend. He was deployed in Iraq at the time and happened to see my maiden name and first initial (FortilusF) and decided to see if it was me. And it was.

Months prior to our reconnection, I requested a consecutive overseas tour assignment back to Germany. While visiting a few friends and checking on my home in South Carolina prior to leaving for Germany, he drove down from North Carolina to see me. During that visit, on October 13, 2008, I found out that my mother, who was living in West Palm Beach, Florida, was given six months to one year to live.

Smiley supported me immensely with the news and assisted me tirelessly with the process of shortening my time in Germany and returning to North Carolina. He helped with finding my mother the best possible medical providers and specialists, which resulted in the six months to one year being almost four years.

He asked my mom for my hand in marriage, and we wed on Saturday, March 27, 2010. His mother, Dr. Norma Wilson-Fogel, officiated the ceremony.

Shortly after our wedding, I was notified that I needed to deploy to Iraq. I filled the position of a soldier who had a heart condition and couldn't deploy. It was a difficult time being away from my family. I left my mother with Smiley, and he rendered phenomenal care of her. He had already retired from the Army. He went with her to her doctor appointments, making sure she was eating healthy.

What is your recollection of your time in Iraq?

Believe it or not, it started with a terrible experience of flying into a blackout and sound-silence area, which placed us in a vulnerable state. If detected, the enemy could attempt to shoot us down if they wanted. That was really scary. Every day we experienced mortar attacks. And we always carried our weapons and our ammo everywhere we went in full combat gear. I was the medical operations officer, so I tracked casualties and the movement of medical assets within the theaters of operation. I was responsible for five soldiers. We would track the wounded, report them, and get them back home.

I was stationed in Balad from 2010 to 2011. I was there for nine months. This was post-9/11, so we were there fighting terror. That's where my training in Korea and Bosnia came in handy. You train for survival skills, self-defense skills, and basically if you're ever captured, how to manage and maintain yourself as a prisoner of war. Everyone is trained as a soldier, regardless of their gender.

In times of peace, in the US, what was your responsibility?

I did the operations, the medical and strategic planning, that were aimed to improve the organizations that I was in. I also did human resources. I enjoyed both of these careers. In North Carolina, I worked as a medical operations officer for the 18th Airborne Corps. I also did human resources for the 261st Multi-Functional Medical Battalion.

I moved on to Alaska and served as the chief of human resources for Bassett Army Community Hospital from 2015 to 2017. It was a great experience and opened my eyes as to what a leader should be, know, and do, as well as not do. I learned a whole lot, especially managing the onboarding and releasing of the civilian staff. Training and development of soldiers and civilians was very rewarding and further enhanced my managerial skills and abilities.

I recently relocated to Fort Benning, Georgia. I've decided to retire earlier than initially planned.

So you're retiring as a major?

Yes, I will not be in long enough to qualify for lieutenant colonel. I'll retire with the Army, but I think I'll still work, but less, because Smiley Wilson IV, our five-year-old son, doesn't want me to work. I've been working since I was fifteen. I'm used to getting up and going. But my hours will not be as laborious. I do plan on working, if even just part-time.

What will you be doing?

Since I already have my bachelor's and master's degree in management, leadership, and military science, I would like to teach online. I would prefer to teach human resources. I love working in the medical services. We're like our own little community. We support ourselves. It's like an army within the Army is the best way I can explain it. But we have all of our support systems internal to the medical service branch.

When you joined the Army, what was happening with the United States?

When I first joined, we had to deal with the after-effects of Operation Desert Storm, from 1990 to 1991, which was the first major foreign crisis after the Cold War. I was in the middle of America's War on Terror following 9/11.

Since the Revolutionary War and on through the First and Second World Wars, women have gradually established themselves not just as seamstresses and secretaries, but also as nurses, parachute-folders, etc. Where do we stand on the debate of women serving in the military?

Women were pretty much limited to those support jobs, but now we are much better integrated into the system. We have more career-filled opportunities available to us. There are still limitations.

There was an important debate about women soldiers joining combat.

Right before I went to Alaska, they conducted a pilot. They allowed the first group of women to train and see if they could qualify for combat arms. This was about three-and-a-half years ago.

In 2013, Secretary of Defense Panetta lifted the ban on women that disallowed integration and allowed for them to join any field they wanted to join. In 2016, it became the law. Apparently, the ban was enforced in 1994, when women were restricted from joining the artillery and infantry, and that rule was lifted in 2016. Speaking of women in the Army, is there sexual or racial discrimination?

As it pertains to racial discrimination, it's becoming more blatant, especially since Trump took office. I've seen it firsthand here in the organization that I'm in; hence, it's one of the main reasons I've submitted my retirement packet.

Gender-wise, there had been the air of "Oh, you're a woman," especially on the operations side, because it's such a male-dominant-type career. Until this day, there are a lot of men who believe that we should've probably remained in nursing and support-type fields. It is accepted for us to be a nurse or an assistant, or even a physician's assistant, but when it comes to more of what's considered male-dominant jobs, there is a conflict. A lot of it is about mindsets and upbringing. Some men are narrow-minded, regardless of whether Army or civilian sector, and you often cross paths with people like that.

Presently, the subject of sexual harassment is everywhere. What is your experience in the Army?
Due to fear of reprisal and/or retaliation, there are sexual harassment classes and training, how to avoid it, how not to be the perpetrator, and how not to be victimized. The Army has a zero-tolerance policy. But there are those who refuse to adhere to the regulations and policies.

Do you think that women and men should serve in the same unit?
We already do, and there are definitely pros and cons to it. But the cons are along the lines of those whose mindset is very biased or of a predatory type. There are predators anyway, regardless if it's the Army or not. So those two mindsets cause difficulties. I've been fortunate enough where I haven't experienced any sexual harassment against me, but I know people who have. That has to do with people who have an upbringing where men think that women are there at their disposal or subservient to them. I include those who do what they do out of "power," whether it be in rank, position, their affiliations, etc. They feel that women are not equal to men or do not contribute equally to the Army.

There's always been a controversy, and two very important women generals in the US Army had a famous debate whether women are fit emotionally and physically to be in combat. Brigadier General Elizabeth Hoisington opposed the service of women in combat and felt that women cannot serve three months in an Army unit and are not mentally, physically, and emotionally qualified. She also felt that women in combat reduce the effectiveness of the military force. And that men's and women's relationships become a problem because they cause distractions.

On the other hand, Major General Jeanne Holm disagreed and said that the time had long come for women to serve their nation in combat units, and they should be integrated in units, fighting in ships and planes, with the exclusion of infantry. She felt that the number one criterion must be in the ability of the unit to perform its combat mission, and everything else is secondary to it. What is your opinion about women participating in combat?

I've had that discussion before with males and females within the Army, as well as with my husband. Based on my experience, the types of female and male soldiers I've met throughout the years, I believe women are more than capable. I've met a lot female soldiers who are technically and tactically more proficient and stronger than some of the males. They would be more qualified than a man to be in those combat arms units, because there are very physically fit women who can outperform their male counterparts.

Do you think that mentally they can endure it?

Yes. We've been enduring our entire lives, between discrimination and the servitude-type mindsets, and we've had to fight for our rights. History has proven that we're mentally tough enough to endure life's challenges, whether it be combat or not.

What do you think about the controversy of having gays and transgenders in the Army?

We've always had gays and lesbians in the Army. It was just not spoken of, and it was a very scary thing for someone who was gay or lesbian to let it be known. I recall a general, I can't recall his name, who was featured in a magazine where he identified more with being a woman and dressed as such after he retired. He had a split image in the Army. He got married and had children because he had to suppress who he was in order for the community he was in to accept him. It has always been there, but now it's just a matter of having an open platform. But I don't think it's something new.

In civilian life, the boss is not supposed to go out with the secretary. What happens when you have a romantic relationship in the Army in the same unit? Do you think it's distracting?

Well, ironically enough, two of the soldiers under my supervision got married. So when I was informed, "Hey, ma'am, our soldiers got married," by my second in charge, I asked, "Oh, which one and to who?" And she said, "To each other." So it is a misconception that you can pick out the sexual identities of people. I said, "Oh, OK, I didn't see that coming." They are not allowed to work for, or in, the same section with each other.

With regards to the distraction of women being in combat arms, I believe it's in our upbringing. Men may get distracted because they feel responsible for being a woman's protector and not their peers, even if the woman can protect herself.

In the twenty years that you've spent in the Army, do you see more acceptance of women as equal peers?

Yes. The rules and regulations have enforced that, regardless of what the leadership's personal viewpoints are. They must afford the same opportunities to everyone regardless of gender, just as long as they meet the qualifications.

Do women have the same opportunity to get up the ranks as men?

I know an orthopedic PA who's a female. She's retired now. But I know, through our friendship and discussions, that she's voiced discriminatory behavior she's experienced because of being a woman, especially since orthopedic surgery is so labor-intensive. She was discriminated against because she's a woman. An example she gave was that, due to the type of apparatuses they [orthopedic surgeons] use, a few of her male counterparts believed the strength and understanding of mechanics required in the field was outside of a woman's scope.

You rank right now as a major. Do you think that proportionally there are as many high-ranked women in the Army as men?

No. First, there are more men in the Army than women. Second, whether the comparison is made on the enlisted or officer side, men are usually selected over a qualified woman due to personal preferences and misconceptions about the leadership abilities of women.

So it's just like in civilian life. There is discrimination in the Army against women in high positions. I want to ask you a sensitive question: How did President Trump's comments about immigrants affect you personally?

Trump saying that Haiti was a shithole country was a slap in my face. It was really hurtful, to the point that it almost validates my decision to retire, because I said, "I don't want to work for somebody like that." The policies in place prior to his presidency said you will not discriminate. You will not violate the rights of human beings who built this nation and the Army. His words and actions—especially his words—have been and continue to be a 180-degree turn, contradictory to what the foundation of this organization is supposed to be. His words throughout his presidency continue to be very hurtful, mean, and degrading to various groups.

Fabiola Wilson (Ret. US Army Major) served in the US Army in many capacities over more than twenty-two years, including as a hospital adjutant and chief of human resources at the 14th Combat Support Hospital at Fort Benning, chief of the human resources division at Bassett Army Community Hospital in Alaska, a medical operations officer with the 18th Airborne Corps at Fort Bragg, and a company commander and human resources officer, also at Fort Bragg. She served in Iraq as a medical operations officer with the 261st Multifunctional Medical Battalion. She earned her undergraduate degree at the University of South Carolina and a

Fabiola Wilson with her husband and son at her retirement ceremony

graduate degree at Webster University. She is now retired and owns an online travel and wellness business. Her main focus is to be present on a continuous basis for her family and friends.

HELENA WONG

BRAZILIAN/CHINESE-AMERICAN INTERNATIONAL BUSINESS
EXECUTIVE AND FINANCE EXPERT

"I feel that my values are Chinese, my heart is Brazilian,
and my pocket is American."

I MET HELENA WONG THROUGH the Women's Forum of New York, an organization of truly amazing leaders. The members, like Helena, take an active role in providing education to women whose careers have been derailed by adversity. They expand the network of women leaders across corporate and civic boards, and they share professional and personal enrichment programs within the group.

I thought Helena looked Chinese, falling for the easy conclusion based on looks alone. But when she introduced herself, I detected a Brazilian accent. Helena wasn't surprised by my assumption. Many times, she has had people in the United States correct her when she tells them she was born in Brazil—even insist that she must be wrong. Rarely is there malice, she said, but there is a bias for people to judge others by their appearance.

What I came to recognize is that Helena's petite appearance and pleasant demeanor reveal a wealth of intelligence, humor, and tremendous strength. Her story draws on her past, growing up in Sao Paulo as the eldest child of Chinese parents who escaped Chairman Mao Zedong and the Communist Revolution. The stories of the atrocities of war in the history of China as told to her by relatives resonate throughout our conversation.

Although she was born in Brazil as a daughter of first-generation refugees, memories of her Chinese past are a vital part of who she is and continue to give her strength. In her young life, Helena had responsibilities beyond what was normal for her age. Growing up in a small town of only three thousand people in Brazil, she assisted her parents in silk-worm breeding and in the sale of cocoons to Chinese merchants to produce silk. She remembers herself as a free-spirited girl who flew on her bicycle everywhere, climbed trees, and played games with her friends and siblings. When the family moved to Sao Paulo, Helena, at the age of seven, helped with bookkeeping and in translation for her parents who did not speak Portuguese and who had a business going door-to-door selling merchandise. At fourteen, she discovered the discriminatory world against immigrants, a system that put her father, unjustifiably accused, in jail for allegedly smuggling foreign goods into the country without paying taxes. While trying to clear her father's name and free him, she was temporarily sidetracked from her plans for an education.

Helena's eyes filled with tears when she told this story. The memories are difficult. But, in retrospect, Helena believes that the events that placed her in charge of rebuilding her family's mental and financial health prepared her for the difficulties she encountered in the foreign environment of The Wharton School at the University of Pennsylvania and later in the competitive corporate world. Helena would hold senior leadership positions at several multinational companies, including Procter and Gamble, Pepsi-Cola and Western Union.

It is clear that Helena's calculated risk-taking grew from the self-confidence she developed from having to "walk into the unknown" throughout her life. Now she helps companies expand, recover after losses, and find new markets. She is a role model to young women, inspiring them to join corporations and become important decision makers in a predominantly male realm. And she has adopted the American philanthropic model of donating her time and money so less-fortunate individuals face fewer hurdles, especially in higher education.

When we sit down to talk about her journey with immigration —first as a daughter of immigrant parents in Brazil and later as an immigrant herself in the United States—it becomes clear how Helena has adjusted and thrived. She is comfortable taking risks and understands the need for working hard—characteristics that are especially vital for women at the top.

Helena doesn't use her financial success to lead an extravagant life, but rather to help the neediest members of her family that were left behind in China. A special moment came when she took her mother to China to reunite with her maternal grandmother after having been separated for thirty-four years due to political unrest. "That," she says, "was the most gratifying of all."

Helena is a remarkable example of how the human spirit can overcome difficulties of the past and still extract the positive aspects that her tri-cultural background and adopted country offer. "I feel that my values are Chinese, my heart is Brazilian, and my pocket is American," she says.

Can you tell me about your childhood in Brazil and how it impacted who you are today?

During my childhood, my family was struggling financially. My parents were new immigrants who did not know the language and were ill-prepared to make a living in a very different kind of environment. My parents were both Chinese. They migrated from China to Brazil, escaping the Chinese Communist Revolution. My father was escaping because he was in the military, in the Chinese Nationalist Party, so if he had remained in China he would have been killed as some of his family members were killed. My parents escaped on a ship to Brazil, and it took three months to get from Hong Kong to Rio de Janeiro.

They landed in Brazil in late 1951. For them to go to Brazil in those days, it was probably like us going to the moon today because there was this big unknown of what to expect on the other side of the world! They thought they were going to the jungle, and they even took needles and thread with them.

I was born in the city of Sao Paulo in Brazil. My parents were much older at that time. My mother was thirty-three and my father was already forty-two when they had me. I was the oldest of three kids. My sister was a year and four months younger and my brother was six years younger than me. My parents did not speak Portuguese. They came to Brazil with a completely different background. The only thing my father knew was to fight wars given that he was in the army all his life. My mother never went to school, so she was totally illiterate. They only spoke Chinese, and having to learn Portuguese, a Romance language, was very difficult for them.

Given that my father was not making enough money to pay the bills, my mother said, "I'm going to go to work." My father was very macho, and so he objected initially. However, she insisted and decided to sell women's clothes door to door. My mother, whose Portuguese was very bad, had a charming personality and became an excellent saleswoman. She became the bread earner of the house.

The reason I'm pointing this out is because she was a role model for me. She actually stepped out of her traditional role, while my father took on more of the stay-at-home-dad role. He stayed home, cooked, and cared for us while my mother was out on the streets, selling door to door and carrying a large, heavy suitcase of merchandise. As my mother became more successful, she turned the front of our house into a small boutique, and my father was able to get a car and drive her around to also sell door to door.

As my parents became more successful in their business, I needed to help them, as I was the oldest of the children. From the time I was seven, I helped my father by writing checks in Portuguese for him, and I also became a young bookkeeper. Since I was born on December 23, around Christmastime, I was never able to really celebrate my birthday, as I was busy helping my mother with gift wrapping in her boutique.

While I was helping my parents with their business, I was also studying very hard. One of the key values my parents instilled in me was the importance of education and doing well academically over anything else. My mother said, "I cannot buy you expensive clothes, but I promise that you will always look clean, and you'll have a good education."

Education was the number-one priority in my life. My parents moved us to a bigger city that offered better school options. I went to a private all-girls Catholic school that was considered the best school in this new town. My mother always said, "We have nothing materialistic to give you. Our legacy is your education." And my father also said, "You have to study English because it's going to be your future." But in the Brazilian school, they didn't offer it until middle school, so I started to learn English when I was seven years old on my own by listening to records that taught English and by reading English books.

What gave you the motivation to study and learn English on your own?
Like any other kid in Brazil, I always considered the United States as the number-one country in the world to go and study, and I always dreamed of going there. When I was seventeen, I decided that I would go to the US as an exchange student. I wanted to travel, and I really wanted to improve my fluency in spoken English. I did go to the United States, and I lived in Philadelphia with a great American family for six months, and I graduated from an American high school. I'm still in touch with this family that became my American parents.

I then returned to Brazil to finish the second semester of my senior year and to also get my Brazilian high school diploma.

What did you do for fun while you were growing up?

When I was a kid, I played a lot of games, climbed trees, and loved riding my bicycle. One of the games I liked to play was to pretend that I was an owner of a newsstand selling comic books. I loved reading and collecting the comic books my father used to buy for me. I would display these comic books like in a stand and pretend to sell them to my "customers"—my sister and other kid friends. When I was a teenager, I loved pop music and dancing like my girlfriends. I played piano and enjoyed reading books. I also liked playing chess. I used to study the movements that Bobby Fischer did in his worldwide chess competitions in the '70s.

Did your parents teach you how to play, and did you play with boys predominantly?

I learned chess in the social club I belonged to. Most of the time, I played with boys in the chess club. There weren't many girls playing chess.

Well, I guess this sort of prepared you for what would happen to you as an adult, when you became an executive in the business world. There are not many women business executives internationally.

As the firstborn child of an immigrant family, I was extremely independent and had to learn a lot on my own. My parents were not pushy and never told me what to do. I was self-driven. I wanted to be a doctor because I loved biology and lab classes where I could spend time looking at cells through a microscope.

When I was fourteen, my father was put in jail, a victim of racial bias and being accused of illegally selling merchandise in the family business. My parents did not speak Portuguese well enough to explain or defend themselves, so my father was in jail for seven days before I could find a lawyer to free him. After two years, he was cleared of all accusations.

During this difficult time, I basically had to hold my family together because my mother was distraught, and my siblings were too young. It was a tough growing experience, but it also made me more self-reliant and more resourceful. I had to figure out how to overcome all these hardships that I had. But that made me stronger. I could have the courage to go as an exchange student to the USA.

Why did you go to business school when your dream was to become a physician?

My parents had two other children to support, and I didn't want to put my parents through the hardship of supporting me through eight years of medical school, so I decided to forgo medicine as a career. Instead I decided to pursue a career in business because it was only four years of university (versus eight for medicine), and that would allow me to intern and work sooner. I did very well in my college entrance exams for Brazil's top business school (Sao Paulo School of Business of the Getulio Vargas Foundation). Four years later, I graduated first in my class.

My first job after college was to work as a treasury analyst for Dow Chemical. That was my first serious job working for an American multinational. I learned how to protect the company's assets against major currency devaluations in a bad macroeconomic situation. I liked finance, and that led me to understand and love foreign currency management.

You say you learned to love managing foreign currency. At that time, did you have a clear vision of how you wanted to proceed using this knowledge?

My dream was to come to the United States and work in international finance for a company in Wall Street. Even though I was barely twenty-one, I didn't want to wait to pursue my MBA. I started to apply to the top business schools, and I was accepted at the Wharton business school, which was my first choice. I was twenty-three years old, and I was one of the youngest in my class. When I went to Wharton, I was among the best and the brightest in the world, and that was exciting but also challenging for me, as English was not my first language and the competition was tough.

The first semester was particularly difficult. I had difficulties listening to the classes and taking notes at the same time. My solution was to record the lectures and when I came home at night, I had to listen to everything again and then take notes. So basically, I had to listen to every class twice. In Brazil, I was used to being the top student of the class, but in the US, I had a lot of difficulties to overcome—including financial challenges.

As immigrants, my parents had absolutely no money to send me to business school in the United States. I needed a total of $34,000 for two years of tuition and board to graduate from the Wharton business school. This is equivalent to $170,000 today. My parents could not help me, and I did not save enough money as I had just worked one year before starting business school. I only had nine thousand dollars. The part of me that has self-confidence said, "I don't know how, but I will figure it out when I get there." But I was very scared and worried! So much so that I spent most of my first two months researching and applying for scholarships, and I was also trying to work on campus. I was a cashier at the bookstore and I was working in the student administration department, so I did not have much time to study. I did have a breakthrough when I got a ten thousand-dollar scholarship from an organization, which was a big help, but I needed another ten thousand dollars to pay my tuition. Being a finance person with experience in foreign exchange hedging in Brazil, I was able to double the scholarship.

How did you do that?

Basically, I leveraged the existence of two foreign exchange markets in Brazil at the time—the official rate given by the Central Bank and another rate in the open market based on supply and demand. The spread between these two markets was two times back then. So, I was able to transform a ten thousand-dollar scholarship into twenty thousand dollars by taking advantage of this spread between the two currency markets in Brazil.

The experience I gained financing my education through leveraging the foreign exchange markets in Brazil helped me to get nine job offers at the end of my MBA—in a recession year.

It's amazing how you learn fast. Every semester, my grades got better because I learned how to be more efficient in my study. My English got better, and I did not have to keep taping everything any longer as time went on.

I actually had the best grades in the last semester when I graduated. I came to Wharton with nine thousand dollars, I paid all my tuition and board so I had no debt, and I still had eight thousand dollars in my bank account when I graduated!

With the eight thousand dollars, I decided to take my mother to China to see her mother (my grandmother) and her family, who she hadn't seen for more than thirty-four years. She had recently found out that her mother was still alive, after Nixon opened the relationship with China, and she was able to write and trace back to her family.

What did you do after your MBA?

After graduating from Wharton, I went to work for Procter and Gamble in their global headquarters in Cincinnati. I worked in Cincinnati for three years and then was transferred to Singapore, where I opened the Southeast Asian markets for Procter and Gamble. I lived in Singapore for three years and was then promoted and moved back to Brazil.

In Brazil, I was also part of the leadership team that opened Procter and Gamble there. This was fascinating because I started the Pampers diaper business from soup to nuts. I led the team that chose the manufacturing site and the ingredients for the diapers—everything had to be locally made, given the Brazilian restrictions for any importation. We launched Pampers behind a very unique marketing campaign against our key competition J&J. We became, within four months, the market leader of diapers in Brazil.

After nine years with P&G, I wanted to come back to the US and live in New York. That was not possible with P&G, as they had no offices in New York, so I decided to leave P&G. That was again a risky move, as I was moving to New York without any job leads. But as I mentioned, I was used to being a pioneer with every move I chose to take. I moved to New York, again saying, "I have no idea how it will work out, but I will go to New York, and I will figure that out."

I worked very hard to find a job. I was very tenacious and did not leave any leaf unturned. I followed any suggestion and any lead given to me. Within six weeks, I got three offers. Out of the three jobs offered, I decided to join Pepsi-Cola. I worked at Pepsi for four-and-a-half years as director of global business development. I supervised about 150 countries, traveled all over the world, and I loved international business. I helped Pepsi to build their beverage business in key markets in Eastern Europe, Latin America, and Asia.

After Pepsi, I took another major career risk. I quit to join Western Union. I left behind the beautiful offices of Pepsi to move into a company that was coming out of bankruptcy. Western Union was looking to hire a head of marketing to build their international money transfer business from the ground up.

Despite the initial challenges, my job at Western Union International was the most fulfilling because it was so transformational. I was the Chief Marketing Officer and the only woman in the C-suite. The business was still struggling, and I had basically no people and no marketing money. However, the rapid expansion into new international markets helped to turn the business around. I was part of the senior leadership team that expanded this business from twenty to two hundred countries in five years, and the business grew ten times in this period.

Later, I decided to work for smaller, more entrepreneurial companies—including working as the global president for a Hong Kong family business in consumer electronics called Oregon Scientific. My last corporate job was with Rosetta Stone, in Washington, D.C., where I was the president of international business. I joined them because I was very interested in languages and in digital learning.

After Rosetta Stone, I decided to make a major change in my life. I remember that it was a sunny day as I was driving in my car when I said to myself, "Helena, it is time for you to reinvent yourself and do something different because corporate jobs don't last for too long." CNBC News was telling us that CEOs were really, really anxious because their jobs would be gone in two, three years. The corporate world was changing fast, and it was not something under my control, and it had nothing to do with me.

Looking back, I was working very hard for these companies, and it was not what I wanted any longer. I decided to quit corporate life and start a new chapter of my life, even though I had no idea in what direction.

I would think that it was very difficult to find yourself in this situation.
Well, it has now been five years since I left the corporate world, and I have built a "portfolio career." That is, I am engaged in pursuing different things versus focused on only one company, which gives me more freedom and diversity. I have divided my time and interests into four main buckets.

The first one is investments. I spend time investing my own money, and I also invest for family and friends. I just like to help people, especially women, to do better in their finances.

I have created a diversified portfolio of different assets around the world, and managing this has taken a big chunk of my time. It is something I really enjoy because it has opened new opportunities and made me learn new things. Within my investments, I also became an angel investor, investing in startup companies, which makes me stay updated with the latest technology changes. In addition to being an investor, I also mentor some of these companies. Managing my own investments is something that I enjoy a lot. It also gives me a lot of flexibility because I can do this online or over the phone anywhere in the world.

My second bucket is my consulting and advisory work, helping businesses to grow and expand internationally. I focus on building cross-border businesses between Brazil, the United States, and China, because those are my three countries.

The third bucket is my board work for profit and nonprofit organizations. I am currently on one for-profit board of a fintech startup, and I would like to join more for-profit boards. I am currently on nonprofit boards like the Women's Leadership Board of the Harvard Kennedy School and the P&G Global Alumni Network.

And the last is my "giving back" bucket. I like to mentor women and young people. I also like to teach at universities. I taught in the MBA program of the Hong Kong University of Science and Technology and also taught international business for the Pratt Institute's School of Design. Teaching for me is a way to share my knowledge with the younger generation.

Finally, I am also involved in a few nonprofit organizations.

What about your personal life, Helena?

While I'm not married and I don't have any kids, I'm very close to my brother and sister and nephews and nieces. I am also very close to my extended family of cousins and their families—both in Brazil and in the US. In the Chinese tradition, your cousins are like your brothers and sisters. And I have eight cousins that are close to me. So, I'm very dedicated to my family, and I have a lot of great friends around the world that I've made through the years. With them, I travel. I go to movies, shows and dinners, and play tennis.

How did you feel as a woman professional in a man's world?"

I basically had to work much harder. At Wharton, 80 percent of the students were men and 20 percent were women at that time. And in the executive world where I spent most of my corporate life, there were mostly men in the C-suites or senior leadership teams. So I learned the tricks of how to make myself noticed. For example, I knew where to sit in the boardroom, I always wore red in major meetings, and since I was petite, I learned how to make my voice heard. I learned how to have more voice projection and to have more of an executive presence. But it did not happen overnight. I always had to work harder.

I was always in operating roles, not taking the staff jobs, in order to climb the ladder. The price I paid was working very hard and taking the hardship jobs. I actually was able to do it because I was single and I didn't have small kids, which allowed me to be flexible and to take international assignments.

My career was a top priority for me. It is really hard for a woman to reach the top positions. There are a lot of things you have to overcome. I was serious, and not flirtatious. Nevertheless, there was a suspicion sometimes that I used my femininity to climb the ladder, which offended me terribly. What I've learned is that women, particularly at high levels, are a target. You're a target left and right. Surprisingly, I also had a few women against me. Not just men, but women.

Did you find cultural differences in America that were difficult for you?

Not difficult, but I want to share this observation. While both Brazil and the US are countries made of immigrants, I am seen very differently in each country.

I was born in Brazil and grew up there. While I looked Chinese, my Brazilian friends would say, "Helena, you're not Chinese, you're Brazilian because you were born in Brazil." I always felt Brazilian, and I was always treated as such. Nobody would call me Chinese. It doesn't matter what the color of your skin is or what you look like, because Brazil is made of immigrants. Everyone came from somewhere.

On the other hand, Americans tend to label you based more on how you look and the color of your skin. When I came to the United States, Americans would ask me, "Where are you from?" And I would say, "From Brazil." And they would say, "But you're not Brazilian. You look Chinese. So you're Chinese." Americans usually label me as Chinese because of the way I look or the color of my skin.

One thing I really admire about the US is the importance of philanthropy, which I learned to appreciate since I have been living here. I now donate my money and time for philanthropic purposes. I think it's very important, and I am grateful to have acquired this in the United States.

Which culture or country influences you the most: Brazil, China, or the US?
Basically, I feel I am a combination of the three. I feel that my values are Chinese, my heart is Brazilian, and my pocket is American. Let me explain. My core values of commitment to family, my value for academics, and for ethics of working hard all come from my Chinese background. My love for dancing and music, my zest for life, my love for the beach and sun, the fun, the colors, and the emotional part are all Brazilian. When I said my pocket is American, it's because my professional life and my way of earning a living are American. I mostly worked for American multinational companies, and I studied in an American business school. My way of looking at business and at investments are very American. That is why I feel I am a combination of all three.

Do you take advantage of the cultural life in New York?
I usually go to many Broadway shows and plays. I like to go to the symphony and to the ballet. I love the city and what it has to offer. I especially like New York in the summer because I love to eat outdoors and enjoy going to Central Park every weekend for biking and walking, or just reading the newspaper on the lawn. New York is the most exciting city in the world, and that is why I am living here.

What do you think about the bans and policies on immigration?
I think it's terrible, because I'm an immigrant. I think, economically speaking, you need immigration in order to grow in any country and

to help increase productivity. I think that the ban against immigration is wrong because this country is made of immigrants. Immigrants have contributed to the greatness of this country. I believe that diversity of thoughts and background breeds creativity.

Helena Wong celebrates her graduation from The Wharton School at the University of Pennsylvania with her parents.

Helena Wong was one of three women to receive the 2018 Highest Leaf Award from The Women's Venture Fund, a non-profit that helps women entrepreneurs launch their businesses. The Leaf Award honors women whose "business or professional contributions significantly impact their industry and exemplify an understanding of the balance between outcome and responsibility in their workplace."

MONICA YUNUS

BANGLADESHI-AMERICAN OPERA SINGER
AND SUPPORTER OF THE ARTS

"I stand on the shoulders of strong women who are immigrants, my mother, and my grandmother, who made sure I knew the value of hard work and of sharing all of my gifts with the community."

MONICA YUNUS WAS FOUR WHEN HER mother first discovered her musical talent. Once nurtured and cultivated with love, that distinctive voice and passion would lead Monica to become one of the most internationally admired opera singers of her generation, with credits from the Metropolitan Opera to the Zouk Festival in Beirut, Lebanon. Her collaborators range from Andrea Bocelli and Plácido Domingo to Jon Batiste.

Born in Bangladesh, Monica came to the United States after her parents divorced. She and her mother lived near Monica's Russian grandparents in New Jersey, where she would come to learn the struggles, as well as the resilience and resourcefulness, that many immigrant families describe.

"Growing up, I did not feel that I was always on solid ground because my grandparents did not speak English, and I could feel them struggle when they didn't understand something—a bank teller asking them a question, or figuring out directions," she says. "In those moments, I became aware of how difficult it was to always have to translate everything, that you were always the outsider."

Monica would graduate from The Juilliard School with a bachelor's and a master's degree. In 2003, she made her principle debut with the Metropolitan Opera in New York City in the role of Barbarina in Mozart's *The Marriage of Figaro*. She has performed in many prestigious opera houses, nationally and internationally, as well as in Bangladesh, where she reunited with her father.

Inspired and encouraged by Muhammad Yunus' tremendous humanitarian achievement as a Nobel Peace Prize winner and founder of a microcredit bank, Monica co-founded Sing for Hope, which mobilizes artists to support arts programming at under-resourced schools, hospitals, and community centers. It is grounded in the belief that the arts have the power to uplift, unite, and transform individuals and communities.

The organization is perhaps best known for its Pianos project. Artist-designed pianos are installed in parks and public spaces in the five boroughs and, after their public residency, are gifted to New York City public schools with coordinated visits from Sing for Hope artist partners.

It was an extraordinarily beautiful spring day when I visited

Twenty-Eight Liberty Plaza in Manhattan, following the music on a breeze from Battery Park. A New York scene unfolded around a dozen of the sixty Sing for Hope pianos, each one painted by an individual artist and each offering a sound as unique as the pianist.

Cathy was playing a piano covered with abstract orange-and-gold design, and I complimented her talent. She said she intends to play as many pianos as possible. The one at the Oculus transportation hub in the World Trade Center is accessible every day after work.

I asked Matt if he chose his piano for the art or for its sound. "I play all of them. They all 'own' different sounds, and that's what fascinates me," he said. "Monica Yunus and her partner, Camille Zamora, conceived this idea, and so they provided us with art available to take us away from the mundane everyday life."

There was a mother playing Mozart's "Twinkle, Twinkle, Little Star" with her little daughter, a man with a white ponytail, and a student with a backpack who noticed me from the corner of his eye, smiling.

I made my way to Monica's office on Eighth Avenue to interview this exceptional opera singer and to learn more about her dreams and her humanitarian contributions. She approached me with a warm smile that reached her beautiful hazel eyes. But it was her walk toward me, graceful but decisive, that set the scene apart: a walk of a woman that says determination and suggests that any dream can become reality once she puts her mind to it.

Monica understands the strength of community, thanks to her mother's dedication and her father's selfless devotion. Her motivation is to use her art to empower others. And so she continues to sing—for herself, for the rest of the world, and for hope.

———

You're a child immigrant, born into a family of immigrants. How do you deal with being from so many places?

My own story began in Bangladesh where I was born. I came to the United States when I was three months old, so I have no recollections of Bangladesh, though now I've been back several times. I was literally born in the Hill Tracts of Bangladesh, very close to a leper colony. The Hill Tracts are full of indigenous people. That obviously made a big impression on my mother, who had been born in Russia and was an immigrant herself. She was a displaced person in Germany and then, with my grandparents, she moved to the United States when she was only six years old. I am really the first generation that has grown up in the US, but my parents and grandparents were also immigrants.

I grew up in New Jersey, very close to my grandparents. I went to a Russian school and spoke Russian. I also attended the Russian Orthodox Church, so my childhood was filled with the music of the church. I grew up infused with that culture. Because my parents divorced when I was a child, I did not have a Bangladeshi influence while growing up. I was a Russian child in America, and I think that was the part that drove the musical portion of my life. My grandmother was such a beautiful singer. But because she was a displaced person post-World War II, she didn't have the opportunities to develop her talent, take lessons, and things like that.

This was because when they immigrated to the United States, they had to work. They had to bring up their children and take care of their parents. It was sort of the typical immigrant story in some ways: working as hard as possible, raising the next generation who are essentially Americans but being torn having left their home country, and making their way in a new country, trying to understand the new customs and cultures. I think that's an important point, because you are never really one thing. I like to think of myself as a global citizen. I have such strong pulls to the countries of origin of both my parents, but I also feel very American as well. So I don't see why you have to choose. I'll say that because I think it's a much more interesting life to have all those different influences. They're beautiful in their own ways.

I've always thought that being an immigrant gives you an edge in some ways. Because my grandparents didn't speak English, I didn't always feel that I was on solid ground as a kid. When I was growing up with them, I watched them not being able to communicate, translating for them and having to be that person for them even as early as four. It gives you perspective and empathy that are extremely important.

Even though you stayed in America since you were just four months old, did you still feel like you were an outsider?

Yes, absolutely. I saw how my grandparents were treated, so I felt that. I don't know how to exactly describe that feeling. It is just not having a sure footing. I can give you an example. My dear friend growing up was as American as apple pie. Her mom managed a deli down the road. Her father was a police officer, and I actually felt very protected by that. But I knew even as a child that there was a difference between her family and my family.

You must have had a culturally rich childhood.

I grew up going to a Russian school on Saturdays, learning about my culture and heritage, and going to a normal, everyday elementary school during the week. I developed a big love and passion for singing. I was definitely one of those kids you could not shut up. I was always singing. I would sing to the trees in my driveway. I'm not making that up. I would sing to whomever would listen. My mom and my grandma noticed it. When I was eleven, I started take voice lessons with a Russian opera singer, Kira Baklanova, who had sung all over Europe and had sung in the 1950s with the NBC Orchestra and Tullio Serafin. I took lessons for years, and I remember my mother would drive me into New York City for my rehearsals at the Metropolitan Opera where I was in their Children's Chorus, and where my love for opera began.

I always loved to sing, but I didn't really know what the world of opera was. But I became enthralled with the stage and the costumes and the orchestra and the instruments and the drama. It had everything I loved about singing wrapped into one. That was my introduction to opera. I did that for several years as I pursued my musical training and tried to focus it in a more concentrated manner. I was at Boston University's Tanglewood Institute for several summers and at the Aspen Music Festival for many summers, too. Those were all summer programs that were audition-only and highly competitive. That's how I would spend my summers, training and exposing myself to a higher learning than what I was getting during the year. Then I ended up in Juilliard. Looking back, I realize how incredibly lucky and privileged I was, and how much of this was driven by my mother's tenacity and dedication to my passion.

You spent a lot of time at The Juilliard School. How was that experience?

It was great; I loved going there. I think the conservatory is not necessarily for everyone. I made incredible friends there. I met my co-founder for Sing for Hope in that school. It was born out of these relationships I built with people at Juilliard.

But it was not always easy. I remember between my first and second year of my master's degree, I had worked really hard on an aria that I wanted to present at an audition. I came back from the break, and at the beginning of the year, the first thing you do is share the new repertoire you've worked on. I was in the middle of my first audition, and it wasn't going so well. I remember I got to the end and missed the high note. I was really mad at myself. I remember running off the stage and looking at my pianist and begging her to play that final chord, which seemed like an eternity until she finally did. So yeah, that wasn't so fun. And you never have a second chance at auditions. You just sing and that's it. You can't say, "Can I do it again?"

Since you were multilingual, did you sing in other languages?

I grew up bilingual, so I never thought about it. I love languages. I sing in Russian, but there aren't many operas that get produced (except at the major opera houses) in Russian, so I don't get to use that as much as I'd like. I had the opportunity to study Italian in Italy through a scholarship offered through Juilliard, and so my Italian is not bad. I would say my weaker languages are French and German. Many of the operas I've sung in are Italian—Puccini, Verdi, Mozart, a lot of Mozart. I'm what they call an "Ina Soprano"—Adina, Zerlina, Despina—lots of Italian light lyric roles.

How do you prepare for a role?

It depends. My system is counting how many pages are in the score that I actually have music on, and then I split it up act by act. Per act, how many pages I need to learn, and I sort of attack it that way. I try to work backward. First, I usually train by myself, and then with a coach. I also try to learn the language and style and then work with the conductor.

Which were your favorite roles?

I love *(The Marriage of) Figaro*. I love the opera *Lucia (di Lammermoor)*. That's a dream role I haven't yet sung.

Growing up, I understand that you weren't close to your father, Muhammad Yunus. But that relationship grew around your first visit to your place of birth, Bangladesh. How was it going back to your homeland?

It was really amazing. I had never been to Bangladesh. I was born there, but I hadn't been back. So this was the trip of my lifetime. I visited in 2005, and when I got off the plane, my father was there to greet me along with his wife and my stepsister and some folks from the Grameen Bank. On that trip I reconnected with my extended family, including twenty-six first cousins that I'd never met. On my mother's side I had one cousin, one uncle, and an aunt. And on my father's side, I had seven uncles and twenty-six first cousins. So just that alone, the sheer volume of family, was exciting.

In Bangladesh, everything was new: the sights, the sounds, the smells. I remember thinking everything was so green, so tropical and lush. I was coming from New York where the predominant color for clothing is black, and here in Bangladesh everything was so colorful.

People dress in massive amounts of colors, and the markets would be overflowing with vegetables and fruits. There were so many flavors I'd never tried. For instance, I tried jackfruit for the first time. That's another thing I love about my singing career, that I get to travel so much. The sights, smells, flavors hit me all at once; it was very exciting, very overwhelming.

We went to the Hill Tracts in Chittagong and to the hospital where I was born. There's a family home in Chittagong where many of my uncles live with their families. It was one of those trips that I'll never forget. And any subsequent trip would be different, because it won't be my first trip.

Have you gone back since then?

Since then I've been back with my husband, Brandon McReynolds.

When we got married, we had two ceremonies—one in the United States and one in Bangladesh, which was great. And one day I hope to go back there with my son.

Did you feel like a stranger, or did you feel like you belonged there?
I have family there, and I absolutely felt like I belonged. In Bangladesh, I felt like there were elements of myself that I got to see in a different way.

Since that first time, your relationship with your father has developed into something truly beautiful. He received the Nobel Peace Prize in 2006 for founding The Grameen Bank, the Bangladeshi microcredit institution. The Grameen model has been replicated in more than 140 countries and helped millions of families overcome poverty. I understand you were a part of the special day in your father's life, when he received the Nobel Prize and you sang "O mio babbino caro." Tell me about the ceremony.
The ceremony is very elite, very royal. They host two ceremonies, the Nobel in Stockholm, and the Peace Laureates are honored in Oslo. I was a part of the Oslo ceremony, where my father received the Nobel Peace Prize. They have a small unveiling ceremony the night before, which is very intimate, at the museum. I missed that ceremony because my flight was delayed. I was so disappointed; I was crying in the airport. And they have a dinner where all the Nobel families are invited, which is also very intimate, maybe fifty people. Oslo City Hall is where the actual Nobel Laureates presentation takes place, which is broadcast to the entire world.

After that they have a massive concert for nearly six thousand people. I performed that night for my father, and Sharon Stone and Anjelica Houston were the hostesses. There were so many well-known people: Yusuf Islam, the Judd sisters, Rihanna, John Legend, Lionel Richie. I have a fabulous poster of that night that everyone signed. After that performance, I had to leave. It was such a quick trip for me because I was in production at the Met Opera, so I had two or three days, and a very small window to go and come back. I have snippets in my mind's eye, pictures of what the actual event was.

I cannot imagine anything topping singing "O mio babbino caro"—so emotional. First of all, it is such a well-known aria, and then it's you singing it with your beautiful voice, and then it's for your dad who you haven't been so close to. It's a gift for him.

It was special. It was definitely very special.

After becoming such a successful artist, you started Sing for Hope with your friend from Julliard, Camille Zamora. What led you to start a nonprofit for the arts?

Sing for Hope was born out of moments of reflections by both Camille and me, whether it was 9/11 or Hurricane Katrina. When Camille lost her dear friend to HIV, that was the turning point for her life. We did a concert in his honor in Houston. That concert raised money year after year for the hospital where he passed away. Then 9/11 happened, and Katrina happened. I wanted to raise some money by singing for the victims of Katrina, which was pivotal for me considering my recent trip to Bangladesh. I had taken a good look at the monsoons and how they can sometimes take down entire villages, and how devastating all of that can be. I wanted to do something with my art. I wanted for it to have a fundraising element. I said to Camille, "Let's do a concert like the one you did in Houston." So we put something together, and we raised a little bit of money.

What was important for me was that this was an example of how the arts are a catalyst for people in so many ways. We were certainly not the first people to say that the arts are important. But in each person's life, these moments can happen, and what you take from that moment is very important. For us, it was the spark that led us to this journey of starting something bigger.

I was just talking to a friend who is a star massively on the rise. I look at him and think how wonderful is it that he gets to use his talent in this way. I've really understood that as much success as I can gain, it's only going to be worth it to me if I can turn around and hand it back to other talented people. That's what we see for Sing for Hope too. For our platform, it is important for us to give the same power to people to use their creativity and talent to pay it forward. For some people, fame and fortune are only for themselves. But I feel that if you reach that level of success, it's about allowing other people to reach it, too.

It's interesting that the people I am interviewing share that ambition of sharing their talent and allowing people to have it too. So what is Sing for Hope?

I like to call us an artist peace corps. We are more than eighteen hundred artists, not just singers, but dancers, instrumentalists, and musicians who volunteer our time and talent to communities in need. We're probably best known for the Sing for Hope pianos. We placed sixty artist-designed pianos throughout five boroughs in New York City for everyone to play. Each one is an individually credited piece of artwork. We're out in the parks and public spaces for three weeks for anyone who wants to play. We have a partnership with the Department of Education, and all the pianos are then placed in schools that don't have instruments. We also partner with around 250 nonprofits. So that means if you're United Cerebral Palsy or you're a veterans' center or an AIDS hospice, we develop relationships with you, and our artists go to those locations and perform.

So you buy the pianos every year?

It's funny that people think that the pianos are the big component. It's actually the moving that's more expensive. You get used pianos fairly inexpensively—around $300 to $500. It's moving them around that's more difficult.

The project has been going on for six years of our ten-year history. All six years, we've had donated space. We've had thousands of square feet of space in iconic New York buildings. One year it was the *New York Times* building, where we were given an entire floor. These past two years, it was the Chinese company Fosun International at Twenty-Eight Liberty. They have generously allowed us to use thirty thousand square feet of space for six months. So that's more than a million dollars of donation in-kind.

How do you manage your time between Sing for Hope and your singing?

I want to continue to sing at a high level and to expand Sing for

Hope. It's funny you're telling me you're from Israel, because we had a meeting recently with someone who said, "This project should come to Israel. How can I make that happen?" We have conversations like that often where people are so inspired by the pianos that they want to know how they can bring them to their city. We're handling that question internally, as to how to replicate Sing for Hope in an efficient manner that still captures the whimsy and fun the organization stands for.

I was very sorry to hear that you lost your mother recently. She was a tremendous influence on you and a strong advocate for your success. What does it mean to look back at a person's life and view it full circle?

There's no easy way to capture it for me. There's not a day that goes by when I don't think about her or her influence and spirit. How she lived her life, how she empowered me to live mine. My mom's general attitude was "You could do whatever you wanted; you're so lucky you have this gift, and what would I do if I had that gift." There was nothing that I couldn't do. Some of my friends would say she was a typical stage mom. But I never saw it that way. I always felt that stage moms were people who push something upon their children that they didn't want. In my case, I very much wanted to do this. And she was helping to make that happen, looking for different opportunities to allow my talent to flourish. I don't consider her a stage mom in the least.

She was a strong role model, tough as nails. Life didn't present her with a lot of opportunities, but she kept going so she could build an incredible life for herself and for me. We would travel! I remember for my sixteenth birthday she told me we could have a party, or we could go to England and Paris. I said, "Let's go!" It wasn't like we had a lot of money, but she made those things happen. Going through her old taxes and going through her paperwork, I'm shocked at how little money she had in those years. She had many different careers. She was a Russian teacher, and later in life she worked for the Department of Youth and Family Services.

Has being an immigrant changed the way you handle things?

Being an immigrant has cultivated a greater empathy in me. I think people take a lot of things for granted in this country. They take for granted that you can just walk into a bank and open a bank account. There are a lot of people who can't do that. That really cuts them off from a lot of things. They have no access to credit, no credit history, and on and on. We can't even understand the implications of that, because we're not in that situation.

How do you feel about the situation we are in regarding immigration?

It is completely un-American. Our country's strength lies in its diversity of people. If we undo that, we are tearing at the very fabric that the United States is built on. Most of us came to the US from somewhere else, or our ancestors did. If you want to pursue immigration reform, fine, let's reform the system. But actively throwing out children who do not know any other home is simply barbaric.

Monica Yunis and her father, Muhammad Yunis, with his Nobel Prize

Monica Yunus is the Co-Founder and Co-Executive Director of Sing for Hope. She has performed with the world's leading opera companies, including the Metropolitan Opera, Washington National Opera, the Zouk Festival, and in recitals in Spain, Guatemala, and her native Bangladesh. She has been named a 2016 Young Global Leader of the World Economic Forum, honored with a 21st Century Leaders Award, as "New Yorker of the Week" by NY1, and named one of the "Top 50 Americans in Philanthropy" by *Town & Country*. A leading voice in the "artist as citizen" discussion, she has performed and spoken at *Fortune's* Most Powerful Women Summit, Skoll World Forum, Aspen Ideas Festival, and the United Nations.

EPILOGUE

THE FIRST TIME I BECAME an immigrant, I moved from my homeland of Israel to Italy to study medicine. I made a decision to exchange the comforts of the known for a demanding education and a risky but rewarding future.

I learned a lot about myself in this new setting. I came from an emancipated world—where I had served in the army with little gender discrimination—to a strict Catholic country. I had self-confidence and a purpose to study to become a doctor. I enjoyed the new culture as an observant and curious outsider, or "the other" that I was. And that was OK. I was welcomed as an individual, not as a member of an amorphous group of immigrants that had to be deemed worthy—or not—of entering a new country.

And when I became an immigrant for the second time, I was already married to a US citizen and was embarking on a residency and fellowships in a stressful but cocooned world. My difficulties were inherent in the medical field, the testing system I had to adapt to, the sleepless nights, and the English language barrier. I worked hard—as I continue to do—and I was lucky.

So, as I interviewed the women for this book, many of whom arrived in America with much less support and with the added burdens of racial, sexual, and religious persecution, their stories filled me with tremendous admiration and joy. I couldn't wait to share their triumphs and their personal and professional accomplishments.

At the same time, I couldn't ignore the circumstances unfurling in the news around me. With pain in my heart, I saw wrenching changes in attitudes and political policies toward immigrants. Fear and distrust took root almost overnight, threatening to overshadow and ultimately obliterate the good will that opened doors for me and the women in this book.

So I kept interviewing, and I kept writing. I found a mission. I believed that what I learned in the course of this journey would be important and worth sharing. What we could glean from these women could prevent us from leaving a negative legacy about immigration, women, and humanity for generations to come.

One of the most striking things I discovered is that these women carry with them traditions, spices if you will, that create a colorful, abstract painting. Taken as a whole, the painting embodies the new land they create together. But when you stand close to this work of art, each swatch retains its integrity. The edges might blur a bit here and there, a new hue might form where edges overlap, but the essence of that original color, the culture and its practices, remains intact.

I worry that some of this uniqueness will fade as fear pushes immigrants to assimilate and shun the cultural gifts of their homelands. Parents bent on "becoming American" could let slip the time it takes to attend traditional dances or prepare beloved foods, leaving children with shreds of their heritage or worse—resentment of a family culture that has made them defensive and apprehensive.

At the other extreme, some immigrants might find comfort from turning inward, hiding in a deceptively safe environment, forming a closed society that becomes isolated from all foreign influences. Many more will simply hide.

We must be mindful of our neighbors and encourage them to cherish their cultural richness while enjoying all the possibilities that this country offers. We cannot let these unique flavors dissipate.

I also learned to appreciate the generation of parents who gave birth to these amazing women. They encouraged their daughters and granddaughters by nurturing self-respect, independence, and a foundation of education to find their own lives in the United States—and sometimes to endure hardships and discrimination.

I discovered that although many women in the United States feel liberated—certainly with exception and room for advancement on all fronts—women in other countries have to grapple with forced marriages, subjugation, invisibility, and barriers to achieve success in male-dominated worlds. For them—and for me, perhaps—the rewards are sweet when they finally achieve their freedom to succeed, create, and contribute. There is an innate sense, a social obligation maybe, to want to give back, to have other people benefit from and enjoy the work we invest ourselves in.

At this particular time, it was important to me to explore the feelings and actions of these women who fought to climb the ladder in a man's world, to fight sexual discrimination, racial discrimination, and other forms of oppression, and to pave the way for others.

I chose to write about these women for their bravery. They strove for professional success in areas where gender inequality was rampant. They were the first ones to sit among mostly men in law school and medical school classrooms, laboratories, and boardrooms, and they held their heads high and became pioneers. I invite you to look at these women as inspiration for your own lives.

Along the way there are also the people some of us choose not to see, the less-skilled or less-famous than the women in this book. These people fulfill jobs as housekeepers, gardeners, waitstaff, and other positions that keep the country moving forward. Documented or not, whether they can vote or not, these immigrants work hard and serve the country.

They feel American, yet these days, they rarely feel free. Desperation and hopelessness have replaced pride and commitment to their adopted country. Can you imagine how it feels to be helpless to plan for your future, to never feel settled, to always look over your shoulder?

We cannot allow this hollow, worthless feeling to creep into the lives of immigrants who look to this country for growth and salvation, for a hopeful and healthy future.

As Hillary Clinton said when she spoke at the Women's Forum of New York, it is our responsibility to be mentors for the women who need our help, to share their stories, and inspire the next generation. This is my attempt to speak up and to provide a voice for those who have not yet found their own. It is up to me and you to stand up and provide examples of greatness, achievement, and perseverance. We need to write down and illustrate what works—and what doesn't—in order to provide a guide for the future.

ACKNOWLEDGMENTS

I AM ETERNALLY GRATEFUL to many people who inspired me and helped me write this book.

My parents, Israeli immigrants from Russia and Poland, whose stories of courage led me to believe that the impossible can be achieved: my father, Aaron, a doctor, whose self-sacrifice and great risk taking allowed him to fulfill a dream to immigrate to a country that did not yet exist; and my mother, Rachel, who named me after my grandmother, whom I never met and who perished in the Holocaust.

My daughters, Jordana and Ariel, who patiently listened to my exciting encounters with the Invincible Women. Steven, Eric, and my grandchildren, who fill my life with love and laughter. And all the sons and daughters of the protagonists in the book who are blessed with more than a single heritage. I urge you to follow the road to freedom that has been paved for you with courage, love, and conviction.

Love and gratitude to Dr. Lawrence Fish, who facilitated my American experience, and to my dear friend Joel Cohen, whose initial and timely suggestion culminated in this book.

I am forever indebted to Lisa Kosan, my talented and indispensable editor, who believed in my project from the beginning and who helped me crystallize my ideas. Amruta Lakhe, my assistant editor, who identified with the life of "the others" who came to this country. Esther Margolis, a dear, loyal friend, whose guidance opened the door to the world of publishing. Dede Bartlett, who recognized the importance of this book and who supported my goals. Dale Degenshein for her guidance and support. And Ruth Cowan, an early advocate who made key introductions for me.

Most of all, the women in this book, for sharing with me their life journeys.

ABOUT THE AUTHOR

BILHA CHESNER FISH, MD, is a board-certified radiologist with expertise in body imaging and musculoskeletal radiology. She founded Manhasset Diagnostic Imaging and then Pathways Women's Health, one of the first privately owned diagnostic and women's health centers on New York's Long Island.

Born in Israel, she served in Naval Intelligence with the Israeli army and earned her MD from the Faculty of Medicine, University of Bologna, Italy. With her husband, whom she met in medical school, she went to the United States and completed her

Bilha Fish with her daughters, Jordana and Ariel, their husbands, Steven and Eric, and her grandchildren Lilli, Shoshana, and Maxwell

training at the New York Hospital-Cornell Medical Center and the Hospital for Special Surgery. She became an expert in the newest technology and accepted a position as Chief of Imaging at Beth Israel Medical Center in Manhattan.

In 1995, when she expanded her radiology practice with an innovative women's health center, she focused on preventative programs and asked volunteer physicians in the community to teach women to be proactive about their health. The center offers group therapy for women afflicted by cancer to provide support through the process of healing.

Dr. Fish also established the Unbeaten Path, which provides age-specific programs for adolescents on topics such as anorexia nervosa, bulimia, sexually transmitted diseases, bullying, and recognizing mental health issues, for which they receive health credit in high school. She sponsored a nationally recognized community awards program for local teens and senior citizens.

Over the years Dr. Fish complemented her science experiences with more creative and artistic endeavors, earning two master's degrees, in art history and studio art, at Long Island University's C. W. Post campus. More recently she enrolled in the master's degree program in Italian studies at Columbia University. She is fluent in English, Hebrew, French, and Italian. She resides in New York City and Sag Harbor, New York.

Bilha Chesner Fish created this painting, The Lift, *2010, as a tribute to her father. "He always gave me the confidence to imagine a world without limits," she said.*

Biltza Itzcowicz, the maternal grandmother and namesake of author Bilha Chesner Fish, perished in the Holocaust. Her memory is a blessing.

CPSIA information can be obtained
at www.ICGtesting.com
Printed in the USA
BVHW041304190520
579966BV00010B/208